SUPERSTARS

SUPERSTARS

TWELVE LESBIANS WHO CHANGED THE WORLD

DELL RICHARDS

Carroll & Graf Publishers, Inc.
New York

First Carroll & Graf edition 1993

Carroll & Graf Publishers, Inc.
260 Fifth Avenue
New York, NY 10001

Library of Congress Cataloging-in-Publication Data

Richards, Dell.
  Superstars : twelve lesbians who changed the world / Dell Richards.
    p. cm.
  Includes bibliographical references (p.   ).
  ISBN 0-88184-955-3 : $12.95
  1. Lesbians—Biography. 2. Lesbianism. I. Title.
HQ75.3.R53 1993
305.9'06643—dc20   93-2151
                                                                      CIP

Manufactured in the United States of America

Grateful acknowledgment is made to New Victoria Publishers, Inc., for permission
to reprint excerpts from *A Perilous Advantage: The Best of Natalie Clifford Barney*
edited and translated by Anna Livia, with an introduction by Karla Jay. Published
by New Victoria Publishers, Inc., P.O. Box 27, Norwich, Vermont 05055.

To Andrea Jackson
Heart's Ease

"It is an act of devotion to honor our dead with a few words by which they may continue to outlive themselves; instead of mute forgetfulness, we can give them some inspiring, courageous epitaph describing what they were. . . . The history of their loves, devotedly recorded, adds to the beauty of our world; it is this that we inherit from their riches."

—Natalie Clifford Barney,
Eparpillements, 1910
"Scatterings"

from Jean Chalou's biography
Portrait of a Seductress: The World of Natalie Barney
translated by Carol Barko.

CONTENTS

Acknowledgments 11
Introduction.. 13
James Miranda Barry.. 21
Florence Nightingale.. 47
M. Carey Thomas ....~~First g to head degree~~....................... 71
Jane Addams 93
Lillian Wald ...~~founder of public health nursing~~113
Alice Hamilton... 135
Edith Hamilton.. 159
Natalie Barney.. 177
Sylvia Beach.. 201
A'Lelia Walker... 217
Anna Freud... 243
Vita Sackville-West 261
Bibliography 287
Index 289

ACKNOWLEDGMENTS

Over the years, gay and lesbian scholars have made me aware time and again of what was being left out of history—and what could be done to fix that omission. Although I cannot name them all here, I would like to thank: Lillian Faderman, Janice Raymond, Carol Smith-Rosenberg, Karla Jay, Blanche Wiesen Cook, and Tee Corinne, as well as Jonathan Katz, Martin Greif, and Louis Sullivan for their insights and lists of gay women.

Nonetheless, this book of biographies could not have been written without the scholars whose extensive research and interviews made this collection possible: women like Noel Riley Fitch, Anna Livia, and Barbara Sicherman; men like Lytton Strachey and Nigel Nicolson. The bibliography gives a more complete listing.

Without the diligence of Joanne Moore and Coletta Suniga, the help of Joan Greenfield, this book would never have seen the light of day. Thanks also to the staff of the Sacramento Public Library who tracked down books that had not been touched, much less used, for more than half a century.

I also owe a great debt to my agent, Malaga Baldi, and my publisher, Kent Carroll, both of whom gave invaluable support.

Jeannine Guttman also deserves special mention for the support and encouragement she has given me. Not only in history but in life do lovers become loving friends. Barb also deserves special mention for putting up with us. "Ex's" may become family, but that doesn't always make it easy.

11

INTRODUCTION

I became gay as an experiment. I was in my early twenties, a radical, a feminist. After doing what I was supposed to do—going to college and getting married—I figured there had to be a better way.

It was the early 1970's. Kate Millett's seminal work, *Sexual Politics*, had just been published. It was a revelation, a book that literally changed my life. Suddenly, I understood—and had a word for—my experience. For particularly abrasive men like my high school history teacher who invariably made fun of women's ideas, who cracked jokes about them not being able to understand because they were destined to be housewives. Or my loving and left-wing husband who felt that I should do the cooking because "it was my job." Sexism wasn't just rampant in literature; it was rampant in life. *My* life.

I began to realize that being raised as an only child might not have been as bad as I had thought. Granted, there were no brothers or sisters to commiserate with about the tragi-comic life of my parents. But if my parents wanted to lavish attention—or expectations—on anything but the dog, I was it. Unlike my friends who had often played second fiddle to brothers, I at least got top billing.

In fact, I sometimes got more than top billing. Because I grew up during the 1950's, a time when fathers worked and mothers stayed home, my mother and I were the basic unit, the female dyad who kept each other company during the day. My father worked all day, came home tired in the evening, and played golf on the weekend. We were so much the unit that we rarely took his wishes into account, and then usually only as an afterthought—when it dawned on us that he might not be particularly pleased with whatever it was *we'd* already decided.

Despite these early feminist advantages, becoming gay wasn't as easy in practice as in theory. Admittedly, my oldest friend, a woman I had known since fourth grade, willingly seduced me almost as soon as I got home from London—and marriage. But she already had a girlfriend who, like most girlfriends, immediately suspected something was up and called first thing next morning. It was a rude awakening for me—in more ways than one.

I also didn't know how to be gay, and I didn't have any role models. I'd heard the rumors about teachers who were "that way" at school but they weren't of any use. Even if they'd been willing to talk, I wouldn't have known what to say. It wasn't so much a matter of behavior as my sense of self that required the most profound change. And that could only come with time. I might have had the privileges of being an only child, but I had still grown up a *girl*, with all the usual psychological foot-binding that entailed.

Only I didn't know that then. I just knew I didn't fit into this new world very well. There was a huge gap between where I was and where I wanted to be.

In some ways, of course, I was well prepared. During high school, I began to see through the myths of mainstream culture, at least as they played out in suburbia in the 1960's. The big myths. Motherhood and patriotism. By then, I was already interested in Europe and "culture" and the arts, those ineffable things that lead to "gay sensibility," things that, indefinable as they are nonetheless connect gay culture to the past and the future.

As a young adult, I also felt like a citizen of a global village. Long before men walked on the moon and satellite photos came back of the earth as this beautiful blue orb hanging in space, I didn't love my country with the usual unquestioning patriotism that was required. I loved the landscape and the earth, but I was critical of my country's many failings and unwilling to ignore its flaws. Even then I was striving for a culture that transcended national boundaries, a gay culture that defies national characteristics despite its citizens being born in different countries.

Oddly enough, the thing people always ask if you say you're a "political lesbian" is: "How did you change your sex life?" But the sex was the easy part.

First off, there was the emphasis, I am proud to say, that my generation—the baby boomers—placed on oral sex. And when you're drunk and stoned, which I usually was at least on the weekend in those days, turning to women's bodies wasn't that much different. After years of conditioning to think of women as the beautiful, soft, loving, nurturing sex, what amazes me today is that any woman ever remains heterosexual. The taboo against lesbianism *must* be very strong and the trade-offs very high not to gravitate to women.

But the difference was greater than the surface. And the differences in gay culture are so subtle that even today I'm not sure what they are. All I know is that I've gone through these profound changes as a result of being gay and living, for the most part, in an environment of women.

There were some obvious differences. One of the first things I learned was that gay women don't giggle or flirt—the standard, unspoken method of communication among heterosexuals—unless they are actually interested. I rid myself of those habits fast.

The other differences were less obvious, however. I noticed how supportive of my ambitions and dreams the lover in my life suddenly was. For the first time, I was surrounded by people who believed it was possible for a woman to succeed. I was surrounded by people who believed in my dream of being a writer. The everyday variety of psychological abuse that is par for the course in the heterosexual world hardly exists among lesbians. When you get rid of the men in your personal life, for example, there's no one who expects you to work *and* cook *and* write. Or at least to organize it all. I don't know what it's like to be a gay man, but when you're a lesbian, there's no one trying to be supportive but so thwarted by their own conditioning and competitiveness that the best they can say is "Yes, Dell, we know you'll be rich and famous someday."

Suddenly, I found that the most important person in my life not only believed in my dreams but was willing to help me get there. So much so that I know I would not be where I am today, that I would *not* be a published writer, if I were still a heterosexual. The women I've been involved with over the past twenty years helped me make my dreams come true by sharing them with me, making them seem less formidable, and even pointing me in the right direction, if not giving me a good kick to get me started!

Of course, there are drawbacks to a homosexual life, too. But I believe that in a sexist society, women only have two choices: internal or external oppression.

If a woman remains heterosexual, she must, by definition if she is to remain even partially sane, internalize much of the horrible self-hate with which our society views women. If she is able to escape her conditioning and become gay, she can free herself of a great deal of that self-hatred, but she must be strong enough to face a society that sees her in even more negative terms. Personally, I would rather have the poisons be external than internal, outside where I can fight them rather than inside my own head.

As I wrote this book, I began to realize that I had to try to define the differences between heterosexual and homosexual culture, especially as they affect women. Little has been written about this, but I can still feel the difference in my bones. I know it's not politically expedient at this time to accentuate our differences. Politically, we are hoping for acceptance by emphasizing our similarities to the mainstream. But that is an illusion that I hope gays and lesbians don't actually buy into. Mainstream society is bound by sexist, class-ridden, racially oppressive, testosterone-poisoned rules that are killing the planet as well as the people in it. To save this planet, we need profound changes, changes of the type I think gay and lesbian people worldwide can give us. We have a culture that is twenty-five hundred years old at least, that, despite the homophobia of much of society, is healthy, wealthy, and wise.

I have attempted to point out some of the differences in this book, but I admit I've only scratched the surface. I do know, however, that gay culture has existed throughout history and is somehow passed on through generations of people who become part of it for one reason or another—genetics or politics, nature or nurture—without ever fully understanding why they must go through the tortuous process of reversing their psychological moorings to become outcasts. Thousands of years separate us from our ancestors, yet we renew this culture every century, passing it on from generation to generation. Though the world view of the planet changes, and the politics of nations change, gay culture remains remarkably cohesive and coherent. If anything, gay culture today has more similarities to the gay culture of ancient Greece, similarities in *weltanschauung*, family structure and lifestyle, similarities which unite it to the past and to the future, than it does to heterosexual societies.

Because we are invisible, however, heterosexual society usually misses both our similarities and our psychological differences. Admittedly, most heterosexuals will never experience homosexual culture unless they spend months, if not years, alone with their gay friends. Any time more than two heterosexuals are together, the dominant culture invariably takes over, no matter how liberal everyone is. Most heterosexuals simply know nothing about our culture, and nowhere is this more painfully apparent than in the biographies I used for this book. There was so much left out, so much misunderstood, that it was shocking. Even understanding something as simple as why two women would push single beds together was a mystery. Although it would seem too obvious to even need stating to any lesbian—they wanted a double bed—it wasn't obvious to at least one biographer. Perhaps the man was never presented with two single beds instead of a double when traveling as a couple. In this world, anything's possible, even simple myopia.

Oddly enough, I don't think this type of innocence was malicious. I used to think biographers were protecting their subjects, but I don't anymore. I'm not even sure it's homophobia except in the broadest sense. Instead, I'm beginning to believe that people can't see what they don't know is there. Even trained academic biographers will go through incredible contortions to explain behavior—in their terms—because they are missing essential pieces of the puzzle.

This blinkering was particularly true of the biographies of cross-dressing doctor James Miranda Barry. Because the biographers did not understand the economic, political, or sexual traditions of female transvestism, Barry's behavior was simply incomprehensible. Both June Rose and Isobel Rae thought it odd that she even wanted to cross-dress. They had no idea what the psychological ramifications might have been, especially had she been a lesbian.

They also assumed that everyone must have known—even though it's perfectly clear that *had* everyone known, they would have never needed two court-martials to try to boot her out of the military. Had they known, Barry would have been kicked out with one simple question and a quick inspection.

But people did suspect *something*. The most plausible explanation was that they thought Barry was a terribly effeminate *gay* man, an even worse turn of events than masquerading as a man!

Because the biographers were seeing her through heterosexual eyes, because her experience was so vastly different from theirs, they could not begin to understand her. They almost seemed to be holding her at arm's length, as if she were some sort of distasteful insect. This led them to assume that she was lonely, frustrated, bitter. But, in fact, we don't know that. We know she probably had a hard life, at least psychologically. Most women who cross-dressed did. But it might not have been any worse than the life she would have faced as a poverty-stricken female with no skills and no prospects. The thing we do know is that she was a fighter who was unwilling to take no for an answer—more marks on the lesbian side of the scale, if we were weighing it. But aggressiveness alone doesn't make her bitter or frustrated.

To most lesbians—who are comfortable with androgyny and cross-dressing at least as it relates to tuxedos at fancy-dress balls—her behavior is not only understandable but laudable. As lesbians, we also assume, as neither biographer did, that if there were at least one jealous husband upset with his wife spending too much time alone with the good doctor, there might have been others.

Another problem heterosexual biographers seem to have is giving enough credence to the person's partner. Mary Rozet Smith is hardly mentioned in most of the biographies of Jane Addams, nor is Ellen Gates Starr. Yet both these women had a profound influence not only on Addams but on Hull House itself. So much so, it might be safe to say that Addams probably would not have started Hull House nor become famous if they hadn't been in her life. Ellen Gates Starr helped her found Hull House and Mary Rozet Smith was one of two women who gave her the constant financial support needed to keep it afloat. Because biographers usually downplay the role of the wife in a man's life, I don't think they understand how much a lesbian's life partner is part of her success. For the most part, the balance in the lesbian relationship is more equal than it is in heterosexual relationships, and this invariably contributes to the woman's success. And it's not just the "behind every strong man" syndrome. (There is also the issue of self-esteem, but that is a massive subject needing so much research that I can't begin to do more than mention it here.)

Yet nowhere is this phenomena of interdependence more apparent than in the lives of Adrienne Monnier and Sylvia Beach. They were like two peas in a pod when it came to careers. Without Adrienne, there would have been no Sylvia. Though it's not quite as clear in the case of Anna Freud, that was probably also true for her. Dorothy Tiffany Burlingham was not just an emotional refuge but a direct, working partner in their psychological enterprise, the woman who helped her start the *kinderseminar* in Vienna, the war nurseries, and the Hampstead clinic in London.

The same is true for M. Carey Thomas. Without Mamie Gwinn and Mary Garrett, M. Carey Thomas might never have been able to do what she did. While these two women *are* mentioned by biographers, their importance is always downplayed or left out. Gwynn is called a temptress and seen as someone who stood in Thomas's way, while Garrett's offer to buy the presidency of Bryn Mawr for Thomas is minimized.

The case of Florence Nightingale is even more complicated, since the women in her life were relatives. Though this phenomena is a fairly common occurrence in a past where female relatives, such as the Ladies of Llangollen or the author(s) "Michael Field"—which was actually the aunt-niece combo of Katherine Bradley and Edith Cooper—could spend months or even years together without anyone thinking twice. It was only when they deserted their families, wanted to have their own residence, or live together permanently that relatives began to question their relationship. Biographers tend to ignore certain implications which, if included, actually add to our understanding of how women lived in the past.

The same is true for even more taboo relationships, such as that of Edith Hamilton and Doris Fielding Reid, a former student of Hamilton. While the women did not live together until Hamilton retired, knowing what went on before that would be invaluable especially given the fact that Hamilton was only fifty-five when she retired, because of "nerves" as much as anything else. We know her deteriorating relationship with M. Carey Thomas played a part but, it also would be very interesting to know how her relationship with the student figured in her decision. Was another reason for her retiring early because it was the only way to avoid the scandal that might have been caused when she and Reid moved in together? At this point, we don't know.

Despite their academic standing and intellectual skills, heterosexual biographers simply don't know what to do with lesbian relationships. Alice Hamilton's are not mentioned. Nor are Lillian Wald's, despite the fact she had both 'steadies" and "crushes."

If a woman marries, like A'lelia Walker did, the situation deteriorates even further. Biographers take marriage at face value, confident that heterosexuality is the only viable explanation. Yet it's clear that traditional marriage had little to do with these women's lives.

When faced with women like Natalie Barney and Vita Sackville-West, women who created families out of their love life, the inability of most biographers to write about this phenomenon which is so common in the gay world becomes especially apparent. Admittedly, the language doesn't even have words for it. For the most part, neither literature nor psychology has offered models or satisfying explanations. Only in history do we get glimpses of similar patterns. Yet here again, few biographers draw analogies or point out this recurrence. The loss is phenomenal, since, in these cases and others, it is the key to understanding the person's behavior.

While biographers do their best, they can't help being blinded by their blinders. The best they seem to be able to do is ignore the phenomena or try to fit the women into the heterosexual models they know, which, unfortunately, destroys the very meaning of them.

Unfortunately, this bowdlerization is so standard and perhaps even inevitable, given the profound differences of the two cultures, that it is rarely seen for the Stalinist revision it really is. In the false name of privacy, the fact that historic figures were gay is routinely left out of all but gay history books. I hope that if nothing else, I have shown in this book how gay the world really was and really is. I specifically added the sexual orientation of every person to try to give a clearer picture of the past, to give more realistic weight to the importance of most of the gay people mentioned—and their contributions—as well as the twelve lesbians I chose to write about in detail. To be helpful to any of us, history cannot be written to satisfy a particular political system. If it tells any truth at all, it must be as whole and all-encompassing as we can make it.

Which brings me again to the exploration of gay culture. We are at a unique period of time. The earliest of gay cultures, the Greeks, took being gay so much for granted that they didn't even need to discuss it. It was so much a part of life, they didn't even have a *word* for it. Being gay, being bisexual, was life itself.

Once Christianity appeared on the horizon with a world view so fascist it could not even let other religions co-exist, gays were forced first to the margins of society and then to fighting for their very existence.

Today is the first time in history that we can look at this gay culture we are creating and ask ourselves what it is; how it is similar, if it is, to the mainstream, and how it is different.

We know now that the creation of gay culture is a truly profound process made all the more remarkable for being hidden for so long. Except for those rare historic periods of sexual freedom when homosexuality suddenly becomes chic, gays have been outlawed and forced to live underground for centuries. Yet gay and lesbian culture has not only survived and thrived but made substantial contributions to the world as we know it today. That is a truly remarkable feat.

Chapter One

JAMES MIRANDA BARRY

In 1809, a young man entered Edinburgh University as a med student. He was really young, barely a teen—plus he was frail and effete. But no one thought anything of it at the time.

If they had thought anything, they would have thought how brilliant, how studious, how serious he was. He'd come up to Scotland with his mother and did nothing but study. Didn't date, didn't make friends, didn't go out to the pub for a drink. With his nose in a book so frequently, he hardly spoke, he walked away with a Doctor of Medicine in three years, somewhere between thirteen and seventeen years of age—a historic Doogie Howser.

So began the distinguished but somewhat eccentric career of James Miranda Barry.

Four years after graduating from med school, Barry joined the British Army and was sent to South Africa as the Colonial Medical Officer, a career highly placed appointment. For the next forty-three years, Barry saw the world, courtesy of the Bulldog Drummond.

Twice he was court-martialed for insubordination. Twice he was acquitted.

He was really good at his job, too good, in fact. He was always questioning his superiors. He couldn't obey orders, unless he agreed with them, nor could he follow channels and deal with the rigid protocol military life demands.

In 1865, Barry died during a particularly bad summer flu caused by London's open sewers. He left no heirs, no family.

Barry would have died in peace, a nonentity, had not one minor circumstance changed his life. When the woman preparing the body for burial took off his clothes, she discovered *he* was a woman.

In one fell swoop, Barry officially became the first woman doctor in the United Kingdom, the first woman admitted to the British Army, and the first woman court-martialed by the military.

Everyone soon found out about the charade. Educational leaders, military colonels, were livid. At a time when women weren't allowed to go to school because their brains weren't large enough to be educated, an unknown woman passing as a man had not only gone to high school and college but flown through med school faster than anyone in her class—and graduated with flying colors.

At the time, women had almost no economic options.

To quote from Rudolf Dekker and Lotte van de Pol's ground-breaking study, *The Tradition of Female Transvestism in Early Modern Europe:* "A man could . . . always become a soldier or a sailor and was thereby assured of at least housing and food. Women, who were already at a disadvantage because of far fewer possibilities to work and far lower wages, had no such last resort. It is true that public charity helped women more readily than it did men, but this was not meant for young, able-bodied, childless women."

To support themselves, women had few choices. They could marry, work as a governess (if they had training in subjects such as singing and drawing), be a domestic servant (a twenty-four-hour a day, seven-day-a-week job), sell themselves on the street—or be an actress, which was only one step above the street in those days. To quote Dekker and van de Pol: "The typical feminine alternative of prostitution involved far less security and much more contempt from society than entering the service of the military or the fleet did for men. In fact, prostitution was as marginal as begging and vagrancy, and was defined and persecuted as a crime."

Unless the woman could pass as a man. Then her economic options expanded enormously. Then she was bound only by the limits of her imagination.

If a woman could pass as a man, she could also have other rights: she could own property and vote. Despite the obvious difficulties, enormous numbers of women chose this option in the seventeenth, eighteenth, and nineteenth century. The 1989 death of Billy Tipton, a saxophone player who decided to become a man in the 1940's because a woman would only be allowed to sing in the band, shows how common this phenomena is, even today.

During the Civil War, some four hundred women are supposed to have fought on both sides. The first woman to be awarded a Congressional Medal of Honor was a gender-bending cross-dresser. A woman with long curly hair, Mary Edwards Walker wore men's trousers (or *uniform* during the Civil War experience that got her the medal), top hat, and tails. Unlike most of the women who passed, Walker was arrested several times because of her insistence on wearing men's clothing while making no bones about being a woman.

The vast majority of women we know about were soldiers or sailors. Despite the added difficulty of hiding one's gender in a dormitory situation, military service was the easiest possible job to get. You didn't need references, you didn't have to prove your age—or sex, obviously. The military took absolutely anyone and paid them a hefty bonus to sign up. What's more, it was the only way to travel and see the world, if you were of the working class.

Nobody knows the number of women who passed then—or now. Most of the women we know about caught the eye of historians because they got caught themselves. But they are the tip of the iceberg. The ones who quietly changed sex by changing clothes are the vast majority. Though they could have been arrested for fraud, not that many actually were. Even though it was illegal to cross-dress until recently—the 1960's in much of the U.S.—and lesbian artists such as Rosa Bonheur had to get special permission to wear trousers, most of the soldiers and sailors were seen as patriots and merely mustered out of the service if they were caught at all.

Many of the women who passed in the 1600's and 1700's wrote autobiographies about their experience. Christian Davies made her pension days richer by writing the true story of her campaign as a foot soldier under the Duke of Marlborough. Mary Frith, also known as Moll Cutpurse, had been a highway robber in the early seventeenth century with a pawn shop to boot where she resold the goods to the very people she'd stole them from—until she realized that an autobiography of her life would add even more coins to the coffers.

Barry passed at what was the height of the cross-dressing era. While she might not have known about the phenomena, the people who helped her pull off the scam certainly did. Henry Fielding's 1746 *The Female Husband* was about the true-life cross-dresser, Mary ''George'' Hamilton. Being a judge, Fielding had heard about her case and wrote a novel about it that was one of the most popular of its day. The phenomena was covered widely in the press and in books of the day. Barry's main benefactor, whether he read Fielding's book or not, would have heard about similar instances.

Others, when they grew too old to pass as a young man whose voice hadn't changed or beard hadn't come in yet, created theatrical acts from their male impersonation and took to the stage. Hannah Snell became, "Bill Bobstay the Sailor," once she realized show business might be an easier life than the military.

Technically, these women aren't necessarily considered lesbians today. The concept of transvestism as a sexual category wasn't invented until 1910. Today they are labeled transvestites. When asked about their sexual orientation, their answers might still create uncertainty. In fact, according to Annie Woodhouse, author of *Fantastic Women*, most male transvestites today are heterosexual, some 85 percent.

But the story for women is quite different. Until recently, cross-dressing women fit the historic definition of a lesbian: a man trapped in a woman's body.

To quote Dekker and van de Pol:

"Sexual desire and love was thought of as something that could only be experienced with a male. We can therefore assume that most women who fell in love with other women (*or wanted to do anything that would be considered male in its day* [authors addition]) could not place or identify these feelings. Therefore, it is logical that those women would think: If I covet a woman, I must be a man."

Or, more importantly in this instance, if I want to do a man's job, I must be a man inside.

Unfortunately, we know so little about James Barry's personal life that it is difficult to know whether she was a lesbian, by modern sexual standards, or not. She had many of the stereotypical characteristics of a butch, but her love life is shrouded in mystery.

Nonetheless, Barry *was* a part of a tradition, an early gay underground that had its height in the seventeenth and eighteenth centuries but has flourished well into the twentieth century. Nobody knows how many women cross-dress or even pass for men today, but it wouldn't seem as common simply because the economic, political, and psychological reasons for doing so aren't as important anymore. Today, every time a woman puts on trousers, she is cross-dressing—or at least would have been labeled as doing such until Garbo and Dietrich made trousers fashionable for women! Whether Barry was gay in the modern sense of the word or not, today's economically liberated, trouser-wearing woman can thank her and others like her for their cross-dressing freedom.

One thing *is* certain. Barry enjoyed passing as a man and did it fairly well. She was known as a flamboyant dresser, who loved the trappings of her uniform. Whether she needed it or not, she always wore her sword as well as her officer's hat. She was athletic.

She was also an outrageous flirt, always honing in on the most beautiful woman in the room. Barry was supposed to have been involved with a Mrs. Fenton, who stopped at Mauritius on her way back to England to have a baby, but unfortunately intimate details of their relationship are scant.

Barry's bedside manner was also very good—so good, in fact, that one husband complained about the time "the doctor" spent by his wife's bedside, alone in the evening on nights he was away.

This lack of knowledge isn't surprising. Few intimate details of women's personal lives are ever available. Diaries are burnt; letters thrown away, at least if they have anything scandalous in them.

One thing we do know about Barry was that she was very intelligent. As such, she was probably well aware that the easiest way to have *everyone* find out was to let *anyone* find out. History books are full of women who turned their lover in because they were jealous, or in-laws who called the authorities when a lover let their secret slip out.

Sophie Bishop, the charwoman who discovered Barry's secret, claimed Barry had the marks of pregnancy. Maybe Barry did. Maybe she also had had a child. But that wouldn't have meant she wasn't a lesbian. Maybe she discovered her true sexuality late in life.

What *is* fairly certain is that Barry was a woman. And before the newspapers got a hold of the story, the woman who discovered her secret was trying to make a buck off it by blackmail. But since no one was falling for the gambit, it's likely she elaborated on the story to make it seem more believable. To quote a letter from the doctor who certified the death about the charwoman who discovered Barry in June Rose's biography, *The Perfect Gentleman*:

"Among other things she said Dr. Barry was a female and that I was a pretty doctor not to know this and that she would not like to be attended by me.

"She then said that she had examined the body and it was a perfect female and that there were marks of her having had a child when very young. I enquired: how have you formed that conclusion? The woman, pointing to the lower part of her stomach said 'From marks here' (stretch marks). 'I am a married woman and the mother of nine children and I ought to know.'

"The woman seemed to think that she had become acquainted with a great secret and wished to be paid for keeping it."

Perhaps the woman not only wanted to add evidence to firm up her story but didn't want to go into the finer details of what was actually missing.

What we do know is that Barry fit into the definition of a lesbian at the time and, as such, can be considered a foremother of today's modern, but quite different, lesbian.

Barry was born sometime between 1795 and 1799. Strange as it may seem today in this information swamped society, massive record-keeping simply didn't exist in the 1700's. Most people were born at home. The church kept records—if you belonged to their parish. Many people had no idea what date they were born on or exactly how old they were. Accuracy wasn't important yet.

Despite the research of two biographers, no one knows who her parents were. The best guess is that she was related to the well-known Irish painter, James Barry, whose name she took to get into med school.

What *is* known is that the London-born Barry was extremely intelligent and extremely poor, a useless combination at a time when women's intelligence was of no use no matter how brilliant she was. If it hadn't been for a group of influential friends who were patrons of her uncle, Barry would have been sunk.

Being broke and having exhausted her relatives' generosity, the woman who was probably Barry's mother took her to meet one of her uncle's best friends—a wealthy Latin American general exiled in London—to ask for help. General Miranda was, to quote from Isobel Rae's biography *The Strange Story of Dr. James Barry*:

"... a fascinating character, this 'Precusor of South American Independence' ... One of his friends was ... the Earl of Buchan ... an 'eccentric Scottish nobleman ...'"

While the mother pleaded their case with the general, Barry wandered into the library. General Miranda was known to have one of the largest private collections of books in London, book collecting being a rare and expensive hobby in those days. Medicine was his special forte. Miranda, seeing Barry's interest, invited her back to use his library. Eventually, he became so impressed with her genius that he hatched a plan to send her to college.

Miranda couldn't have done it alone. Two other men helped: statesman Edmund Burke and Lord Buchan, a staunch believer in women's education who had been a patron of Barry's uncle.

To show how history works, most of this information is put together from Barry's full name: James Miranda Steuart Barry. *James Barry* is thought to be taken from her uncle, *Miranda* from the general of the same name, and *Steuart* from the family name of the eleventh Earl of Buchan.

Though people take education and job opportunities for granted today, that wasn't the case two hundred years ago. Class lines were rigidly drawn. No one moved up the ladder unless they had a patron. Neither welfare, unemployment, or government grants existed. If you were an artist or unemployed, you starved unless more affluent relatives or a patron took you in.

When her uncle died, leaving a destitute but intelligent niece who would have wasted her life in domestic servitude, or worse, if someone hadn't come to the rescue, it made perfect sense to transfer the patronage to the niece. Luckily for Barry, the Earl of Buchan had just collected an annuity of £1,000 for Barry's famous but poverty-stricken uncle when the painter died in 1806. The painter never lived to see a penny. It was probably decided to give the money to the niece, send her to med school, and see what happened.

It's not that surprising that influential people took an interest in her, or that they came up with the idea of passing her off as a man. What *is* surprising is that they decided to put their radical theories on women's education to the test. Barry went to med school before John Stuart Mill or Mary Wollstonecraft argued for the rights of women, much less the idea of women's education. Three liberal men, with Barry's consent, devised a scheme to test the thinking of the day.

Barry never took off her disguise once she donned it, but she did succeed beyond anyone's wildest dreams to become a very successful doctor. Over the years, she was one of the first doctors, male or female, to use preventive medicine. She was known to throw away prescriptions for dying patients and open the windows, saying all they needed was fresh air. Since the medicine of the day was often more deadly than the disease, she was often right.

She was a vegetarian and a teetotaler at a time when the three food groups were meat, bread, and alcohol. She advocated a varied diet during an era when people were lucky to get anything other than salted meat, booze, and gruel.

She was also one of the first doctors to perform a successful Caesarean section.

Whatever her medical theories, she was a fighter who never gave up, who fought for the rights of others, for slaves, for prisoners, and the mentally ill at a time when these groups weren't even considered human. Although her reforming crusades made her enemies wherever she went, her fighting spirit never hurt her reputation as one of the best doctors of her day, though her farsightedness was barely recognized in her lifetime.

Barry had asked to be buried without a postmortem examination, without preparation for burial. Had her dying wishes been granted, the world would have never known that the first woman to graduate from med school beat all the others by more than half a century.

But when Barry's body was washed, and it was discovered that the esteemed gentleman was none other than a lady, the scandal took England by storm. To quote from Rose:

"If Sophia Bishop had kept silent about what she discovered on the death-bed, the scandal would never have spread. But she was outraged, stunned . . . For two weeks no word of the story reached the public. But in the new London clubs on St. James's and Pall Mall, in the pot houses and the gin shops, tongues wagged and the gossip grew.

"By the 14th of August *Saunders News Letter*, a Dublin paper, broke the story of 'a female army combatant.' The *Manchester Guardian* reprinted the article a week later, and the *Whitehaven News*, a Cumberland paper, picked up the scandal on the 24th of August. Rumor had flown so far that the authorities could no longer afford to ignore it."

Even today, controversy still exists about Barry's identity—whether she was really a woman, an undeveloped man, or a hermaphrodite. One thing we do know, James Miranda Steuart Barry was not what she seemed. But what she seems to lesbian eyes today is quite close to the androgynous gender-bending that is becoming more and more common among younger lesbians in the gay community today. And to us, she looks very familiar.

The Career of a Doctor

Barry was brilliant—but she stood out. Not only did she have bright red hair, but, like most passing women, she was short. When she became an Army surgeon, she tried to fix that by having high heels made to make herself seem taller. She also wore padded shoulders to give herself a more masculine body. Whether she liked uniforms or was just proud of what she'd done with her life, she always wore her uniform. Lest anyone forget her rank, she was never caught without the elegant, peacocklike military apparel of the day: a tri-colored hat with feathers, gold shoulder epaulets, and a sword almost as tall as she.

As if that weren't eccentric enough, she also had African or Jamaican servants whom she took to England with her, which *really* made her stand out. And she kept a series of poodles which, like Gertrude Stein's Basket, was named Psyche dog after dog after dog.

By the time she arrived in Edinburgh, Barry already had the M.O. figured out that would protect her all her life. She used her eccentricities to draw attention from the irregularities of gender. In Scotland, she managed to put people off by playing up her age. Because she was too young to be enrolled in college, much less graduate school, it worked. When it came time to graduate, the deans never asked her whether she was a man or not; they just worried about her age. She only scraped by that one because there were no rules governing age yet. Those were instituted a few years later—after Barry left.

At college, Barry threw herself into her work. She had been given a tremendous opportunity and wanted to make the most of it. (If she failed, it would have been back to the streets.) She took subjects such as chemistry, botany, anatomy, surgery, midwifery, medical law, Greek, Latin, and philosophy. She had been sent to one of the best med schools of her day and studied with some of the most brilliant medical minds of the time. As a result, she had a solid understanding of the most advanced medical theory and technology available by the time she graduated, which would not only come in handy a few years later but make her famous to boot.

She also was able to dissect bodies in class. Although typical of med schools today, most students at the time never got closer to an organ than a sketch in a lecture or a book. By dissecting bodies firsthand, Barry learned what the human body actually looked like, inside and out.

In two short years—much faster than it usually took a medical student—Barry was ready to write her thesis. She chose to write on the hernia of the groin. One can't help but wonder what influenced her to choose such an odd subject. Was she fascinated by an injury that mainly happened to men and rarely women? Or was the choice—a subject so near the genital area, in an era of incredible squeamishness about the

body—another ruse intended to keep suspicious officials busily on the
scent but searching the wrong track. Whatever her reasoning, she passed
the examination with ease, including an oral in Latin. She dedicated
her thesis to her benefactors, another clue to their identity.

With an M.D. under her belt, Barry returned to London to study with
one of the most famous surgeons of the day. She worked as a "pupil
dresser," watching surgeries and accompanying doctors on rounds.
There, too, she put her nose to the grind, and in a few months, passed
the regimental surgeon's exam for the Army. They waived the physical
since they were even more desperate for doctors than for soldiers. A
glance would show that she was in good health, the only *real* qualifica-
tion. If anything, the authorities were more concerned about her age
than her sex.

For the next four years, Barry worked in hospitals in England. Then
came her chance: she was appointed to the British colony at Cape
Town. So began her posts abroad. From then until the day she retired,
Barry would see the world—from the tropics to more inclement zones,
from plum posts to pits.

Choosing to work abroad was a smart move for a passing woman.
In a foreign country, there was less chance of someone recognizing her.
Given the time period, she might have even heard of James How, nee
Mary East, born some forty years before Barry. East so successfully
passed as a man—in order to marry a childhood girlfriend—that she
eventually became quite a well-to-do pub owner. That is, until someone
who recognized her began to blackmail her. She had to turn to the
authorities to get the blackmailer off her back. He was imprisoned, but
the notoriety was too much. East sold the pub and retired. Barry was
probably shrewd enough to realize that going away was safer. She might
have missed England, but being with colonial officials who did not
know her (or knew her powerful benefactors if they *did* know of her)
was much less risky than being in London.

Barry made the most of her new post. She quickly became the doctor
to the governor, the highest official in the colony, and thereby aligned
herself with the most powerful person in South Africa. And she immediately became known for her medical expertise. Three events cemented
her reputation: Saving the life of one of the governor's daughters; healing the son of a political exile; and saving the life of a mother and
newborn when she performed a Caesarean section.

Although healing the governor's daughter proved useful later because
it put the governor in her debt, healing the exile's son and performing

a Caesarean brought her fame. In both cases, she did something truly remarkable for the time.

Although doctors thought he was dying, the son of the exiled count was just depressed at the situation he found himself in! He was imprisoned with his father and had no company other than the old man. He was also working as secretary to his father who was dictating his autobiography.

At a time when people simply did not understand the tremendously powerful effects the emotions can have, Barry prescribed hydrotherapy (baths), a window to look out of, and the companionship of some young women his own age rather than being cooped up alone with his father.

She prescribed light and air—and threw away his medication.

Barry's idea of opening windows was a concept so advanced that it wouldn't be accepted until well after Victorian times a century later. Over the years, she became known for this unbelievable cure. Somehow Barry knew the restorative power of fresh air and sunshine at a time when houses that hadn't had a window opened in years were hotbeds of germs. Actually, Barry understood the concept of germs long before the idea was common knowledge.

Barry's "air cure" added to her reputation for eccentricity, but her successful Caesarean section brought her reputation as a doctor. Though it's not certain, it was probably the first one in British history performed by a doctor.

Whether a first or not, it was certainly an amazing feat for the time. News traveled quickly through the colony and back to England of how she had cut open a woman's body and pulled the child right out of her stomach! What was even more amazing was that Barry would even have the confidence to try it. She was probably desperate, given the fact either the child or the woman was going to die if she didn't. The only thing she knew about the procedure was what she had learned in a lecture by a doctor who had performed it twice but hadn't succeeded either time. In 1820, the Caesarean section was almost unheard of, and was performed successfully—the mother and child both having lived—only in Switzerland. No one else would be successful at it in England for more than a decade. In payment, Barry asked that the child be named after her, which it was.

In addition to her more illustrious clients, Barry also had military patients, who included more than six hundred soldiers brought down by cholera one year. Though she didn't realize it at the time, knowing how to treat cholera would come in handy when she got to the Crimea three decades later.

But Barry didn't just earn accolades in South Africa. She also made enemies, powerful enemies who not only stood in the way of advancement but would eventually see her court-martialed.

One such instance was an influential family in the colony. She refused to allow the son of a pharmacist who had been dispensing medicines for years to continue practicing. As the Colonial Medical Inspector, it was up to her to license pharmacists. She refused, arguing that no one should give out drugs who didn't understand the diseases they were diagnosing. Since he wasn't a doctor, he shouldn't dispense.

Whether right or wrong, she fought tooth and nail. But she only succeeded in making herself unpopular. She was great friends with the governor by then, but it wasn't enough. The family was too influential—and willing to put everything on the line to win. After all, their livelihood was at stake.

This wouldn't be the last time Barry clashed with those above her, either in the military or in society. Barry also got into trouble for pointing out that a conflict of interest could arise if government physicians also accepted private patients over and above their regular career ones. Though she sometimes saw private patients, she usually asked for a token favor in exchange. When she wouldn't accept payment, people often sent presents. One pleased woman sent Barry two black horses from her stud farm.

But the fight with the pharmacist was just the beginning. Perhaps because she was so bright, because she had come so far, she took her responsibilities very seriously, too seriously. Everywhere she went, she found incompetence, ignorance, and injustice. And everywhere she went, she had to fix it. Barry made even worse enemies when she found injustice.

At the Cape, she was also given the job of overseeing the leper colony, the town jail, and the prison.

What she found was appalling. The lepers, most of whom were black, were kept in conditions not even fit for animals. Their quarters were filthy and they were given inedible food. Worse, children who hadn't caught the disease were allowed to live with parents and other people who were dying of it. Rather than removing the children and stopping the spread of the disease, they were forced to pass it on to the next generation.

As soon as Barry saw the conditions, she immediately called for changes. The things she ordered are now standard, even minimal, requirements, but they were revolutionary at the time:

"The bedding and clothing must be frequently changed, and [the lepers] must bathe twice a week at least. . . . The sores must be washed twice daily with tar water and dressed with tar plaister," she wrote, via biographer Rose.

She also wanted the people fed properly. Again she wrote, showing ideas which were far ahead of her time but which, unfortunately for her, raised immediate hackles:

"Nothing salted such as fish, meat etc, should be permitted. Milk, rice, vegetables, and fruit should be used as much as possible."

The manager of the leper colony threatened to resign immediately rather than take orders on how to run his hospital. How dare this upstart doctor tell him what to do. He'd been running the colony for years. And at half the cost! The reforms would break them!

The prison was even worse. Conditions, even for the sick, were positively medieval. In a *dungeon*, she found a man:

". . . with his thigh fractured—without clothes, without a bed, or pillows, or blankets, dirty in the extreme, without a single comfort . . . that he had neither been furnished with medicine nor proper diet, nor attendance so much required in his helpless and painful state— but that once in twenty-four hours, the keeper brought him a bucket of water . . ."

When the governor finally stepped in on Barry's behalf to order the prison to create a sick bay, it was one of the first in the world.

Because of her constant efforts, conditions improved at the leper colony. But in the process, she ruffled too many feathers of the men in charge who, it turned out, had longer memories than elephants, at least when it came to revenge. That was the pattern wherever she went—demanding reforms, fighting for what she knew was right, even to the detriment of her own career. In this respect, she was the opposite of Florence Nightingale, who knew how to bide her time. Though Barry had laid her life on the line, giving up her gender and possibly her sexuality, to become a doctor, she never thought of the consequences to herself or of the trouble she could get into by fighting for others. She had recited an oath, which she took to heart. All that mattered were her patients.

Life as a Man

The personal life of James Miranda Barry is almost a complete cipher. Barry's papers consist of official letters and documents about her career or the battles she fought. Though her professional life is fascinating, we want to know more. If only she had kept a diary, if only we had her thoughts to answer the questions: Why did she do it? What did it feel like?

Barry passed as a man from early adolescence until death. To know what she experienced, to know what she thought and felt about the incredible subterfuge would be priceless. It's no wonder romance novelists had a field day with her life. They made her the illegitimate daughter of a lord, a jilted woman who followed her man around the world, to name just two characterizations.

But the most burning question is that of her love life. And if questions about her motives are murky, answers about her love life are completely opaque.

Barry was known to flirt with the best-looking women at any party. And she appears to have had some kind of serious flirtation with at least one woman in addition to Mrs. Fenton. We know about the other because her husband complained that Barry was always visiting his wife at night when he was gone. We don't know what happened. But we can imagine.

What's surprising is not that Barry *didn't* leave a record of her love life but that there's *any* mention of it at all.

Becoming romantically involved with anyone was one of the quickest ways to get caught at passing. For a woman who cared more for her career than anything else, it's doubtful she would have risked everything for love. In fact, it appears that she was so fearful of getting caught that she never even wrote her mother once she entered the military. She didn't want to give anyone any lead.

Many lesbians did have liaisons with other women, some even took wives. However, according to Dekker and van de Pol, passing as a man was often seen as the first step to becoming gay:

"Transvestism must not be seen as a disguise for the world, but as a step that psychologically enabled a woman to court another woman. In other words, while nowadays lesbianism is not felt as a problem of gender, in the seventeenth and eighteenth centuries it was."

But love was dangerous. Romance was the downfall of many of the women. Look what happened to "George" Hamilton. She might not have gotten posthumous fame and a novel written about her had she not tried to marry. It might have been seen as patriotic to pass as a man, but to take a wife (or a lover) pushed it beyond the pale if you got caught. To quote Dekker and van de Pol:

"Cases of cross-dressing drew most attention when the disguised women courted or married other women."

But some did. And some were successful.

The hunter Lucy Ann "Joseph" Lobdell married another woman; Ralph Keriwinieo married twice, and Edward de Lacy Evans married three times.

But just as often, love backfired. Ralph Kerwinieo was exposed by a jilted girlfriend. Both Ethel "James Hathaway" Kimbal and Lillian Arkel "Col. Sir Victor Barker" Smith were discovered when a sharp-eyed court clerk realized they were impersonating men when they applied for a marriage license.

If the women succeeded, that only created another whole set of problems: mainly what to do on the wedding night, at least if the other woman wasn't already in on the secret.

Billy Tipton claimed he had a "war injury" that prevented "him" from having sex.

But many women tried to pass in this arena, too.

Anne "Jean Baptiste" Grandjean's wife claimed not to know her husband was a female. Over the centuries, dildos have been fashioned from leather, wood, and ivory, among other materials, with pig's bladders tied to the end to make the impersonation complete. And certainly, with the prevalence of "strap-on" tools, it's easy to understand how the cover of darkness could be a great aid to disguise even in this most intimate of settings.

The problem with a dildo, however, is that it really got the woman into trouble if she got caught. The few women, like Catharine Linck, who have been burned at the stake as punishment for lesbianism were convicted on evidence of dildos. Women caught for such transgressions as "being lewd on a bed" generally got lighter sentences—a whipping, for example.

No matter what the bedchamber solution, relatives were an even greater cause of stress for the passing woman. Catharine Linck's mother-in-law turned her in after her daughter and Linck had a fight and the distraught woman had turned to her mother for comfort—or for revenge.

Of course some women such as Henrica Schuria, were so good at passing that even once they were caught, their lovers said they would gladly marry them if they could.

Martin Grief in *The Gay Book of Days* says Barry had an affair with a woman who stopped at the island of Mauritius when Barry was stationed there in 1829. Pregnant when she left for New South Wales from India, Mrs. Fenton gave birth to her baby, a girl named Flora, in Mauritius. Mrs. Fenton was already intrigued by Barry.

"There is something about this same Dr. Barry," she wrote in the journal that was published ten years after Barry's death.

Prior to meeting Barry, Fenton said she had been told by a nurse also stationed in India that Barry was a woman. After Fenton gave birth, she records that she and Barry were both at loose ends. Apparently, they often toured the island together because it seemed "both agreeable and natural."

Perhaps Mrs. Fenton knew so much about Dr. Barry because she had firsthand knowledge that she wasn't about to admit. After all, her husband was nowhere near and they were both "on the wing," as she termed it.

The affair was cut short by the news that Dr. Barry's closest friend in South Africa, Lord Charles Somerset, the former governor of Cape Town, was dying. Barry rushed to the scene. Even though she went AWOL, she did not get into trouble. But she never returned to Mauritius or Mrs. Fenton.

There were also rumors about Barry's relationship with Lord Somerset during the years at the Cape.

It was a time of particularly volatile political intrigue—the governor might have been a friend, but he was also a despot. A flyer was put up that said he and Barry were lovers. It was pulled down immediately and a reward offered but no one was ever caught.

Most biographers attribute the incident to political intrigue. But there is another possibility, far worse than the fact biographers think people suspected her of being a woman.

After meeting her at dinner, Lord Albemarle wrote Barry had a "certain effeminacy in his manner which he was always striving to overcome."

If people didn't suspect Barry of being a woman, they undoubtedly thought "he" was gay. As such, the flyer linking Barry and the governor would have been very disturbing. The reward offered—eighty-five hundred rix dollars, which was many times Barry's salary—makes it seem so. An affair between a man and a woman might be cause for comment but it would hardly be enough for a scandalous flyer. If the implication were that they were homosexual lovers, however, the flyer would make more sense. Other references to Barry and Lord Somerset also reek of the same homophobia. Barry was often called Somerset's "little wife."

Biographers have tried to construct a time period during which Barry could have disappeared long enough to have a child. Rose thinks it was during the time she went AWOL but Rae feels that once Barry's career was established, there are no gaps in the record during which she could have remained isolated long enough to hide a pregnancy.

Try as she might, and despite the subterfuges she took to prevent people suspecting the truth, there were always suspicions about Barry's gender—or sexual orientation.

After her death, when the true nature of her sex became known, people said they had always suspected her of being a woman. And they might have. But Epimetheus was always a lesser god than Prometheus for good reason. Hindsight is of little use to anyone. It's always easier to say you know something when the secret is out.

No one, however, seems to have confronted her. Whether they couldn't be bothered, whether her reputation as a doctor, or her friendship with the most powerful official in the colony protected her, we'll never know. But here, too, there is another possibility, a gayer possibility.

Cross-dressing women were a fairly well-known phenomena, enough so that people felt there was a precedent, a tradition even, as Dekker and van de Pol argue. It might not have protected them from prying eyes or vicious gossip, but it *might* have protected them from direct accusations.

Barry did play the part well. At a time when physical exercise was thought to be harmful for a woman, Barry was considered an accomplished sportsman. According to biographer Rose, Barry always led the hunt, was considered a "superb marksman," and was good with a whip.

"She could often be seen driving her carriage with four high-spirited greys through . . . town," wrote Rose.

Barry also was known to follow up any affront to her "manhood" by challenging the offender to a duel, although she probably only fought one duel in which neither "man" was killed.

It gets harder and harder to hide a woman's gender as she ages. At best, Barry was short, beardless, and effeminate. "Passing as a beardless lad" only works so long. The older she got, the more eccentric she

seemed. Perhaps she knew and understood this—and created another
ruse to stop people from inquiring: in her old age, she was considered
argumentative and querulous.

We will never know the true story of Barry's private life, but given
her amazing accomplishments that hardly matters. Despite the lack of a
"love interest," she pulled off many amazing feats. And, like Florence
Nightingale, she fought for the dignity of people less fortunate than
she, no matter what their class or race. By the end of her career, she
had brought antiseptic conditions to hospitals and sickrooms, introduced
indoor plumbing in at least one locale, as well as abolishing the open
sewers in the area.

Keeping up with the latest medical advances—without the aid of
magazines or computer bulletin boards—she also used the smallpox
vaccination nearly two decades before it was introduced in England.
Had she been better at public relations, that, in addition to some of her
other accomplishments, might be in the records books today.

Barry Meets Nightingale

Whatever the oddities of her gender, it didn't seem to endanger her
career. Barry seems to have done that all by herself.

When the chance came, the officials she had fought over the treatment
of prisoners in Cape Town blocked a promotion that, by rights, should
have been hers. It was the first of many career setbacks caused by her
belief that right triumphed over might.

When Barry made enemies, she made enemies who were out for
blood. She not only lost at least two promotions but even got court-
martialed—not once but twice! She got through unscathed, but it broke
something in her. As she got older, she started playing the game and
learned more about using "channels," but until then she went "over
the boss's head" whenever she met a bureaucratic brick wall.

Perhaps because she led such an extraordinary life and had overcome
such incredible obstacles, she felt nothing could stand in her way. Her
life certainly seemed proof that she could get away with anything. But
quietly carrying on a masquerade was quite different than bucking the
system at every turn.

At St. Helena, the British colony just off the coast of Africa, Barry
had to pay the price.

In fact, Barry ran into the same set of problems Florence Nightingale later had with the British Army—a bureaucracy that only thought about cost, and the sick person's welfare be damned.

In Barry's case, the year was 1836, twenty years earlier than the time Nightingale served in the Crimea. There were no reporters at St. Helena; no one in England had any idea what was going on there. And no one cared. Unfortunately for Barry, she wasn't the diplomat Nightingale was and the results were disastrous. Once the wheels began turning, there was no saving her.

Faced with an intractable bureaucracy, Nightingale bided her time until disaster struck. Then she stepped in to save the day.

Barry did just the opposite. She no sooner arrived on the island than she took charge of the hospital and began demanding reforms. She had just set foot on the island when she found cases of dysentery in massive numbers—caused by something that could easily be fixed: the terrible food.

She recommended a varied diet. The officials in charge thought she was mad. How could diet have anything to do with illness? Where would they get the extra food anyway? They could barely afford to have the existing rations shipped in.

As if that weren't enough, Barry also found a high rate of venereal disease at the hospital, compounded by the fact that men and women, as well as the mentally ill, were housed in one facility.

In fact, most of the women had been forced into prostitution when the East India Company, one of the world's largest trading companies in its day, left the island and took the women's jobs with it. Barry demanded a separate hospital for the women and another for the mentally ill. And all hell broke loose. Asking for fancy extras in the diet was one thing, but asking for two brand-new hospitals was beyond comprehension.

Barry wouldn't give in. She fought and fought, writing letters to everyone she could, going to the very top, the Secretary of State at the War Office in England. But she was only in charge of the hospital, not the island itself. The governor of the post, who was also the head of the military on the island, threw her into the brig for questioning his authority.

Ironically, she was cited for "conduct unbecoming the character of an Officer and a Gentleman" in her court-martial. If only they had known what they were saying!

Barry was held for two weeks without trial. She was eventually acquitted, which only made her more certain of her cause, not less. She kept up the fight, and less than a year later, got at least one of her demands—a separate wing for female patients at the hospital.

Barry might have triumphed in the end, but she hadn't learned anything about working the system. Less than a year later, she was in trouble again.

The second court-martial involved her salary, though the real reason must have been her unwillingness to follow protocol. According to biographers, the records have been lost, so we will never know what the actual charges were. It seems that officials were simply tired of her unyielding persistence and planned to get rid of her once and for all. This time they sent her to London for trial when she was arrested.

In her defense, she said something truly striking:

"If for a single instant, I could imagine I have lost sight of the character of a gentleman I should have spared this or any other tribunal the task of investigating my conduct."

Barry's definition of a gentleman was undoubtedly broader than the usual, encompassing traits of compassion as well as everything else. But if Barry didn't think of herself as a man, this was certainly a great plea. Which worked.

Despite the biographic brouhaha about her gender, the court-martial brings us to the firmest piece of evidence we have that no one in the Army suspected Barry of being a woman. If questions about her gender existed, she would have been court-martialed for that immediately. It would have been simple to prove—and it would have gotten her out of the military fast. This glaring historic omission leads to the conclusion that Barry's sex was not questioned. She was seen not only as a bitchy troublemaker but a cranky little Nellie. No wonder people were so relieved to find out she was *only* a woman! That solved the whole problem very neatly, with much less disruption to society than if she had been gay.

Barry gave a spirited defense and was acquitted. But her departure from the island, under court-martial, shows a marked contrast to the doctor who arrived less than two years earlier in all her military glory.

An eyewitness said she looked:

". . . faded and crestfallen. He was in plain clothes. . . . His blue jacket hung loosely about him, his white trousers were a world too wide, the veil garnishing his broad straw hat covered his face, and he carried the inevitable umbrella over his head so that it saved him from the general gaze."

She might have been bent but she was not broken.

Not even fear of causing trouble stopped Barry from practicing medicine. And she did help change the world. She was one of the first modern dieticians, one of the first people to advocate a healthy, varied diet as a means of preventing illness.

A vegetarian who brought a goat with her for milk and gave her daily ration of meat to her dog, Barry was only ill once in thirty-two years—thirty-two years of living in foreign countries and being exposed to germs and diseases for which she had no built-up immunity. Ironically, as she got older people said that her short stature and feminine demeanor were caused by her vegetarian diet.

No matter where she was posted, she constantly pushed for better food for hospital patients—including fresh vegetables, which were almost unheard of at the time. Although she drank nothing but water in an era when wine and ale were considered essential, she understood the benefits of moderate wine consumption as a source of vitamin C, if nothing else.

Barry's understanding of the concept of germs again places her far ahead of her time. One of her many ''eccentricities,'' she would wash fruit and vegetables before eating them to get rid of the ''animalculae'' on them. At a time when people never even washed their hands, this was probably one of the simplest actions anyone could do to protect his health.

At a time also when bathing was thought to be dangerous, she knew that cleanliness was essential. She demanded that the sick be bathed, an unheard-of idea then. She also said that their clothing as well as their bed, needed to be changed often. She demanded wounds be cleaned daily (often with alcohol, an antiseptic) and the bandages changed. Surprising as it seems today, this was another revolutionary idea.

Though Barry was born twenty to twenty-five years before Florence Nightingale, both women shared an understanding of medicine that was far ahead of its time. To them, the bottom line was hygiene, hygiene, hygiene. Both knew that people could not get well—and would only get sicker—in conditions of filth. Despite their differing ages and differing paths, one wonders what would have happened if the two women had been able to combine forces. Florence, the ultimate feminine charmer and Barry, the masculine, unrelenting fighter. What a powerful duo that could have been!

As fate would have it, they did meet.

Barry *was* posted in the Mediterranean during the Crimean War, not far from Nightingale and the fighting. During a vacation, Barry went to visit Nightingale's hospital under the auspices of Lord Raglan, the youngest brother of Barry's old friend, the governor of Cape Town. Though Raglan might have been a great hero to Barry, Nightingale hated him. Nightingale saw Raglan, the Commander-in-Chief of the Crimea, as an aristocratic blowhard and a major impediment to her reforms. Which put her at immediate odds with Barry.

For all the trouble she had with the military, Barry still identified with it. It was not only her career, it was her life. She had sacrificed everything for it.

By the time Nightingale and Barry met, the military was under severe attack in England for its handling of the wounded. For the first time in the Crimean War, a journalist had gone out with the troops. And what a difference it made. Writing back to England, the reporter made the public aware of the horrible conditions the troops not only lived in but died under. Though the sanitary conditions were typical of the era, that—combined with the complete lack of medical supplies—created a tremendous uproar. Nightingale had gone out to Scutari under the blessing of the Secretary of War. But she had no idea what she was getting into. Conditions were much worse than even the reporter had let on. There was nothing but bare walls at the hospital, no equipment, no beds, linens, bandages, tools for surgery—nothing. There wasn't even decent food. And to make matters worse, there was open sewage in the hospitals. A setup for disaster.

At Corfu, Barry had already instituted many of the reforms for which Nightingale later won fame. Of the 260 veterans Barry treated at Corfu in 1855, only 17 died. Total. By contrast, at Scutari—where Nightingale was waging her battle to institute the same reforms on a more massive scale—the death rate was 23 *per day*.

When the two women met, Barry was the old hand, the official representing the military. Newly arrived but already exhausted, Nightingale was the do-gooder, the outsider who didn't know what was going on.

Barry was sixty years old, a world-reknowned expert in her field, confident in the knowledge of her expertise, while Nightingale was just starting out. Young, relatively inexperienced, overworked, and facing the might of the British Army, Nightingale was none too happy to see this spy of Lord Raglan's descending on her.

We don't know what Barry said, but whatever it was, it rubbed

Nightingale the wrong way. Nightingale wrote, as quoted by biographer Woodham-Smith:

"I never had such a blackguard rating in my life—I who have had more than any woman—than from Barry sitting on [her] horse while I was crossing the hospital square with only my cap on in the sun. [She] kept me standing . . . during the scolding I received while [she] behaved like a brute."

Nightingale called Barry "the most hardened creature I ever met throughout the army."

It's too bad they didn't realize that despite the differences of age, affiliation, and temperament, they had two important things in common. They were both not only women, but women fighting the same cause.

Barry's last position was in Canada, as the Inspector-General of hospitals there. If the military wanted to get rid of her, Canada was certainly the way to do it.

She was approaching what would have been the age of retirement for most people. Nonetheless, Barry faced two furiously cold winters in Canada before she became so ill, she had to be sent home.

Despite her advancing years, she still made an impressive sight in the white snows of Canada in winter.

"Wrapped in musk ox robes, she travelled round the city in a magnificent red sleigh, complete with silver bells, coachman and footman," writes Isobel Rae.

Although Barry rarely got sick, her last illness forced her to retire. Being the scrapper she was, she appealed that, too, for it cost her some of her pension.

She might have retired from the military, but she didn't retire from life. She lived another six years and traveled during much of the cold, damp English winters. She often went to the Caribbean, whose tropical climate she had loved so much when posted there. She also spent the occasional season, as was the custom of the day, at Whitehaven Castle as the guest of a friend, the Earl of Lonsdale.

By then, she was somewhat bitter. She was known, at least in circles where ease and politeness were valued, as caustic and argumentative. After so many years, the subterfuge must have taken its emotional and mental toll. Anyone who has ever been in the closet knows how hard it is to lie, to omit some facts and change others, day in and day out. Barry must have been prey to some of the same fears: the fear that discovery would lead to the loss of livelihood, humiliation, and scandal.

What Barry suffered in this regard must have been at least as bad, if not worse, than being in the closet.

After years of working in the tropics and living a man's life, Barry probably also found the drawing rooms of England stifling in more than one way.

Ironically, Barry died during what was called a flu epidemic, from the open sewers which Barry herself had gotten rid of in her postings abroad. But in 1865, they still existed in England and were particularly dangerous during the summer.

Although she expected to die as quietly as she had lived, it was at her death that word of her amazing masquerade got out.

For months, the papers were filled with stories of the woman who became a doctor and rose to the rank of Major-General in the British Army by passing as a man. For those who did not believe in women's education, who said, as Samuel Johnson did of women preaching that like a dog walking on hind legs, it is not that it is done well but that it is done at all, the discovery must have been quite upsetting.

For those who believed women were inferior, that their brains were too small to be educated, Barry's discovery must have been quite a shock.

James Miranda Barry

1795 Barry probably born in London between 1795 and 1799
1809 Enters Edinburgh University as a med student
1812 Awarded Doctor of Medicine
1816 Appointed Colonial Medical Inspector, South Africa
1826 Performs successful Caesarean section
     Court-martialed and acquitted
1828 Posted to Mauritius
1831 Posted to Jamaica
1836 Appointed Principal Medical Officer, St. Helena
     Court-martialed and acquitted a second time
1839 Demoted to Staff Surgeon, sent to West Indies
1842 Promoted to Principal Medical Officer, Trinidad
1845 Returns to England
1846 Appointed Principal Medical Officer, Malta
1851 Posted to Corfu as Deputy Inspector General

1855 Visits Florence Nightingale at Scutari
1857 Appointed to Inspector General of Hospitals, Canada
Invited to join the newly formed, all-male St. James Club in Montreal
1859 Becomes ill with bronchitis; is sent back to England
1861 Dies of summer flu epidemic in London, thought to be between 61 and 66 years of age

Note that dating events exactly is extremely difficult, as biographers often disagree on year. I have tried to use dates from the most credible sources, where available.

Chapter Two

FLORENCE NIGHTINGALE

Because she couldn't pass as a man, Florence Nightingale had to fight her family for fifteen years to do what she wanted with her life. Luckily for her, she was a drama queen of the most magnificent sort. Like her mother and sister, her emotional displays were grandly operatic! She had hysterics, she fainted, she got ill. When she came home in triumph from the Crimea, she took to her bed permanently. It was the only way to get rid of her family once and for all.

Throughout her life, Nightingale used emotions as weapons—the only weapon, really, women had at the time. She was never going to speak to her mother again if she didn't get to study at Kaiserworth Hospital, in reality, a three-week jaunt during the summer to see how it was run, hardly a life-and-death matter. After the Crimea, she thought she was going to die if her family didn't leave her alone and let her live in peace. After her great love, her aunt Mai, left her, Florence took twenty years to forgive her.

In the midst of all this drama, Nightingale got a lot done. She fought a major battle with the British Army to change the way military hospitals were run. She introduced the idea of hygiene into civilian hospitals in Great Britain and India. And she changed the profession of nursing from one that only drunkards and hookers fell back on to one of dignity.

And Florence had many people in her life: three women she loved passionately, two female mentors, and a man who became her friend and "front," the man who helped her change the course of the British Empire.

Her first love was Marianne Nicholson, a cousin. She wrote, to quote Cecil Woodham-Smith's biography, *Florence Nightingale*:

" 'I have never loved but one person with passion in my life and that was her.'

"Marianne was dazzlingly beautiful. . . . She had exceptional musical gifts, an exquisite soprano voice, and possessed a confidence in her own charm which enabled her to dare anything."

Well, almost anything. Neither Florence nor Marianne had the courage of the Ladies of Llangollen, cousins sixteen years apart who defied family not once but twice by eloping when the youngest became of marriageable age. The two women went to Wales, with a servant known as Molly the Bruiser, to live happily ever after and to become the model for the romantic friends movement of the eighteenth and nineteenth century.

Though Florence was passionately in love with Marianne, she wasn't sure Marianne felt the same. If anything, Marianne only seemed to care about her family, especially her brother Henry.

Florence was meeting many men and had expected to find a husband. But she soon began to realize that what she really wanted was to be left alone to study.

In trying to see Marianne, Florence invariably ended up seeing Henry, who began to fall in love with her. Not knowing what to do, not wanting to give up Marianne, she encouraged Henry. She even thought about marrying him. In fact, many women did end up marrying brothers as a way of becoming part of a desired sister's family. If she didn't have any choice, if she had to marry anyway, if the married couple could live in the family home with the sister, it was often the best of a bad situation for less hardy lesbians.

(Lesbian poet Emily Dickinson had encouraged Susan Gilbert to marry her brother in order to have Susan near her. Only later did she realize it wasn't a very good solution and turned her affections to others, such as Kate Scott Turner.)

But according to Woodham-Smith, Marianne was dangerous.

She was unpredictable, swinging from cruelty to kindness, truth to lies without apparent motive.

Perhaps she wasn't in love with Florence the way Florence was in love with her. Woodham-Smith writes of Florence:

"She was deeply, furiously, discontented, with life and with herself. Her infatuation with Marianne was perpetual torture. She had let Henry fall more in love with her than ever. . . . Her life at home was hateful;

impossible that God should have bestowed the gift of time on His female creatures to be used ... 'faddling twaddling and the endless tweedling of nosegays ...,' " as Clarkey, the woman who would become her mentor, called it.

For six years, Florence encouraged Henry in order to be close to Marianne. Then Henry made a fatal error: he proposed—and demanded an answer.

Florence had to decide what she was going to do. She couldn't continue to string him along. But she realized she couldn't marry him just to be near his sister. She had to break it off. She said no. She wrote another cousin, who would also figure in her life:

"I was not true either to her or to myself in our friendship. I was afraid of her: that is the truth."

Furious with the betrayal of her brother and the embarrassment a rejection after six years of courtship caused, Marianne ended the friendship.

Florence was in agony. Ever dramatic, she wrote that she paced the garden in the evening and asked why God had forsaken her.

Florence was so distraught at losing Marianne, she thought of becoming a nun. But on learning a bit about Catholicism, she decided it wasn't for her. She was much too independent-minded for organized religion.

Marianne didn't speak to Florence for more than a decade, and when she did, it was in revenge. Interestingly enough, Marianne's attempt at revenge only succeeded in catapulting Florence into her dreams.

Whatever Florence's dreams or the fight it took to achieve them, Nightingale's training ground for combat strategy was her family, with whom she battled for fifteen years before she was allowed to do what she wanted.

In Nightingale's day, it was unheard of for a middle-class woman to have a career. A woman going out to work who didn't need the money was unthinkable; she would only bring disgrace to the well-to-do family. The battle Nightingale fought with her family is almost as fascinating as her love life.

The youngest of two daughters, Florence was her father's favorite, a fact that would come in handy in the last years of the familial war. At a time when formal schooling for girls was nonexistent and their "education" consisted of such geishalike attainments as playing the piano, she and her sister, Parthe, were tutored by their father. W.E.N. taught them Greek and Latin, as well as French, German, and Italian.

As such, Nightingale had a classical education almost unheard of for a woman of her day.

Flo worked hard, and at a young age became her scholarly, introverted father's intellectual companion, discussing history and philosophy with him while her sister planned parties and dinners with her outgoing and vivacious mother, Fanny.

Florence tried to please her mother and wrote that she was "trying to learn to curl her hair." But her heart wasn't in it. At fifteen, she already knew that she craved some regular occupation, "something worth doing instead of frittering time away on useless trifles." But it would take her nearly twenty years to be allowed that.

A year later—the point at which she was about to debut in London society—Florence heard the voice of God. He told her to dedicate her life to service, though unfortunately for her, he didn't say what kind.

Florence thought about joining a convent and turned to another woman who became her mentor for a few years. Marianne's aunt Hannah was a very devout woman, the perfect person for Florence to turn to once she had seen God. In long letters, Florence poured out her heart to Hannah who encouraged her to hold forth, hold on to her vision. In letter after letter, Hannah kept reminding her that God would speak in time and guide her.

Although Florence still didn't know what she wanted to do, she knew what she *didn't* want to do: She didn't want to get married. Her family had no idea she had seen God nor did they believe she could find a life different from that expected of her. And the family was none too pleased when they began to suspect they had a rebel on their hands.

At the time, getting married was the only way to have any independence or freedom. Marriage not only could merge family wealth but it often united families of lower standing, bringing them into a higher realm. Florence's mother hoped to seal the family's position in society by making a good marriage for her daughters.

Florence, the brightest, was at the top of the family list. Her mother Fanny had no suspicion that anything was amiss. Everyone who met Florence was impressed. Social butterflies were surprised by her wit and charm. Serious reformers were astounded by her immediate grasp of issues and problems. Florence would have had no trouble finding a husband who would make Fanny happy—if that's what she had wanted.

Prior to her "coming out," Florence's family spent eighteen months in Europe waiting for their house to be rebuilt to accommodate the eighty extra people who always came to stay when a daughter debuted. There were masked balls till dawn and private plays directed by well known Shakespearean actors.

A frantic amount of gaiety was had by all except Florence. It did nothing but wear her out.

In Europe, however, the world began to look different, broader. For the first time, Florence got a taste of what was going on outside her mother's circumscribed realm. For the first time, Florence met Italian patriots and French bohemians. For the first time, she saw the intellectual world of the famous Parisian salon held by Mary Clarke, who would become a mentor for life.

Clarkey, as Florence dubbed her, held a salon where women were seen not only as the intellectual equals of men but were also regarded as friends, instead of wives and lovers.

Clarkey had a deep friendship with a man named Claude Fauriel. They met daily. It was obvious they respected each other in addition to being devoted to each other. They weren't married, but it was still perfectly respectable. This relationship made Florence realize that women could work with men, something she had never seen before. It set the pattern for her relationships with men for the rest of her life.

In Europe, Florence also began to lay the foundation for the network of friends who sent her the documents to study in secret that would make her an expert on health care. But first she had to escape not only the marriage market but her own self-doubts.

Nightingale was up against every barrier imaginable. Unlike Jane Addams who realized very early that she wanted to help the poor, Nightingale didn't know what she wanted to do. Because her family wouldn't allow her to do anything but socialize, she saw herself frittering away time in a meaningless social whirl, in balls and parties, dinners and visits. While she enjoyed the attention that her beauty and wit brought, it wasn't enough. No matter how much fun it was, socializing only left her frustrated and depressed. And she worried she wouldn't be ready—or worthy—if God ever deigned to let her know exactly what he wanted.

Once back in England, Florence became ill—which was to become a pattern throughout her life. Depressed, fearful that she would never escape her family, physical illness overwhelmed her.

At this point, a woman twenty years her senior, a woman Florence would rely on to save her again and again over the years, rescued her.

Her father's sister, Mai, visited at Christmas. Seeing Aunt Mai and spending time with her brought Florence out of her lethargy.

The difference of two decades in their ages hardly mattered. Emotionally, they were perfectly suited to each other. Both were intellectual as well as spiritual, a rare combination in those days. What was more, Mai recognized Florence's gifts, her ability to lead and inspire others.

Despite the age gap, Mai was soon the pupil, Florence the teacher. To quote Woodham-Smith:

"They were now close friends, no longer fond aunt and adoring little niece but equals reveling in closest intimacy. . . . In spite of their difference in age [Mai] worshiped Florence with the worship of a disciple of a master. She placed Florence above ordinary humanity, above the claims even of her husband and her children, and became her protector, interpreter, and consoler."

Just as important, Mai began running interference with Florence's family, taking Florence's side in the growing battle, slowly helping her escape their hold and fulfill her destiny.

Married with a family of her own, Aunt Mai was only to become Florence's companion for a few years, moving in with her and caring for her when Florence thought she was dying. Until their break some years later, they were devoted to each other.

Of Mai, Florence said they were "like two lovers."

Finding Herself

The summer Florence lost Marianne, she found a way out of her depression by turning to action. And through action, she found her calling. She began simply enough, by nursing family members who were ill—a suitable occupation for a woman as long as it did not interfere with her one real obligation: socializing. She took care of her aging grandmother and an old family servant. Then she expanded and began to nurse sick people in the surrounding villages. During the autumn, she was present at a birth and two deathbeds, an almost unheard-of thing for a woman of her station. In the process, she realized her calling.

But nursing wasn't a respectable occupation in those days. It was the last resort of drunken women who couldn't keep a job and part-time prostitutes. There was no training, no schools. Women simply sat with the ill or dying, if they weren't actually in bed with them or passed out drunk on the floor. When Florence suggested to her family that she go to a hospital to study nursing, they were horrified. To quote gay historian Lytton Strachey's *Eminent Victorians*:

"A 'nurse' meant then a coarse old woman, always ignorant, usually dirty, often brutal, a Mrs. Gamp, in bunched-up sordid garments, tippling at the brandy-bottle . . . they could hardly be trusted to carry out the simplest medical duties."

What was even more horrifying, nurses were expected to be *in the same room* as naked men—and worse, *touch* them.

Florence's father, who had spent his own time on her education, was infuriated. For this, he had spent years teaching his beloved daughter, his star pupil, Latin and Greek?

To quote Strachey: " 'It was as if,' " she herself said afterward, " 'I had wanted to be a kitchen-maid.' "

But Florence's mental state was getting worse. Her family was adamant that she follow the prescribed route of upper-class women of her day into a good marriage. Working was out of the question.

Florence began to escape by dreaming and falling into trancelike states. Bored to tears with frivolous conversation, she found herself escaping into reveries, not only in the privacy of her own room but at dinner parties. There was no question she preferred fantasies to table talk, but when she started doing it in public, she got scared. She was afraid that if she was forced to continue her life the way it was, she would never come back from one of her trances. She knew of the mad women "locked in the attic" because they couldn't cope.

In addition to massive letters and voluminous diary entries, Florence wrote a story appropriately entitled "Cassandra." It described the life of a young woman as she went through her trivia-filled day—and the exhaustion and depression that eventually kills her. At age thirty-one she wrote, quoting Strachey, "I see nothing desirable but death."

As if that weren't bad enough, Florence was being courted by the most eligible bachelor in all of England, Richard Monckton Milnes, editor and publisher of the first collected poems of Keats. He was perfect for Florence. In addition to his literary learnings, he was a reformer whose work eventually led to British juveniles being sent to reform school rather than jailed with adults. What was Florence's problem, her family moaned? She wasn't going to have those beautiful reddish-brown tresses forever. If she didn't marry someone soon, she would be too old and decrepit. At twenty, a woman was considered past her prime!

Florence had to admit she was drawn to Milnes's politics and to his keen mind. But she was scared of marriage. True, it would have gotten her away from the stranglehold of her mother and from the day-in, day-out socializing. She knew she would lose her independence, however. She also feared no one would take her seriously if she were Milnes's *wife*. What about her dreams, her calling? Marriage wasn't part of God's plan.

Just as she had done with Henry, Florence held Richard off as long as she could. After waiting for seven years, Milne demanded an answer. Florence said no, even contemplating suicide at the thought of a life that could only be a continuation of what she was then living.

Writing the book probably got the fantasy of suicide out of her system. And nursing sick relatives had given her a vocation. Which was a good thing because when Florence rejected Milne, all hell broke loose.

For her mother, it was a simple question of making Florence obey. Allowing her to rebel would bring disgrace on everyone. For her sister Parthe, who didn't attract beaux the way Florence did, it meant more waiting while Florence toyed with perfectly decent young men. If Florence, the family's pride and joy, disgraced herself with this ridiculous idea, the scandal would be so great Parthe would never be able to catch a husband or marry well.

For Florence, it was a matter of life and death.

Florence refused to give in, her mother refused to give in. It was a standoff. Pulling out all the stops, Fanny wept and accused Florence of having a secret love affair with a surgeon. She began telling friends what was going on, even weeping in front of them. It was most embarrassing for all concerned—especially the audience of friends and family.

Florence and her mother weren't the only hysterics in the family. Her sister threw her bracelets in Florence's face and screamed so violently, Florence fainted. The battles and high drama continued more or less unabated for eight years.

Parthe took to saying that she couldn't live without Florence. She would fall into hysterics whenever Florence mentioned going anywhere—even out of the house. Friends and relatives began to question whether Parthe didn't have a "morbid" attachment to Florence.

The theatrics got so bad, her father moved into his men's club in London to escape.

By the autumn of 1847, Florence collapsed and took to her bed after writing to a friend that she could not face "the prospect of three winter months of perpetual row" with her family.

The only thing that saved her were friends of the family who offered to take her to Italy to recuperate. There, surrounded by liberal reformers who wanted to change the world, she began to come to life again.

And there, she met Sydney Herbert, the man who would later become the comrade-in-arms she was looking for—and Secretary of State. She also determined that she was going to get what she wanted. She just had to make her family see it was the only way.

Her buoyancy lasted until she returned to England. But this time instead of worrying and becoming ill, Florence got up at dawn to read reports on hospitals and public health, preparing herself by studying in secret. She not only read about England but used the liberal-minded contacts she had made in Europe to obtain reports from other countries. She still did "housekeeping" as required, making an inventory of the food, linen, china, glass, and other necessities of an estate that consisted of servants and visiting relatives as well as an extended family. But she saw it differently. Now, her chores were giving her the training she would need when she was finally able to run her own hospital and order supplies by the thousands.

She studied and waited. There was no job in sight, her family was being as pigheaded as usual. Florence came up with suggestions. She visited a hospital while her mother and sister were "taking the waters" at a nearby spa. But the cost of the emotional damage was high. Liberal friends and family, including Aunt Mai, began to intervene. Florence was extraordinarily intelligent and determined. They decided they had to get her away from her home.

On a trip to Greece, Florence was able to make a detour to visit hospitals in Berlin and Kaiserswerth. For the "inspection," she spent two weeks. As soon as she got home, she wrote a thirty-two-page essay which was printed anonymously in 1851 about the training nurses received there.

In the Mediterranean, she acquired a baby owl which she named Athena. Florence hypnotized it to calm it. It eventually became so tame, it traveled in her pocket everywhere.

By 1851, she had decided there was no point in trying to persuade her family—she needed just to fight.

"I must expect no help or sympathy from them," she wrote.

Her father ended up saving her. He had originally been against her "throwing herself away." But during the years that the battle raged, times changed. Friends and relatives began to side with Florence. W.E.N. tired of the battlefront that his home had become. To his wife's horror, he agreed to give Florence £500 a year to live on, a lot back then. Enough to give her economic freedom.

In April 1853, Liz Herbert (Sydney Herbert's wife, who had also become one of Florence's friends) heard of a position as superintendent of a hospital for women, excruciatingly called the Institution for the Care of Sick Gentlewomen in Distressed Circumstances.

Florence, in her mid-thirties, was considered extremely young to be taking charge of a hospital. But since it was going under anyway, the hiring committee probably decided they didn't have much to lose. She impressed them with her knowledge and her enthusiasm, but to get the job she had to agree to bring a personal attendant, a "superior elderly respectable person" as her chaperone.

Nightingale probably never would have been hired if it hadn't been for her old flame, Marianne. Her family was still against it; Nicholson let it be known to members of the committee that the very thought of the job had caused a tremendous break between Florence and her family, that there were daily rows. Though everyone knew it, Florence's mother was infuriated at having her dirty laundry aired in public by someone else. She and Parthe, as well as W.E.N., rallied behind Florence—and after nearly a decade of opposing her every move for independence, publicly said they were behind her.

Florence got the job but she got no pay. She even had to support her chaperone. But she was able to leave the family home to live at the hospital. (It was unthinkable for her to live alone. Decades later when Virginia Woolf moved to Bloomsbury with her brother, it was considered scandalous that an adult wasn't present to chaperone, and protect, her.)

Florence was in charge of everything at the hospital but its finances. She could finally start to put all her theories into practice. Sixteen years after realizing she had to create a career in a world where careers for women didn't exist, Florence was finally on the road to starting one. And what a career it was! Before she was through, she would take on the might of the British Army as well as the colonial government in India and succeed.

The Crimean War

Stereotypes sometimes have little, if any, connection to reality. Seen as a pure, self-sacrificing angel—the Lady with the Lamp—Florence Nightingale was in reality a workaholic who drove herself and her associates to exhaustion and a visionary with a mind like a steel trap who could remember minute details from thousands of documents, yet not lose sight of the larger issues involved.

Nightingale never actually worked for any length of time as a nurse. But she became a legend in her own time. Thousands of soldiers returning from war who had been treated like dirt until Florence arrived, thousands of wounded soldiers hospitalized in appallingly dirty conditions told of her fight to treat them like human beings, to give the wounded simple necessities like blankets and bedding, clean clothes and decent food—and amazing as it may seem today—a floor to walk on that wasn't covered in excrement.

Thousands of survivors, thanking Nightingale for their very lives, returned to England telling the tale of the woman who insisted on dignity for the wounded. Had Nightingale not been there, they would have died or been treated like dogs.

The legend came not from the fight with military to give the men dignity but from a simple vow that no one should die alone. To meet that promise, Nightingale went without sleep for days on end, staying up night after night with her lamp to keep watch and give comfort at deathbeds.

From this continuing act of charity, a legend grew. At age thirty-five, a few years after getting her first job, there were songs about her; newborn daughters named after her; even ships given the name *Florence*. England's most famous statue maker, Staffordshire, did a tabletop ceramic of her that sold thousands. A biography fed the public's craving for details—though pictures of Florence had almost no resemblance to her since she wouldn't allow a portrait to be used.

In other words, the Crimean War changed Nightingale's life. At the time, the British Army was thought, at least by the British, to be the best in the world. But conditions for the soldier were deplorable; conditions for the wounded unimaginable.

When Nightingale arrived at Scutari, at the British Army hospital on the outskirts of Constantinople, there were no bandages for wounds, no splints for broken bones. Soldiers were laid on bare ground—or on straw mixed with manure—like animals in a barn.

There was no kitchen, not even cups or buckets to bring water, much less food. Doctors were in such short supply, the wounded were lucky if they ever saw one. Nightingale calculated there were four miles of beds—and no supplies.

Anesthesia for surgery had just been discovered and wasn't used much. Army leaders argued *against* it, giving examples of courageous acts by generals that they thought everyone should follow. They argued that if a British aristocrat such as Lord Raglan chose to have his arm amputated without anesthetic—and shouted afterward: "Bring that arm back! There is a ring my wife gave me on the finger"—everyone should have that kind of courage.

Someone had set the stage for Nightingale, however.

Prior to her departure from England, William Howard Russell, the first journalist to cover a war from the front, had already written back to England. To quote from the journalist who brought it all home:

"It is with feelings of surprise and anger that the public will learn that no sufficient preparations have been made for the proper care of the wounded . . ." Russell wrote in *The Times*. "Not only are there not sufficient surgeons . . . not only are there no dressers and nurses . . . there is not even linen to make bandages. . . . Not only are the men kept in some cases for a week, without the hand of a medical man coming near their wounds . . . but now . . . it is found that . . . the men must die through the medical staff . . . having forgotten that old rags are necessary for the dressing of wounds."

When the public heard of the deplorable conditions, considered usual by Army generals, it created a huge outcry. The minute Nightingale began reading the stories Russell sent back, she knew she had to go.

By then, her remarkable ability to draw important people into her circle had begun to pay off. Her friend Liz's husband, Sydney Herbert, was now Secretary of War. Herbert not only knew how brilliant Nightingale was, but he had also seen what she had done in less than a year at her first job. She had turned things around so fast at the Distressed Gentlewomen's Hospital, it made everyone's head swim. They could barely keep up with her innovations.

Organization was Nightingale's strong suit. One of her many innovations was to order supplies en masse, which saved the financially troubled institution tons of money. She also had begun to make a name for herself by actually nursing the sick, including prostitutes, during a cholera epidemic so fearful few nurses had the courage to stay. Although

Nightingale already was getting known for her selflessness, Herbert did not want to waste her by using her as a mere nurse. He knew that her true talents lay in administration.

Herbert gave Nightingale a much greater task: to superintend the official introduction of the first female nurses at British military hospitals in Turkey. From the start, she was seen as an administrator with official standing taking charge of a disaster.

Even with that official order under her belt, however, the Army didn't see it that way. They saw her as a upper-middle-class busybody who had never seen war and couldn't possibly know what she was doing. Although under immense public pressure, they did what bureaucrats from time immemorial have done best—they waffled and waited, used red tape, and passed the buck to keep the boat from being rocked.

Not that anyone wanted the wounded to suffer. But each bureaucrat had his own fiefdom that he didn't want anyone encroaching on. No one wanted to take the blame for "silly schemes" that might fail and explode in their faces. By the time Nightingale arrived, the bureaucratic tangle in the Army was so deep, it even made getting necessary supplies to the soldiers impossible.

According to Woodham-Smith's biography, military records show that twenty thousand pounds of lime juice arrived in December but weren't given out until February. And then only after twelve hundred sick soldiers had been shipped to Nightingale's hospital, eighty-five percent of whom had scurvy of such malignancy that they were losing not only teeth but toes, which the vitamin C in lime juice would have prevented. One of Nightingale's first victories was simply to get provisions already available distributed!

There were other obstacles. The only nurses that existed at the time were nuns. Nightingale said they flitted about like useless angels worrying about souls while leaving the bodies dirty and neglected.

As long as the soul was saved, the body was negligible.

Even given a charter by the Secretary of War, Nightingale wasn't sure she could find enough women of "unreproachable character." Eventually she found forty women: fourteen had worked in hospitals, the other twenty-four came from religious orders.

When they arrived, they were greeted with the patronizing attitude men so often use against women. Col. Anthony Sterling of the Highland Brigades wrote that he did not approve of *ladies* doing the drudgery of nursing, calling Nightingale's plan "a new scheme."

The flowery language of welcome overlay a hostility that would keep

Nightingale twiddling her thumbs until a catastrophe so terrible struck, it couldn't be ignored.

The Army knew the women were coming but made absolutely no provisions for them. The only place for the forty middle-class women used to a fair amount of luxury to sleep were four rooms, including a kitchen and closet.

When they arrived in November, there were no beds, bedding, or dressers for clothing. There was no way to cook or wash. Fourteen nurses ended up sleeping in one room; ten in the other. Nightingale and another woman took the closet. The cook and her assistant took the kitchen.

In one room, the women discovered the body of a dead general, unattended and unburied since his death. Besides the sick and the dead, fleas and rats were the only objects not in short supply!

Under Nightingale's iron will and constant pressure, the women set themselves to surviving under almost unbearable conditions. Nightingale wouldn't allow the nurses to touch the wounded until the military hierarchy recognized her authority. The women began making shirts, pillows, slings, and stump rests, the simple but desperately needed supplies that were missing.

While Nightingale waited for an official order that would allow them to work with the men, she began using her own money to cook special food for the ones with cholera and dysentery. The Army, with its usual cavalier attitude, expected to feed even desperately ill men on a diet of meat, bones, and gristle dropped in a pot of water with "rags, buttons, nails, and odd bits of uniform" tied on to the meat to identify what regiment it belonged to.

As winter approached, disaster began to pile on disaster. The men at the front had no coats, no boots, no shelter, no fuel for fires. Lack of sanitation became a major problem. Arms and legs amputated and thrown into the harbor for disposal began to pollute the drinking water.

Another epidemic of cholera struck. If starvation, exposure to the elements, and simple exhaustion didn't get the men, cholera did. Suddenly, there were so many patients that even the men at the top couldn't ignore them. By mid-December, eight hundred more sick and wounded arrived at the hospital. For the first time, the doctors began to realize what they were up against. They turned to Nightingale for help.

While the nurses set to work on the wounded men with the bandages they had sewn, Nightingale did what she had been trained to do at home. She began ordering and bringing in supplies in massive numbers: six thousand shirts, two thousand socks, five hundred pairs of underwear in the first two months. She brought in plates, cups, knives, forks, and spoons, in addition to trays, tables, clocks, operating tables, scrubbers, towels, soap, and screens.

"I am a kind of General Dealer," she wrote to Sidney Herbert, "in socks, shirts, knives and forks, wood spoons, tin baths, tables and forms, cabbages, and carrots . . . small tooth combs, precipitate for destroying lice, scissors, bed pans, and stumps pillows."

Although few people realized it, in organizing supplies Nightingale surreptitiously took control of the hospital.

A month later, there were twelve thousand men in hospital and only eleven thousand on the battlefield. By then, everyone was turning to her for everything. Because she could get supplies, Nightingale had made herself indispensable.

Nightingale was not content to merely run the hospital. In the "spare" time left over from 20-hour days, she wrote lengthy private letters to Sidney Herbert, detailing not only the running of a hospital but creating a plan for the systematic central organization of the Army hospitals.

Like every problem she ever encountered, Nightingale saw the big picture and found the solution in a comprehensive conclusion. Here in the Crimea was formed the beginning of a vision which would eventually include a reorganization of the whole British Army.

Although the wounded were being fed and treated, they were still dying in massive numbers. Nightingale finally began to question the appalling conditions that everyone else took for granted—the lack of functioning toilets, plumbing, and local sewers.

In Nightingale's time, the idea that cleanliness destroyed germs didn't exist. People didn't understand that you could get sick from unclean water or open sewers. There was no longer a foot of excrement on the hospital floor—Nightingale had already seen to that—but the water storage tanks had been built next to leaking toilets and burial pits. The wounded, as well as the doctors and nurses, were dying in droves as a result of it.

When the courtyard of the hospital was finally cleaned out, the gunk filled 556 baskets and included 24 dead animals as well as two horses. Once the area was cleaned, sewers flushed completely, and walls washed with lime, the mortality rate dropped. By the time the war was over and Nightingale left the Crimea, the death rate at the hospital was

2.2 percent, down from 42 percent at its best and 63 percent at its worst during six months of the cholera epidemic.

It was a simple lesson but one Nightingale never forgot. She would come back to it time and again in her fight to improve the lot of the poor.

Coming Home

In 1856, Nightingale returned to London in triumph. Thanks to her insistence on the dignity of the individual, no matter how lowly his station, a change had not only taken place in the public's perception of the soldier but also in the nurse. Woodham-Smith wrote:

"Never again would the picture of a nurse be a tipsy, promiscuous harridan. Miss Nightingale had stamped the profession of nurse with her own image. . . . The nurse who emerged from the Crimea, strong and . . . controlled in the face of suffering, unself-seeking, superior to the considerations of class or sex, was Miss Nightingale herself."

The soldier, too, was seen in a different light no longer the scum of the earth but a man of courage and loyalty.

Nightingale's image was at its peak, but she was exhausted, shell-shocked, and depressed. Even though all London was at her feet, she was still beating herself for what she *hadn't* done. Her efforts had lowered the death rate in the Crimea, but the system was still in place.

"I stand at the altar of the murdered men," she wrote.

Nightingale had accomplished an amazing amount, but it wasn't enough. She was tortured by the fact that she had only changed conditions on one battlefield. The system would continue to churn out disaster after disaster if it was not completely revolutionized.

She was in a terrible state. The sight of food made her nauseous. She couldn't sleep or rest. In her mind, nothing had been accomplished. Despite physical exhaustion from Scutari, she threw herself into twenty-hour days, into the frenzied activity that would mark the rest of her life.

Though Nightingale was probably the most powerful women in England, she still had not rid herself of her family. Now that she was back in England, they expected her to live at home again. When she refused, *they* moved into *her* suite in London. Even after the London season ended, they wouldn't go home. Florence couldn't be left alone in London all by herself. It was unthinkable—especially with all those famous people around her.

Florence finally pushed the drama into high gear. She collapsed, took to her bed, and said she was dying. And she probably thought she was. She constantly pushed herself to exhaustion and did have very real illnesses. But collapsing and becoming an "invalid" also had some very real advantages.

Most biographers accept her invalidism at face value, but the fact that she never stopped working places serious doubt on the accepted explanation. Whether she was really ill, whether she had psychosomatic illnesses brought on from overwork, or whether it was a cleverly calculated move, taking to her "bed" gave her the only control she would ever have over her life. It freed her from her family—and it freed her from the social round her mother and sister were pushing her into. Since she became famous, even more exciting doors had opened to them. Taking to her bed even freed her from having to waste time traveling to see people. Suddenly, people were forced to come to her. And she was such an important force by then, they did so gladly. For as long as she lived—some ninety years—the Queen of Holland, the Duke of Cambridge were among the aristocrats and nobility who trooped to her door.

She might have been on her deathbed but Florence still couldn't live alone. If she was dying, she needed not only a chaperone but someone to take care of her. Aunt Mai, who had been Florence's emotional refuge for years, whose home had been like her own, who had pleaded her cause since she was a teenager and had even negotiated for her with her parents, decided to come up to London to be with her.

Aunt Mai wanted to spend Flo's last days with her. Despite protests from her husband and family, Aunt Mai left them to care for Florence. To quote Woodham-Smith:

"Aunt Mai broke up her family life. She shut up her house, her husband and girls went to stay at Embley [Florence's family home], and she came to the Burlington to make Florence's last months on earth easy. Her son-in-law, Arthur Hugh Clough, became Florence's slave. He came to the Burlington every day, wrote notes, delivered reports, fetched letters, tied up parcels, and was content, she wrote, 'to do the work of a cab horse.' The Nightingales remained at a distance."

Mai stayed and acted as the go-between, sending reports on Florence's health back to her family, who were instructed not to contact Florence directly. Mai moved in, pleased to be near Florence, excited at being able to be a part of the great work her niece was doing. During the time she was at Florence's, her husband refused to see her because, he said, he was a third wheel, superfluous and unwelcome.

Despite Nightingale's popularity among the public, she was up against tremendous obstacles. She might be a folk hero, but she was still a woman. Although the poor might worship her, she had no title or official standing. Among government bureaucrats, all but a few liberal, reform-minded officials saw her as a meddlesome pest.

But those few men were some of the most powerful ones in the country. Even those who were apathetic or hostile were overwhelmed by her knowledge and diligence.

To combat these barriers, Nightingale made a momentous decision. Within a year of returning to England, she decided to retire from the public eye and find a "mouthpiece."

From 1856 on, at the peak of her fame, Nightingale turned down all invitations to speak, lecture, or attend honorary dinners. She answered little of the "fan mail" she received, leaving the acknowledgments to her sister, who enjoyed basking in Florence's borrowed glory.

Determined to work behind the scenes—where she would be able to accomplish more with less hostility—she continued to push for reform. She began to compile statistics and was a shadow member of a commission which helped create major changes in the British military. She was also one of the first people to use pie charts to explain percentages, even claiming she had invented them.

She also chose Sydney Herbert as a front. Nightingale couldn't have picked a better person. Herbert soon went from being Secretary of War to Secretary of State. Because of her behind-the-scenes work, Nightingale could say that she had "appointed Cabinet ministers." Through Herbert, she also saw many reforms relating to sanitation put into place.

Some biographers have tried to make Sydney Herbert the "love interest in Nightingale's life." But biographers who assume they were anything other than colleagues misunderstand the true nature of their relationship.

Since Nightingale had met Clarkey in Paris, she had known that men and women could be partners, not just romantic attachments. The "band of brothers" who gathered around her called her The Commander-in-Chief. Her suite at the Burlington was called The War Office. Herbert was the general in Nightingale's own private army, an army that consisted not just of Herbert but of other men, who over the years, might have been in love with her but invariably ended up being her "fag," as it's called in England, her "Girl Friday."

After Herbert's untimely death, Nightingale wrote that she was his "real widow." She meant that they had been comrades-in-arms, fighters for the cause. She wrote:

"Sidney Herbert and I were together exactly like two men—exactly like him and Gladstone."

Herbert's widow, Liz, agreed. When Herbert died, Florence became her support and consolation. But they had always been close. When asked if Liz had ever been jealous of the massive amount of time Florence and Sidney spent together, Liz replied that she had never been worried about Florence. She didn't have to be. Florence, she said, was "one of the boys."

And Florence was. Though technically a spinster, she reversed the roles. The powerful men who gathered round her called themselves her wives. They might have been leading the charge, but she was the one *in charge*. Lord Panmure called her "a turbulent fellow."

Although Nightingale took to her bed, she didn't let that stop her from directing one commission of inquiry after another, advising one government minister after another and lobbying them until they did what she wanted. Refusing to see anyone she didn't want to see, Nightingale continued to do what she did best: collecting facts, creating surveys, and tabulating statistics to give an accurate, scientific view of everyday conditions that could be compared with other countries. She continued to come up with new and innovative solutions to minuscule as well as overwhelmingly large problems. For the first time in her life, Nightingale was in her element, working at full capacity, using her truly magnificent mind in a way that awed everyone she came into contact with.

After two years of ill health on the part of Florence but no death, Aunt Mai's family tried to force her to go home. The family wrote to Fanny, Florence's mother, to help in separating the two.

Not only had Florence brought Aunt Mai into her immediate circle but also Aunt Mai's son—who had left his wife to help Florence in her hour of need—and her great cause.

But nothing happened. Mai remained with Flo. The next summer, Mai's daughter, who was getting married, begged her mother to come home to help. It was three years since Florence was supposed to have died. Finally, Mai could bear the pressure no longer. She realized it was, to quote Woodham-Smith, "her duty" to return.

Florence was devastated. On the one hand, she saw her aunt Mai as a mother figure—her real mother, the psychological mother, as Anna Freud would later term it, the one who was understanding and sympathetic.

On the other hand, she also loved Mai in the romantic sense and didn't care that there was twenty years age difference or that they were relatives.

Florence was furious at Mai's betrayal. So much so, it took twenty years for her to forgive her aunt. As a therapist might say, talk about abandonment issues!

But Florence had other helpmates. When Mai left, she turned to an old friend, a cousin, Hilary Bonham Carter, a painter of such talent that Clarkey had tried to convince her parents to let her to stay in Paris to study. Her parents wouldn't hear of it—she couldn't be "spared." Though they had servants, they needed help with the house, the younger girls, the flower arranging. Hilary was permitted to join a ladies' atelier—as long as it didn't interfere with her social life.

Because Florence needed her help, Hilary was allowed to come to live with Florence. Hilary had loved Florence since childhood. Hilary had a "passion" for her, Florence wrote.

Years earlier, when Florence had dreamed of doing something special with her life, she had turned to Hilary. They spent hours talking to each other of their dreams and the difficulties entailed with being women. On one two-day visit, they walked and talked all day "from breakfast until sunset."

The two women corresponded and saw each other over the years. At a young age, Hilary had taken over the responsibility of her family when her father died. Her mother was too "nervous" to cope. But now Florence needed her. Hilary flew to her side, glad to be free of *her* family and more than willing to devote her life to Florence. Florence, however, knew what it was like to waste one's talent, to be forced by circumstance to waste one's life, having spent fifteen years wasting hers. She didn't want to be responsible for Hilary wasting herself as Florence's wife. She wanted Hilary to paint.

They devised a scheme where Hilary would work on her art so many hours a day. Hilary decided to do a bust of Florence.

It was not a particularly wise choice. Though the bust was finished and exhibited—and apparently considered "one of the best likenesses" of Florence—being forced to take herself seriously was too much for Hilary. Though she had dreams, she didn't have the drive to fulfill them. It strained their relationship to the breaking point. Hilary went to Malvern, a spa, for a "cure."

Her family also wanted her back. They were saying she was being "victimized" by Florence; she needed more time to work on her art—anything to get her home.

While Hilary was away, Florence sent a letter detailing her plan of how they could live together. Florence wrote:

"If you would like to come back—as my guest and friend—oh my very best and dearest friend—but not as my letter-writer and house-keeper . . ."

Hilary's family wouldn't let her attend the atelier; they wouldn't let her come back. Florence wrote that losing Hilary was like amputating a limb.

Hilary's family, once they got her home, was not so understanding. Between the duties of running a house she worked on her art whenever she could. Given no serious opportunity, her career as an artist amounted to little. When she died, Clarkey wrote to Florence that "Hilly is devoured by . . . relations just like Fleas."

Florence called the family murderers who sent Hilary to a slow death.

Ironically, Mai's husband ended up having to help Florence. Upon the death of Sydney Herbert in 1861, a year after Mai had gone back home, Florence suffered a collapse. Uncle Sam was forced to take charge of Florence's affairs.

Nightingale chose to avoid the public eye to work more efficiently behind the scenes, but she still understood the value of publicity. At the start of the Crimean War, she had seen the effect one journalist had in rousing the indignation of a nation over a war thousands of miles away.

In England, she turned to lesbian journalist Harriet Martineau. Between 1852 and 1866, Martineau wrote story after story for the *London Daily News* about the deplorable conditions of the poor with information supplied to her by Nightingale. Over the years, public opinion slowly began to change. With Nightingale and others pushing from the inside, Martineau and others pushing from the outside, the government was forced to respond.

During Nightingale's long career, she fought for the introduction of hygiene that lowered the infant mortality and death rates in hospitals; helped bring the concept of sewage treatment and clean waters to India; helped standardize diseases and injuries so that hospitals could be compared to one another and hospital practices regularized; helped revise

Army medical procedure; and what she is best known for, set up the first teacher training college for nurses.

Even though Nightingale thought she was dying for years, she lived to be ninety and didn't give up working until the very end. In fact, she didn't slow down until her seventies.

She never gave up her interest in politics, nursing, or nurses who showed exceptional promise. She continued to be generous, giving away money to people who needed it, rarely living within her means.

As she got older, visiting dignitaries still asked to see her but it was more like an audience with a queen.

In 1907, she was given the Order of Merit, the first woman to receive one. Congratulations poured in from as far away as Japan.

On August 13, 1910, she never woke up from her afternoon nap. Despite her self-imposed isolation, her "invalidism," Florence Nightingale was known throughout the world for the changes she had brought about.

Florence Nightingale

1820 Born in Florence, Italy
1837 Has vision of God calling her to His service
1838 Begins studying hospital reports in secret
1845 Proposes to train at Salisbury Infirmary; family is horrified and goes ballistic
1849 Visits Lutheran Hospital, Kaiserswerth, Germany
1953 Hired to run the Institute for Sick Gentlewomen in Distress
1854 Appointed for the Crimean War as Superintendent of Female Nursing Establishment to the English General Hospitals in Turkey
1855 Cuts death rate from 42 percent to 2.2 percent
1856 Returns to England a hero
1857 Writes government report on British military hospitals
      Refuses to see family, collapses, and is on the verge of death
      Aunt Mai comes to live with Florence in her last days
1859 "Notes on Nursing" published
      Drafts model statistical forms for use in hospitals
1860 Nightingale School of Nursing opens
1861 Establishes training school for Midwives

Since Florence is still alive, Aunt Mai is forced to return home to family

Sydney Herbert dies

1907 First woman awarded the British Order of Merit

1910 Dies at age 90

Chapter Three

M. CAREY THOMAS

Lesbians have to fight for political and social acceptance today but that wasn't always the case. Until the 1930's, when lesbians were branded as evil, sex-crazed predators, no one thought twice about romantic friendships between women. M. Carey Thomas's life is a perfect example of this.

Her first partner, Mamie Gwinn (also sometimes spelled Gwynn,) went to Europe to be her companion during Thomas's stressful student years as the first woman in the world to get a graduate degree. If she had had to go it alone, it might have been impossible. As it was, with Gwinn at her side studying and keeping her company, believing in her and cheering her on, she succeeded.

When Thomas was hired as the dean of the newly opened women's college at Bryn Mawr, Gwinn openly moved into the Deanery with her. No one batted an eye. When the two women broke up twenty years later, a long-time friend, Mary Garrett, moved into the Deanery almost immediately to be with Thomas. The response? Everyone seemed glad that Carey had so easily found someone to replace her beloved Mamie.

The scandal came not from Thomas and Mary but from Mamie running off with one of the other professors. After six years of trying to decide what to do about her love life—whether to remain with Carey or leave her for a married man—Mamie chose the latter. Mamie and her future husband fled to Europe, where Americans and Europeans such as Oscar Wilde and Radclyffe Hall have often gone to wait out tempests in teacups. In Paris, they visited Gertrude Stein.

71

But the major battle in Thomas's life was not about love affairs but education.

Nearly a century after James Miranda Barry passed as a man to get a degree, the "woman question" was still up for grabs. With all the time that had passed, M. Carey Thomas still had to fight to go to college. As a result of that battle, she would fight for a woman's right to be educated for the rest of her life. For her—as for women today—education leads directly to economic freedom.

Thomas was a pioneer who went to one of the first colleges in the U.S. that "allowed women." After graduating, she scoured Europe for a university that would not only admit women but give them a graduate degree.

By following her dreams, she set the stage for her life's work: creating a woman's college whose requirements equaled those of men's and whose graduates would show the world that women could not only learn as well as men but be strong, independent-minded individuals in their own right.

In fact, college marked the beginning of Thomas's independence. The first thing "Martha" did once she got to Cornell was change her name. Her middle name, "Carey," could conveniently be male or female. At Cornell, Thomas also began to shake off her strict religious upbringing. She did not dance, but she made up for that by falling in love with Alice Hicks, a woman she first spied during the entrance exams. She saw her again at the President's tea and was delighted that she was smartly dressed (with a feather in her hat) and intelligent.

One of the first people she ran into on arriving at Sage College, Cornell, was the woman with the wing in her hat. They decided to take rooms on the same corridor and gradually began to spend time together. Shy at first but gathering courage over time, Carey eventually wrote that her heart wouldn't stop "racing in Alice's presence."

Carey and Alice began to study together and went on day-long walks. When it got dark, they sat under Alice's blue shawl. They sold their used textbooks to hire a carriage for romantic drives in the country. They both eventually became so enamored with each other, they barely went to class and rarely opened a book.

Despite the time-consuming nature of her love life, Thomas still finished her degree in two years. Mastering all the subjects came easily—which was lucky since Thomas had to force herself to study. She did well even when she only applied herself marginally, but she would rather be outdoors than having her nose to the grindstone. With little study, Thomas finished her dissertation and was granted a bachelor's degree in June 1877. She later became the first woman trustee of Cornell.

During her first foray into graduate school the next year, Thomas met the two women she would spend the rest of her life with: Mamie Gwinn and Mary Garrett.

Her cousin Bessie had already made friends with the more worldly wise Baltimore aristocrats whose lives had been vastly different from Carey's strict Quaker one.

They had been to plays, galleries, concerts. And they had traveled regularly and extensively.

Carey, on the other hand, was one of the first women to be admitted to Johns Hopkins as a graduate student and "surrounded by the glamour of academic achievement."

The daughter of one of the three executors of Johns Hopkins's estate, Mamie Gwinn was haughty beyond measure but a true intellectual, who would also become a lecturer at Bryn Mawr. To quote from Edith Finch's biography, *M. Carey Thomas of Bryn Mawr*:

"To talk with her exhilarated Carey. In appearance, too, Mamie charmed her irresistibly. She was slender and delicately boned, white skinned and black haired, and her dark eyes were intensely alive. Her movements were light and languid. Again, she was the opposite of the robust and instinctively headlong Carey."

With Thomas joining them, the five women met every other week to discuss literature and feminism. They read the intellectual liberals of the day—Wollstonecraft, Godwin and Shelley.

At first, Thomas couldn't decide who she was most fond of. Both Mamie and Mary were terrible distractions from her studies. Garrett loved to ride, agreed with Thomas on most points, and had "a sort of sweet strength about her." The daughter of a railroad magnate, Mary Garrett was self-effacing but aware of her responsibilities as the daughter of wealth. Carey dedicated her first sonnet to Mary.

But with Mary there weren't the fireworks there were with Mamie, who was "so delightful that [Thomas] wished constantly to be with her." Eventually, Mamie won.

Nearly twenty-five years later, Mary would take Mamie's place. By then, Carey was more appreciative of the compatibility Mary had to offer. They spent one decade, until Mary's death, together. Apparently Thomas weathered the loss of Mamie rather easily. But at Mary's death, she was inconsolable.

Thomas was supposed to be studying. After all, she was one of the first women admitted to the graduate program and she was supposed to be making the best of it. Her father, a member of the board, had been instrumental in lobbying for women's admission. Thomas had gotten in by special vote.

The conditions under which women were admitted to the university were almost insurmountable. Thomas was only allowed to sit in on certain lectures and given a list of books to read for the others. She was not allowed to attend seminars or private tutorials, the heart of a university education.

She soon found that even though she had been accepted for a graduate degree, Johns Hopkins probably would not grant her one—even if she fulfilled the requirements.

For a woman who had a hard time forcing herself to study anyway, it was too much to bear. After one year, Thomas decided to drop out and try her luck in Germany, the center of higher education in those days. Since a few women had been admitted to classes there, Thomas was willing to take her chances. It had to better than Baltimore.

Thomas also had her first and only real "beau" during these years, even though she said she had "declared against such weakness."

Men could only lead to trouble—marriage and, without birth control, the inevitable children. She would never be able to show that women were the equals of men intellectually if she married and gave up the idea of a career. If she was ever seriously tempted, she quickly squelched the idea.

Before Thomas could go to Germany, she had to convince her father to allow her to go—and to foot the bill. At first, he refused. Dr. Thomas was a highly educated and respected man himself, a trustee of college boards and a believer, in general, in women's rights. But his daughter was carrying it too far. Nonetheless, after much hysteria, Carey won.

Mamie had to resort to fainting to persuade *her* parents to let her go with Carey to "pursue her studies." But she, too, was successful.

The two women picked the University of Leipzig because one lone American woman had been admitted there. Once convinced, her father did what he could to help them, using his vast network of connections to place them with a family in Germany.

In 1879, they set off. Life in Germany was harder than they expected—financially, emotionally, academically. Although Thomas was used to being broke, she had to be even more frugal than usual. Gwinn's family had more than enough money, but Mamie refused to support them. Rather than raising Carey to her standard, they both should be frugal and live at Carey's. They bought no clothes, just kid gloves, which every woman of any standing had to wear.

It was a far cry from the life Thomas would lead with Garrett, who bought kid gloves by the dozen.

Thomas was the butch and Gwinn the hothouse flower. Carey did everything from planning trips to cooking and sewing. A typical femme of the era, Mamie often fainted and became exhausted while Carey slaved away.

Things were difficult academically, too. First, Thomas was refused a degree. Then, in 1880, the minister of culture of the province demanded they both apply for permission to attend the university. The American ambassador intervened and they were given permission to continue, but the good burghers decided that no other women were to be admitted.

When the King of Saxony visited, the women hid rather than risk the wrath of someone even higher up the ladder who could change the course of their lives in a whim.

Sexism was also rampant. Male students stared at them bug-eyed wherever they went. If they so much as dropped a pen during class, all eyes turned to watch their every move. If Mamie dropped her muff, the professor ran to pick it up. If Carey was sitting in the sun, the professor would close the blinds.

Afraid of doing anything that might jeopardize their position, the two retreated into an isolation that would set the tone of their life together.

After the landlady berated Thomas for letting an American friend sit next to her on the sofa, they permitted no men to call on them. They decided not to speak to them socially nor even talk to them about academic subjects after class. When they met a fellow student on a walk in the woods who mentioned the class they were in together, they fled without answering.

But they had each other's company which, like many female couples, was more than enough. The only other person they allowed into their circle of two was Gertrude Meade, a friend of Julia Rogers, one of the original five from Baltimore.

Finch calls Mamie a "time-consuming temptress," but Gwinn loved studying and spurred Thomas on academically. Given all the difficulties of studying in a foreign language in a foreign land, Thomas might not have made it if Gwinn hadn't been at her side. She certainly wouldn't have done as well.

Thomas continued to study in Germany. But when she was outlining her dissertation, she found out that she was not going to be allowed to take the final examination. Like Johns Hopkins, no German university would grant her a degree.

Finding themselves back at square one, Thomas was undeterred. She heard that the University of Zurich might give a woman a degree. She and Gwinn packed their belongings and moved to Zurich.

In 1882, she began her dissertation but found the Swiss standards even higher. In addition to a dissertation in German on "Sir Gawayne and the Green Knight," she discovered she would also have to do a dissertation on a modern English poet. Undaunted, she chose Swinburne.

During the six weeks Thomas geared up for one of the hardest tests of her life, Gwinn went to Florence to let her concentrate. With Mamie gone, Thomas got even more stressed out than usual. The professors said they were impressed with her thesis, but that made no difference. She had spent her whole life working up to this moment, what if she failed? She was a nervous wreck.

Thomas had to take three days of written exams, pass another six-hour exam, plus defend her thesis during a three-hour oral with the professors. As if that weren't bad enough, the vote had to be unanimous.

Thomas passed the written exam with flying colors but even that didn't make her feel any better. Two men had failed, another barely passed. What if she blew it after all the time, the money she'd spent?

She worked herself into a fever pitch. Her nervous energy began to take its toll. She couldn't eat or sleep. After six days, a friendly professor gave her strychnine and valerian, the tranquilizers of the day, to calm her down—plus two cups of strong black tea to get her through the exam. By then, Thomas was probably higher than a kite.

"From the moment she approached the green baize table she had felt perfectly calm and had been able to answer with perfect distinctness and, as far as she could tell, with almost no mistakes.

" 'All the laws of the development of Gothic out of Indo-Germanic *were never clearer to me* [italics mine] than at the moment of the examination.'

"But the five minutes of waiting . . . [after the exam] were torture:

" 'I have never felt such a sensation of choking anxiety.' "

Almost impressed beyond measure, the faculty gave her the highest honor it could—*summa cum laude.*

At the time, only one other person in living memory had been given that designation. Thomas got it not only as a foreigner working in a foreign language but as the second woman to have ever been granted a doctorate of any sort from a university in Europe.

Local papers published a story that she had won a doctorate, along with an account of her life. The news began to spread, first among the Quakers where her mother wrote about it in a newsletter, then among the general populace.

Eventually, *tout le monde* heard. Everywhere she went, people stared at her. She got letters from women all over the world congratulating her on her achievement. Susan B. Anthony asked to meet her in Paris.

She and Gwinn traveled the Riviera, the Rhône Valley, and London for nearly a year to savor her triumph and take a well-earned rest.

Once she talked her way into the deanship of Bryn Mawr College, Thomas would not have another vacation of that length until she retired nearly four decades later.

Getting an Education

Like many rebellious women, Thomas was already a "handful" at the age of two. She remembered her aunt sticking a mint in her mouth to make her be quiet so her mother could get a few minutes rest.

At age three, bored with needlework, she began teaching herself to read. She asked her mother to pin letters on a huge cushion and as the woman called out the letter, she'd stab it with a pin. Later, Cousin Bessie and she taught themselves Greek to prepare for college—a pipe-dream in those days since too much "intellectual stimulation" for a girl was thought to be harmful.

By adolescence, Thomas could picture her future. She wrote of her friendship with Bessie, who *would* become a lifelong friend, and their future together: They would live together and "live loving each other and spurring each other on to every high and noble deed and action till all who passed should say 'their example arouses me, their books ennoble me, their deeds inspire me, and behold they are women.' "

Life didn't work out exactly as she envisioned, but it came close. Same scenario, different women.

Once Thomas set her mind to something, nothing could stop her, nothing could stand in her way. As a child, there was no lock she couldn't pick, no building she couldn't find a way into. Barriers that would be insurmountable to most people only whetted Thomas's appetite. A challenge made her more determined to succeed, more determined to triumph. Being allowed to go to college was a prime example.

Thomas's father was a distinguished Baltimore physician from a long line of Quakers who believed in education. If anything, he prided himself on his advanced thinking and freely discussed his theories with his eldest child, Martha. Little did he realize his words were encouraging her—and giving her ammunition. In truth, he believed in education in principle—for all *men*. For *daughters*, the "sacred shrine of womanhood" fitted them for the supreme responsibility of bearing children. Nothing more. In the days before birth control information was legal, the only certain way of not having children was not marrying.

It didn't matter that Minnie, as she was called, was dead set against having children. She called child care "utterly unintellectual." And quite rightly.

When it came to "the woman question," her father was of the old school with sweetness and grace topping the list of female attributes, strength and intellect the male.

To which Thomas responded (in her diary):

"Oh it is too unjust, too horrible. I believe that I have as much sense as any boy I know . . . and more too. It seems to me I'd die if I could do anything to show that a woman is equal to a man."

Thomas had other plans. She used her cousin Frank, four years older and college-bound, as a model for her education. No matter what her father said about marriage, she planned to become a doctor. What Frank mastered, Minnie mastered.

"More and more every day I'm making up my mind to be a doctor for when I grow up I can't be dependent on father or mother and I ain't going to get married. . . . I can't imagine anything worse than living a regular young lady's life," Thomas scrawled in her diary in a moment of passion.

Their friendship was so close that for many years the family considered Minnie "Frank's girl." Frank *was* one of the two young men Thomas ever considered loving. In fact, Thomas might never have made it to college if Frank hadn't suddenly died leaving Minnie utterly distraught. To console her, her family let her join Bessie at a Quaker girl's school in New York—to see if it would lift her spirits. If Frank hadn't died, even finishing high school would have been a much bigger battle than it was.

Both her mother Mary and her aunt Hannah, a well-known children's author and suffragist, were strong-willed women. Dr. Thomas had not been in favor of high school, but nonetheless, Minnie was sent to boarding school to be with Bessie. At the Howland Institute, Thomas studied history, literature, science, and the arts, much like high school today but unheard of in that day, at least for girls. In 1872, the school was even further ahead of its time in having a gymnasium during an era when physical exercise was also thought to be harmful for women's fertility.

Though her father hadn't wanted her to go to the school, he expected her to be first in her class once enrolled. She rarely studied; she had little need to. Her mind seemed to take in facts and figures without even trying.

Which gave her time for other things—including her first "smash," the word for lesbian crush at the turn of the century. Finch doesn't mention the girl's name, but her cousin Bessie, whom she'd been planning to spend her life with, was so jealous, they battled for weeks. It got so bad that they weren't even speaking to each other though they were roommates. Eventually, Aunt Hannah was dispatched to help them patch things up. Her mother wrote:

"I guess thy feeling is quite natural. I used to have the same romantic love for my friends. It is a real pleasure."

"Romantic friends" were still the rage in 1872. Sexologists hadn't hinted that women who loved women might be falling in love and shunning marriage for a life with someone of the same sex. Thomas took it a bit far, even for a schoolgirl infatuation. Carey's mother wrote, warning her of carrying "crushes" too far.

Little did Mary Thomas know that her daughter's love of women was not an adolescent phase.

As if falling in love with other girls wasn't enough, Thomas also got into trouble for cross-dressing and playing the man in an opera given by the school. In later life she never took to wearing trousers; that seemed to have been part of her tomboy youth, a part that was quickly squelched by her mother:

"Thee knows how I feel about thy dressing up as man ... I do suppose it is great fun but I think it is not nice."

On hearing that Thomas had played the man at a mock wedding, she wrote again, saying she would not have it. She warned Minnie that she would withdraw her support for Thomas's remaining at school if she continued to cross-dress.

Being a Quaker, Thomas's mother was probably as upset about it being a drama as anything. Quakers did not think much of the theater in those days and their strictures against plays would be a bone of contention years later when Thomas was the dean of Bryn Mawr, a Quaker-founded college.

Though she did well at Howland Thomas probably would never have gone to college if her well-known father hadn't been asked to give the commencement address for her graduation. In the speech, he said:

"Who shall deny to women the opportunity of obtaining advanced intellectual training?"

Fateful words that would soon come back to haunt him.

Thomas was already well on her way to being a scholar. The classical course she had finished at Howland was equivalent to sophomore work at college. The headmistress, Miss Slocum, spurred her on. Having concluded that Thomas was the only student she had seen with " 'the power of mind' to advance women's position in the world, she told her at graduation that she expected 'great things' of her." In that regard, she was right on the money. As an adult, Thomas would help create a world where women were not only allowed to go to college but *required* to compete with men intellectually when doing so. But first, Thomas had to get her family's permission to take the entrance exams and go to college herself.

After graduation, she returned to Baltimore to study Greek and Latin, algebra and geometry to prepare for the college entrance exams. (She had already begun to master the German she would need for graduate work.)

She tried to study but it was difficult to concentrate. Her father was adamantly opposed to her plan. He worried that she would become an intellectual or, worse, a "bluestocking." He also worried that she would lose her faith. Even though Thomas called herself a Quaker for the rest of her life, she was already questioning Christian dogma and its oppression of women.

And there were other concerns. Money was tight and always had been. With ten children, the family often relied on money from Mary's side of the family to get them through tight spots. If there were any money to be spent on education, it should go on the boys. They would have to earn a living, unlike his eldest daughter, who, no matter what she said about careers, would eventually marry and have children.

" 'Many and dreadful are the talks we have had upon this subject,' [Thomas] wrote later. 'Father was terribly opposed and . . . said never while he lived would he give his consent.' "

All the Baltimore relations took sides against Thomas, all except

Cousin Bessie. Sometimes the opposition was so strong she doubted whether she could persist. Her father felt just as strongly and they both "suffered tortures."

Her father faced a formidable foe, not just in his willful and determined daughter but also in his wife. Mary had also heard the commencement speech. She never complained about her life, but as with most intelligent women of the day, she wished she had had more from life than just raising children. She got her solace from religion, but she knew her daughter would never be satisfied with a life like hers. Her daughter was obviously brilliant. It would be a waste to confine her to child-rearing, especially if she didn't want it.

Mary began to use her husband's own arguments against him and finally persuaded him, three weeks before the exam, to let Carey apply at Cornell, one of the first American colleges which, in 1868, had opened its doors to women.

After Cornell, Thomas faced even worse intractability from her father when she wanted to go to Germany to study. But Thomas was even more independent by then—and more outspoken.

Though she had had to go home to live after college it was obvious the arrangement wasn't going to work. Less a Quaker than ever, her parents were beginning to see it, too. They were worried about her influence on her younger brothers and sisters who looked up to her as if she were a god. Carey had become more and more worldly, less and less religious. Arguments soon started. And continued, with Carey's mother calling her "selfish," Carey calling her mother "cruel."

"What a religion that makes a mother cast her daughter off!" she wrote.

As the differences mounted and the arguments escalated, her family realized that having Thomas at home was not the solution. There were no suitors in sight, *no* obvious solution. Thomas's plan, a young woman alone going to Germany to study, was beyond the pale. But unlike Florence Nightingale, she had convinced her mother. Her mother tried reason, but that didn't work. Eventually, they resorted to proven "feminine wiles," crying.

" 'There is nothing for it, thee must cry thyself to Germany,' " Mrs. Thomas said.

Two weeks of Thomas's hysterics did the trick, finally convincing the doctor that his headstrong daughter must be allowed to do what she wanted if he was ever going to get any peace in the family. No matter how much scandal might ensue, he must hold up his head and back her. Later, when Thomas succeeded beyond everyone's wildest dreams, when she became known worldwide, her family would be very proud of *their* decision.

Romantic Friendships

When Gwinn left Thomas to run off with a married man, an incredible scandal ensued, so much so that Mamie Gwinn and Alfred Hodder had to go to Europe until it was forgotten.

Gwinn never had been sociable, which made her departure all the more surprising. Despite Thomas having to raise massive amounts of money as the dean of Bryn Mawr by entertaining wealthy Philadelphia benefactors, Gwinn invariably wolfed down dinner, then glared at everyone without saying a word for the rest of the evening. Though she was known to be painfully shy, her behavior was still unnerving to the guests.

And Thomas was little better. She ran social occasions like a classroom, leading discussions as if she were testing pupils. Luckily, when it came to fund-raising, Thomas's growing prestige counted more than their less-than-perfect social skills.

Despite her aloofness at dinner, Gwinn was no shrinking violet. She received a degree from Bryn Mawr and began to teach there once she and Thomas settled in.

But like her socializing, her teaching was eccentric at best. Not wanting to lecture, she only had students turn in papers—which was fine because they were as intimidated by her as she was of them. For instruction, Gwinn wrote massive comments on the margins of the paper. There were no class meetings, no reading list, no discussions.

Gwinn did eventually begin to lecture, and this woman Finch describes as "languid and indolent" attracted not only students but other faculty to the seminars because of her brilliance.

In 1898, Gwinn began falling in love with the new professor at the college, a philosopher whose dissertation was widely discussed in its day. Though Gwinn downplayed it, the attraction was obvious to everyone, including Hodder's wife, who probably informed Thomas. Hodder was eventually forced to resign.

That didn't stop the affair, however. Gwinn tried to be true not only to her companion of more than two decades but her ideal of an intellectual woman's life. But it was eventually too much. Cupid won. Six years after his resignation, Mamie left to join Hodder. Soon after, he divorced his wife and married Gwinn.

The scandal was so well known, at least in academic circles, that the triangle became the subject of one of Gertrude Stein's earliest works, *Fernhurst*. She changed the names but the triangle remains the same. The only difference is the ending. In the Stein version, the man leaves, the woman stays with her partner. By reversing the ending, Stein effectively kept the lesbianism intact. In a sense, it mirrored Thomas's life without having to add another character, for Mary Garrett joined Thomas soon after. But the happy ending was one of the reasons Stein did not want the novel published for years. What was acceptable in life obviously was not acceptable in literature, at least in Gertrude Stein's mind. And given the fact that Natalie Barney, writing in French from French soil, was as badly trashed as she was in the U.S. for her lesbian sonnets, Stein was justified in her assessment of the book's impact and the damage it might do to her future literary reputation.

Strange as it may seem in this homophobic, post-Freudian era, romantic friendships between women were acceptable then. A century ago, two women could have lived their whole lives together, slept in the same bed, held hands in public, and even danced together without anyone thinking twice. If anything, they would have been admired and respected since they aspired to the highest ideal a woman could: the love of another woman.

Of course, everything was assumed to be "platonic." No one would have suspected the women of having sex, no matter how affectionate they appeared to be in public, no matter how few beds were in the bedroom or the house. Even today, no matter how many references to two women "holding each other in bed," historians and scholars are loath to "jump to conclusions."

Middle-class women simply didn't do "that" except as a duty to that beast, their husband. Left to their own devices, no decent woman would have even thought of such a thing, much less *wanted* it.

At least that's what everyone believed until sexologists such as Havelock Ellis began saying that women not only had sex but enjoyed it. Once that idea spread to the public, romantic friendships took a public relations nose dive. You mean those two women were living as "man and wife?" The horror of it!

The two women who epitomized the romantic friends movement and were idealized and looked up to by *tout le monde*, the ladies of Llangollen, are clearly a butch-femme pair.

Male homosexuals have always borne the burden of hostility toward
gay sexuality. Unmarried women could always pass as the maiden aunt
who "never got asked." Because they did the asking, men couldn't
hide behind such a ruse. Even unmarried men were seen as sexual
beings, a burden which single women escaped from the time of the
convents until the 1930's.

Even though women such as M. Carey Thomas are obviously foremothers of the current love- and sex-based *heterosexual* definition of
lesbian, it's probably easier to call them romantic *friends.*

It's pretty clear, however, that Thomas was a butch in the modern
sense and that her relationships with both Mamie Gwinn and Mary
Garrett fell along a romantic friend-lesbian continuum.

Thomas was a tomboy and a hell-raiser from the start. As a child,
she was willful, brave, courageous, hardly the usual characteristics of
a girl. And she was "clumsy," another oft-used description of women
who don't fall into the heterosexual gender definition of girls as "grace-
ful." Carey stomped around the house, determined in what she wanted,
assertive even as a child.

" 'I feel as if I needed help and advice in training little Minnie,'
wrote her mother anxiously, 'she is such a handful.' "

How often have mothers of lesbians said that when faced with a
young girl who can't (or won't) fit into the usual stifling gender
stereotypes!

For Thomas, no dare was too frightening, no adventure too scary.

Wanting to test the new girlfriend of a cousin, Thomas led a wild
chase across the rooftops of the neighborhood to see what the girl was
made of.

Another time, Thomas led her younger brothers and sisters in burying
a cousin in the sand at the beach to punish him for a tantrum. After,
the group returned to their game and promptly forgot him. As time
passed, the tide crept in, and soon the waves were breaking over his
head. If some adults hadn't heard his screams and rescued him, he
probably would have drowned.

"Clumsy" or not, Thomas was good at sports. She hunted, fished,
and spent most of her time outdoors. She and Bessie rode in summer
and ice-skated in winter. They also went to "unladylike" places to test
their athletic prowess where only "roughs" hung out.

"*Respectability is nothing* [emphasis author's]," Thomas wrote.

Even if Thomas was afraid, it didn't stop her. Fear only made her
more determined to plunge ahead. Minnie and Cousin Bess killed and

dissected a mouse though they nearly fainted from the attempt of trying to let it drown, since the trap hadn't killed it. When they tried to cut it up, "it made us sick and our hands trembled so we couldn't do a thing, but concluding it was feminine nonsense we made a hole and squeezed his insides out. It was the most disgusting thing I ever did. Eventually they put its organs under a microscope to have a look and felt triumphant.''

All her life, Thomas hated being told she couldn't do something because of her gender. When her mother said she couldn't construct a telegraph "because she was only a girl,'' Thomas wrote in her diary:

"When I heard that, I ground my teeth and swore ... that no one should say that of us—as if we hadn't as much sense, invention, and perseverance as boys.''

In fact, Thomas acted the part of the butch, organizing raids and pranks until the more cultured and sedate Mamie Gwinn got her into line. On a visit, Gwinn once laid into Thomas for her "unfeminine'' habits: sitting with her legs crossed—which proper ladies didn't do— and being too animated when she talked.

In grade school, Thomas led the girls into valiant battles against the boys, to prove they could, to get back at them, or just to have fun.

"Her enterprise seemed endless.... Many a hand-to-hand tussle was only broken up by Miss Marble's [the teacher's] entrance, when the boys 'scattered like chaff' leaving the girls, Minnie in the forefront, to receive the reprimand,'' writes Finch.

Once, when the boys squirted water at the girls, Minnie led a raid against them with buckets—and soaked everything in sight.

Her love of adventure, her fearlessness, her intrepidness would serve her well in later years when the battles weren't merely with squirt guns, but with the biggest "gun'' of all, knowledge.

Bryn Mawr

By the time Carey Thomas became the first dean of the new women's college at Bryn Mawr, she knew exactly what should be required of a college graduate, male or female, having had one of the best educations possible in her day. But before she could put her theories into practice, she had to get hired.

She and Mamie were vacationing in Europe when she first heard that a teaching position might be available at the new college. She had originally planned to be a teacher, but by the time she had been through the odyssey of graduate school, she'd realized that she couldn't have enough impact in that position. Having seen firsthand the difficulties women faced, she wanted to run a college.

She faced a number of obstacles, not just her father. Though well known by then, she was still a woman. And she herself had accidentally created another obstacle. In getting rid of a one-time suitor a few years earlier, she had tried to soften the blow by recommending *him* for the post.

But her imagination was on fire, her mind working at white-hot heat. Even before she wrote to her father to ask him to broach the subject of appointing her dean of Bryn Mawr to the other trustees, she'd begun researching women's colleges. In England, she visited Cambridge where fifty-three women were attending Girton College and doing just fine, even though colleges were still supposed to be bad for a woman's health.

At Girton, she also began thinking not just of the academic side she had challenged but other, important details: whether colleges could offer fellowships to attract the best graduate students; whether class attendance should be voluntary; whether they should have individual dorm rooms with small living rooms instead of the Army-style barracks of the day—all innovations that would create today's college atmosphere.

While this attention to detail helped land her the job, it would also get her into hot water in later years when she was accused of being too dictatorial and autocratic.

But the more she thought about the way she would run a college if given the chance, the more she wanted a hand in shaping this exciting experiment in women's education.

Despite her youth and lack of experience Bryn Mawr couldn't have picked a better person. Thomas had spent years listening to her father and other relatives discussing education in all its arcane detail. With uncles and cousins as well as a father on the boards of the most prestigious universities in the nation, the debates were not merely theoretical but brass tacks. What they decided would influence the course of education in the country for years to come.

Thomas's father had also contributed to her desire by asking her to research the new university at Johns Hopkins when she was an undergraduate. She had reported back to him in minute detail.

She began working behind the scenes, quietly asking her father what chance she had. Not only did she have to persuade them to think of her as a candidate, but she had to convince them to hire a woman. Thomas was nervous about offering herself, someone who had just finished graduate work and hadn't even taught, but she had her reputation going for her. Why would Carey Thomas, the world-famous doctor of philosophy, be involved in anything that wasn't the very best? She wrote her father begging him to take her side, saying that if he didn't, no one else would.

Her father did, and began lobbying for her. By December 1883, the trustees agreed.

Buildings weren't even finished when Thomas began researching East Coast women's colleges. As the newly appointed dean, she set off four months later on a tour. Using introductions from Dr. James E. Rhoads, the president of Bryn Mawr, and other influential people, she began looking at what made colleges work—and what didn't.

The first stop was Vassar. There she saw the "elective" system which had also been introduced at Johns Hopkins and is the basis of most modern colleges in the U.S. today. It was startlingly new in its day, however, to think that, with the exception of some basic requirements, the rest of the subjects could be chosen by the student themselves. It was also a radical change from the European system, which even today relies on required courses of one to three subjects for the major and few, if any, electives.

From Vassar, Thomas visited other Seven Sisters schools—Smith, Wellesley, and what would later become Racliffe but was then Harvard Annex—gathering data as she went. When she got to Boston, Mamie Gwinn joined her.

When she filed her report, a massive document that included everything from the detailed information on buildings and finance to academics, in September 1884, the trustees accepted most of her ideas, many of which were the opposite of their original plans. The most important were the entrance requirements to Bryn Mawr, which were originally considered low. By the time Thomas finished, they were head and shoulders above those of most other women's colleges of the day. According to Finch, by raising the standards of education for women at the university level, Thomas also helped raise the standards of American education for both sexes, in all the grades that lead up to college.

Thomas didn't see her appointment as a triumph only for herself but as a triumph for all women. All her life, she championed the cause of women's rights, especially women's education. She spent most of her life in academia, but in her later years, she turned to other women's issues, including the right to vote as well as the right of all women, even working-class factory women, to be educated. In the 1920's, she helped set up summer schools for working women.

Bryn Mawr opened on September 23, 1885. Though Thomas was to travel intermittently and go through a major break in her relationship with Mamie Gwinn, for nearly forty years, she lived and breathed her dream—a place where women could receive the best education available. Thomas also oversaw the growth of a skeletal campus to one filled with Gothic-style buildings, spreading trees, ivy-covered walls, and the natural beauty that makes a campus look truly classical.

It wasn't easy. She also battled with the Quaker trustees to round out the curriculum with such forbidden subjects as theater. But she did have one ally all these years: Mary Garrett. Even before Mamie Gwinn left and Garrett moved in, Garrett was promoting the cause of women's education and helping Thomas's career.

The wealthy daughter of a railroad magnate, Mary was a philanthropist who used a great deal of her inheritance to further the cause of women's rights. The year after Thomas was appointed dean, Garrett and Thomas opened the Bryn Mawr School for Girls in Baltimore with Garrett's money. The prep school used the Bryn Mawr entrance exam as a graduation requirement and hired Edith Hamilton as the first actual headmistress. (Thomas worked as headmistress *in absentia* during the first years, safely instituting unpopular reforms and requirements by long distance from the suburbs of Philadelphia.)

Five years later, in 1890, Garrett also used her money to see that women were admitted to the new medical school at Johns Hopkins. The Baltimore fund-raising committee for the fledgling med school (which raised most of the money for the school) was made up of the original "five friends." Garrett initially helped the other four raise more than sixty thousand dollars of the five hundred thousand needed. But when it became apparent that no more money was going to be raised, Garrett donated the rest.

Her gift wisely came with strings attached. She not only demanded that women be admitted to the med school but that the standards be as high as the medical schools in Europe, standards so high that one of the teachers joked that they were lucky to get in as professors because they couldn't qualify as students!

Garrett also used her money to help further Thomas's career. When Thomas was campaigning for the presidency of Bryn Mawr in 1893, Garrett offered to give the college a ten-thousand-dollar-a-year grant as long as Thomas remained president and Garrett lived. After donating twenty-six marble busts of Greek gods and Roman emperors plus a well-known private classical library she had purchased for the Bryn Mawr collection, she wrote in a letter to the trustees:

I plan, "whenever Miss M. Carey Thomas should become President of your College, to pay into her hands the sum of ten thousand dollars yearly so long as I live and she remains President."

It was a huge windfall but it still took months for the trustees to decide to actually hire a woman as the president, especially one who was only thirty-six and who, during her tenure as dean, had taken the college further and further away from the Quaker principles on which it was founded. They were also concerned that the money would give her even more power than she already had.

But eventually they relented. They saw the wisdom not only of hiring "one of the brainiest women in this state," as a Pennsylvania newspaper called her but one who came with a handsome yearly gift from her girlfriend.

Ten years later—soon after Gwinn's departure—Garrett joined Thomas at her home on the campus, the Deanery. Friendly, sociable, and wealthy, Mary Garrett made a tremendous difference in Thomas's life.

They remodeled the Deanery, adding a wing for their comfort and more lavish entertaining. In the process, they turned it into an Art Nouveau fantasy complete with Tiffany lamps and William Morris-inspired floral designs. It cost more than fifty thousand dollars at a time when fifty thousand dollars was a fortune. They also laid out a garden.

While Thomas and Gwinn had traveled like vagabonds, Thomas and Garrett not only traveled in style but began bringing back European antiques and architectural ideas to the college. They also brought back items of enormous extravagance which nonetheless fit into a lesbian sensibility and culture, such as "silver and enamel" headdresses for the annual May queen.

When Garrett died in 1915 after only a decade together, she left her entire estate, nearly five hundred thousand dollars to Thomas. It was a grand gesture, but it meant nothing to Carey who only wanted Garrett back. Thomas became incredibly depressed. Even her work no longer mattered. Friends at the college had never seen her like this, not even when Mamie left. They feared for her sanity. Eventually she began to come to, but it took a long while.

Some years later, she wrote to a friend whose spouse had just died:

"I never let myself be a moment without a book, I did not dare. And in time, wonderful, incredible as it seems—life comes back and peace and even joy. . . . Travel is a help in filling one's thoughts and in tiring out one physically."

Until Thomas herself died twenty years later, no one replaced Garrett in her heart.

In 1894, after ten years at the college, Thomas was promoted to the presidency. She served until she retired in 1922. After that, she became a trustee.

Before she retired, her single-minded devotion to the cause and single-handed rule caught up with her. Over the years, she had encountered a lot of criticism of her dictatorial style. So much so that even Margaret Hamilton, Edith's sister who taught at the Bryn Mawr School for Girls, was concerned about alienating Thomas and jeopardizing *her* position when Edith wanted to retire as headmistress there against Thomas's wishes.

Being such a strong-willed woman, Thomas had made enemies, including a much-publicized one: Woodrow Wilson, who had taught at the college before he became president of the U.S. Like Barry, the list of enemies eventually got so long, charges were brought against her. Like Barry, Thomas had to defend herself against charges of double-dealing—not once but twice over the years. Like Barry, she also was acquitted both times, but it was still shocking to a woman who had lived for the college, and the college alone, all her career.

By the time she died in 1935, however, those events were forgotten. Her purpose, decided as a young girl, had been fulfilled. Year after year, an "army" went into the world to "spread her doctrines of true scholarship, freedom of the mind and equality of women," wrote Finch.

Thomas started the army and for nearly forty years, she added to the troops more strong, dedicated women who eventually won the battle of women's education. In fact, Thomas succeeded so completely that today, "the woman question" is such a fact of academic life, it's not even a question anymore.

M. Carey Thomas

1857 Born in Baltimore, Maryland
1877 Graduates from Cornell University

1879 Leaves for Europe with Mamie Gwinn; attends the University at Leipzig and Göttingen but leaves after finding out she will not be granted a degree

1882 Receives doctorate from University of Zurich

1884 Becomes Dean of Bryn Mawr College for Women

1885 "Five friends" open Bryn Mawr School for Girls with Mary Garrett's generosity

1890 Mary Garrett and five friends offer $100,000 to Johns Hopkins Medical School if it will admit women; eventually raise $500,000 needed to open school

1892 Mamie Gwinn begins to lecture at Bryn Mawr

1893 Mary Garrett offers Bryn Mawr College $10,000 per year if it will appoint Thomas President

1904 Mamie Gwinn leaves with a married man; Mary Garrett moves in; Gertrude Stein writes *Fernhurst* about love triangle

1915 Mary Garrett dies of leukemia

1922 Thomas retires from Bryn Mawr; becomes President Emeritus

1935 Thomas dies at age 78

Chapter Four

JANE ADDAMS

Two women in Jane Addams's life made all the difference in the world. The first, a childhood friend named Ellen Gates Starr, traveled to Europe with her and helped her found Hull House. The second, a Chicago aristocrat named Mary Rozet Smith, poured in money, hit up her own wealthy friends for donations, and generally helped Addams keep Hull House afloat.

Despite starting the field of social work, Jane Addams was no Goodie Two-Shoes. Quite the contrary. She was a fiery, union-organizing radical who founded and then spent her adult life in the mostly-female commune, Hull House. For the record, Hull House did have male residents, but they were the exception, not the rule. And they included such intriguing specimens as Englishman George Mortimer Randall Plantagenet Twose—"or something of that sort," as journalist Francis Hackett deemed him—who liked to sunbathe nude—an unheard-of eccentricity for the day. Or better yet, Frank Hazenplug, described by Hackett as "almost unbearably aesthetic, dancing pliantly, hard at work in the Hull-House Theatre, painting, nailing, doing make-up, with a nervous giggle to hide his inarticulateness."

Hull House was so radical that by 1933 at the beginning of the red-baiting that would culminate in the McCarthy era witchhunts of the 1950's, Elizabeth Dilling wrote in her book, *The Red Network*:

"It is of utmost significance that practically all the radicalism started among women in the United States centers about Hull-House, Chicago, and the Children's Bureau, at Washington, [headed by Former Hull House resident Julia Lathrop] with a dynasty of Hull-House graduates in charge of it since its creation." (Taken from *Eighty Years at Hull House* by Davis and McCree.)

If she only knew they were dykes, too. But homo-hunting wasn't added to the list until the 1950's.

Even though neither Addams nor Starr had jobs, the first order of business once they settled in was to help working women. One of their first major efforts, deviously dubbed a "club," was to help women factory workers set up a commune where they could share living expenses and save the money that would help them survive during strikes.

Jane Addams was no Lady Bountiful, bringing food and culture to poverty-stricken neighbors. She believed people should earn a living wage—and fight for it, if necessary. She also believed that everyone had the right to decent food and living conditions, child care, medical treatment, education, even parks.

Her ideas may seem terribly recherché today, at least in the light of media pronouncements that communism is dead, but Addams believed that society had a responsibility for all its members, the poor as well as the middle-class and well-to-do.

Addams was not alone in her thinking, then or now. The vast majority of industrialized countries have embraced a philosophy of socialism similar to that of Jane Addams—and Karl Marx. With the exception of the U.S., South Africa, and a few other countries, most first-world governments accept responsibility for the problems of society, not just for its philosophical underpinnings. They also direct, if not actually control, the means of production—another basic tenet of socialism.

Addams had known since she was seven that she wanted to "help the poor." But twenty years later, she still didn't know exactly how.

Like Florence Nightingale she *did* know what she *didn't* want. She had already refused an offer of marriage and refused to become a missionary even though the religious college she attended pressured her, and everyone else, to join.

Like most young women of her class and day, Addams went to Europe to fill the time. She'd already done one tour, but in 1887 she decided to return to study early Christian socialism. Ellen Gates Starr went with her to study art. Starr was a follower of socialist craftsmen such as William Morris, who had an almost mystical belief in the transcendent nature of art for everyone, even the poor.

They had become close friends during Starr's one year at Rockford

Seminary, a women's religious college in Illinois. Because her father could only afford one year's tuition, Starr had to take a teaching job at Miss Kirkland's School for Girls in Chicago instead of returning in the fall. As a teacher of art appreciation to the daughters of the Chicago aristocracy, she met the wealthy families of Chicago society, an asset that served her well when the two women set up Hull House a few years later. Despite nearly a ten-year absence between their year at Rockford and going to Europe together, Ellen and Jane stayed in touch, writing "frequent and earnest letters," according to the entry on Starr in *Notable American Women, 1607 to 1950*. They also visited and had long talks about what to do with their lives. They realized that most of the roads open to women were filled with aimlessness and futility. Neither wanted to travel those particular paths.

While visiting the Catacombs in Rome, Addams was suddenly struck with the idea of renting a house in a poverty-stricken part of town with "many primitive and actual needs." There she felt she could create a place where young women like herself—who had "studied too much"—could restore balance in their lives through activity. Ever the pragmatist, they could also, she wrote, "put truth to the ultimate test—of the conduct it . . . inspires."

In Madrid Addams revealed her plan to Starr. From what she wrote in her autobiography, *Twenty Years at Hull House*, it is clear what an uphill battle it was for women in those days even to *dream* of doing something.

"I told it in the fear of that disheartening experience which is so apt to afflict our most cherished plans when they are at last divulged, when we suddenly feel that there is nothing there to talk about. . . . As the golden dream slips through our fingers we are left to wonder at our own fatuous belief."

Instead of telling Addams she was a lunatic for thinking up such a crazy scheme, Starr was excited by the idea of moving to a slum to use their middle-class skills to help the poor meet their needs. Addams wrote:

"Gradually the comfort of Miss Starr's companionship, the vigor and enthusiasm which she brought to bear upon it, told both in the growth of the plan and upon the sense of its validity, so that by the time we had reached the enchantment of the Alhambra, the scene had become convincing and tangible although still most hazy in detail."

The "enchantment of the Alhambra . . ." Addams and Starr were fired with the notion of fixing the world, but they were still young, in love, and in Europe.

For a month they discussed the plan. Then, fired with enthusiasm, finally knowing what her goal was, Addams went to London to investigate English attempts at ending poverty there. Starr went to Italy. Addams wrote Starr love-filled letters which Geoffrey Johnson brought to light in a 1989 *Chicago* magazine article. They not only had each other, they had a dream they both wanted:

"I need you, dear one, more than you can realize."

But the world was calling. Addams's most important stop was Toynbee Hall, the settlement founded by a group of men from Oxford University. There, Addams immersed herself in the radical movements of the day, studying Bernard Shaw and the thinkers of the Fabian society. She also attended a strike of London match girls who were protesting low wages and the use of phosphorus, which led to "phossy jaw," one of the many industrial diseases of the day.

The next winter, Addams and Starr were together again in Chicago looking for a suitable house. By summer, they had found what they wanted—a dilapidated mansion that had once been a country estate but was by then in the middle of a slum. In September 1889, Addams and Starr moved into the house on Polk and Halsted that stood between an undertaker's and a saloon.

After their first night in Hull House, Starr wrote:

"I don't know, just at this point, how I should live my life without [Jane]. I couldn't do *this* without her, and I couldn't very well *not* do it."

While Addams started up a soup kitchen and child care center, Starr hung reproductions of classic European art on the walls and put sculpture in the studio—a Venus de Milo, a Winged Victory of Samothrace, a Madonna and Child. While Addams attended to the physical needs of their neighbors, Starr tried to meet the aesthetic ones: to create beauty even in the midst of the ugliness of poverty.

Starr was appalled that the local immigrants had nothing in the way of art. They no longer made the folk art of their own country yet were unfamiliar with the "great works" of the classics. In fact, one of the later triumphs of the settlement movement was to get museums opened on Sunday, the only day of the week the workers had off.

Starr started the first "club," a reading group. One evening each week, Starr would read from novels to anyone who wanted to come to the house to listen. Starr began with George Eliot's *Romola*, a popular novel at the time. While the idea of listening to someone read seems unimaginably boring by our technological standards, having somewhere to go to relax and be entertained (other than a saloon or a church) was an incredible luxury for the residents of the area. Listening to a story was free—and fairly common—entertainment of the day. It also epitomized Starrs desire to help the locals escape the back-breaking toil of their lives. As soon as they finished *Romola*, a neighbor began Hawthorne.

Starr's contacts from Miss Kirkland's school also helped. The first major donation—five thousand dollars for an art gallery—was from Edward Butler, someone she knew from her teaching days.

There's no question that the Starr-Addams partnership helped make Hull House a success. Starr organized art classes. Her photographs of paintings from those classes were later sent to the public schools as a loan from the Hull House collection. In 1894, five years after she helped found Hull House, Starr helped found—and became the first president of—the Chicago Public School Art Society.

But no matter how much anyone at Hull House immersed themselves in culture, they never forgot the basic realities of working-class life. Most of all, Starr hated the effects of industrialization, the ugliness of poverty, the alienation and emotional deadening that rote work brought. So much so, she wrote an essay in the 1895 "Hull House Maps and Papers" that said, in Margaret Tims's biography of Addams:

"For the children of the 'degraded poor,' and the degraded rich as well, in our present mode of life, there is no artistic hope outside of [a] miracle."

When the Illinois branch of the National Women's Trade Union was founded in 1930, Starr was there. Like Addams—and all the residents of Hull House—they were not only there for the founding of organizations but the front lines of street-fighting radicalism and strikes.

In 1914, Starr was arrested for "interfering with a police officer in the discharge of his duty" during a restaurant workers' strike. The jury acquitted the frail, 100-pound, pince-nez-wearing Starr, citing the implausibility of the charge. The fact that she had a posh accent probably also helped get her off. After the 1915 textile workers' strike (made up mostly of women), Starr was made an honorary member of the Amalgamated Clothing Workers of America.

Some forty years after Addams and Starr met, they parted company. By then, Addams was deeply involved with Mary Rozet Smith, a supporter of Hull House from the first. Starr left Hull House after her conversion to Catholicism but still continued to visit Addams. After a 1929 operation on her spine which left her a paraplegic, she moved into the Convent of the Holy Child in New York.

Until the day Addams died in 1935, however, they continued to correspond. Starr wrote every year on September 14. Though neither woman could remember exactly which day it was, it was important to keep a remembrance of the day they started their great venture together. In 1933, a bed-rid invalid, Ellen wrote Jane a special note:

"This is the date that I keep as the anniversary of our going to Hull House."

An anniversary they kept all their lives.

Hull House and Its Residents

Jane Addams grew up in an era when people assumed that problems such as poverty could be solved. In some respects, the problems people faced then were even greater than the ones we face today.

Child labor is an example. "Childhood" as a separate and distinct time in a person's life during which they played, had fun, and were educated, didn't exist. That concept is a twentieth-century invention. Children of the poor worked from the time they were old enough to hold objects in their hands. In Chicago, Addams saw children as young as four and five work alongside their mother in home industries such as the rag trade. When they were old enough, these youngsters graduated to dangerous jobs in factories where they worked unrelenting hours. A child could work all day and night for wages that were much less than those paid to an adult. Once at Hull House, Addams saw children maimed and killed in factories. A twelve-year-old girl she knew died of exhaustion; another teenager committed suicide when she couldn't pay off a debt.

Addams's belief that problems could be solved created many of the amenities we take for granted today: an education for every child no matter how poor, laws limiting the hours children can work, city parks, libraries and other urban services.

In fact, the turn of the century was a time of great social ferment— and the cities, as always, were the great proving ground of ideas. By then, a large middle class, born of the industrial revolution, existed that could implement democracy on a much wider scale than idealistic aristocrats of the past ever could. Settlements and utopian communities dedicated to different ideals sprang up all over the United States and Europe in the form of communes.

While many of these failed—or were so successful their efforts were no longer needed—Hull House endured, probably because Addams was a pragmatist who always asked not what people *could* do but what they *would* do. Many of the services Hull House first offered were in direct response to what neighbors said they needed. This ability to recognize the limits of human nature and work with it rather than against it was one of her greatest assets.

A tireless fighter for the rights of the poor and the working stiff, Addams is considered the founder of social work—though her fiery radicalism bears little resemblance to the bureaucratic system we have today.

Addams was one of the first middle-class Americans to choose to live among the poor. She used her own modest income to create services for her neighborhood.

Addams took many of her ideas from two other settlements—Toynbee Hall in London founded five years earlier and the New York East Side Neighborhood Guild founded three years prior.

Though Addams gets much of the credit, she didn't work alone, either. Her courage and enthusiasm immediately drew other strong-willed women (and a few men) to her side. For the first five years, they had fifteen residents, women such as Alice Hamilton, her friend Julia Lathrop, and Florence Kelley, a socialist who would join Lillian Wald's Henry Street Settlement when she got a job in New York.

Addams and Lathrop just missed each other by a year at Rockford Seminary. Lathrop transferred to Vassar after a year, from where she graduated. And for the next decade, she worked for her father, a lawyer who served one term in Congress. But Addams had made an impression on Rockford alumni, even one like Lathrop who only met her when she came back to visit. During her college days, Addams was already pushing for women's rights in subtle yet important ways, such as being the first woman to actually get a degree from Rockford. Even though the college offered a degree, no one had ever bothered to get one. When she took the courses required to earn a degree, including mathematics, which was then thought impossible for a woman, Addams set a new standard and opened up new vistas for women at the school. To mark the importance of the occasion, she gave her commencement speech in Greek.

Not that Addams was a complete drudge. In her autobiography, she also writes of trying opium during her collegiate days.

Lathrop and Kelley were two of the most important residents, close friends who worked together for years. Both were reformers, even if their approach was as different as night and day. James Weber Linn, Addams's nephew, wrote of Lathrop (and Kelley) in Addams's biography:

"[Julia] sparkled, as did Florence Kelley; their talk was a firework. Her wit was never mordant. Florence Kelley could be terrifying, and when she chose to be, was so; but Julia Lathrop, who could have been quite as terrifying, never chose to be so. She was not so much detached as restrained."

Addams's last book was the biography *My Friend, Julia Lathrop*. She was working on a biography of Florence Kelley when she died.

Lathrop and Kelley, as well as Hamilton, were just two of the many rabble-rousing women at Hull House. For many of the women who came from influential and proper families, Hull House was the answer to their prayers—a way to escape marriage and have a career at a time when women had few career options.

It might have taken Addams many years to realize that founding a settlement to serve poor neighbors was the way to help them but she understood injustice at an early age.

Addams came from a liberal, idealistic family. Her father had been a friend of Abraham Lincoln's in Lincoln's Illinois days. As a state senator, he was known to be so incorruptible he was never offered a bribe at a time when money greased the wheels of most legislatures. He instilled in young Jane a tremendous sense of social responsibility. A Quaker, Jane displayed a tremendous social conscience, even for a Friend. At seven, seeing poverty for the first time in the form of workers' tiny tenement houses, Jane said although she would live in a big house one day, it would be among tiny houses just like those.

Addams stated her life's goal as a child of seven, but it took her many years to remember those words—and to realize she could do it. As a result, she felt she wasted many years in the "snares of preparation." After graduating from Rockford Seminary, Addams did what most well-heeled young people of the day did: she took a tour of Europe in order to familiarize herself firsthand with America's cultural heritage.

While most Americans used a tour of Europe to immerse themselves in art and literature and were oblivious to any signs of poverty, Addams was keenly aware of the destitution around her—and she ended up in some very unlikely tourist spots, such as the poorest section of London where she went for a Saturday-night food sale.

Rotting fruits and vegetables that would not last till Monday market were being auctioned off. One glance at the "mass of ill-clad people clamoring around two hucksters' carts . . . the myriads of hands, empty, pathetic, nerveless and workworn, showing white in the uncertain light of the street . . . clutching forward for food which was already unfit to eat," haunted her the rest of her life.

She later wrote in *Twenty Years at Hull House:*

"I have never been able to see a number of hands held upward, even when they are moving rhythmically in a calisthenic exercise, or when they belong to a class of chubby children who wave them in eager response to a teacher's query, without a certain revival of this memory, a clutching at the heart reminiscent of the despair and resentment which seized me then."

The image not only haunted her but haunted the happiness of a tour that was supposed to prepare her for the elegant and cultured life free from the cares of the "real" world that lay ahead of her. Instead, Addams despaired of ever being able to make a difference.

She kept a journal with entries like, to quote from Linn:

"Blarney Castle . . . 'Owner said to have an income of thirteen thousand pounds a year; ordinary man six shillings a week."

Addams finally decided that, despite her indecision, she would act where she could. In Germany, she took to task the owner of a brewery whose women workers could barely carry massive tanks of ale on their backs. Their hands bore white scars from the scaldingly hot liquid spilled on them as they fought to maintain balance. Everywhere she went, she got off the beaten track to see the real world, the world as working people lived it—and she did what she could to change it.

When she returned to the U.S., she learned that some of her inheritance had been invested in a farm. Addams immediately visited the farm and was horrified to discover that the family lived in abject poverty from a mortgage on which she was making money.

Appalled at her involvement in their suffering, she promptly sold the investment, even though she wasn't sure whether the sale would cause further hardship or not.

By the time she realized she wanted to found Hull House, she had had some experience. At Hull House, Addams came to help but she also came to learn. Mary Kenny, a working girl and union organizer, later wrote about her in *Eighty Years at Hull House:*

"One day, while I was working at my trade, I received a letter from Miss Jane Addams. She invited me to Hull-House for dinner. . . .

"I had been a member of [another] working girls' club and I was much disgusted with the talk of the group. . . . I thought that helping to get better wages was much more important. . . .

"I decided that I would not accept the invitation to Hull-House. No club people for me!''

Her mother convinced her to go.

"Miss Addams greeted me and introduced the guests from England and all the residents. My first impression was that they were all rich and not friends of the workers. . . .

"By my manner Miss Addams must have known that I wasn't very friendly.

" 'Is there anything I can do to help your organization?' she said.

"I couldn't believe I had heard right.''

Kenny told her that her union was currently meeting in quarters over a saloon and could use a nicer place. Addams offered Hull House. Kenny said they needed someone to help distribute flyers. Addams not only distributed the flyers herself, going up high, narrow stairs in back alleys to find women workers during their lunch hour when she could actually talk to them but paid for the flyers to boot.

When she got older, Kenny was invited to live at Hull House. There, she began studying diligently, especially English.

"I realized for the first time how handicapped I was and how handicapped the children of other wage workers were that left school at fourteen.''

Kenny later started the Jane Club, founded the Book Binders' Union, the National Woman's Trade Union League. She also was the first woman organizer for the American Federation of Labor.

Addams said, again and again, that anyone who came to Hull House must have a genuine preference for living in the area. In other words, Addams was one of the first middle-class people to return to the "downtown,'' though gentrification was the last thing on her mind.

At South Halsted Street, the poverty was unlike anything Addams had grown up with. Hard-working but intelligent immigrants with very little understanding of their rights made up the majority of the neighbors. It was the perfect place for an experiment in life.

"The streets are inexpressibly dirty, the number of schools inadequate, sanitary legislation unenforced, the street lighting bad, the paving miserable . . . and the stables foul beyond description . . . Many houses have no water supply ... there are no fire-escapes, the garbage ... is placed in wooden boxes which are fastened to the street pavement,'' wrote Addams.

In the first few weeks, Addams and Starr set up a day-care center. A kindergarten was added for working mothers of the area, whose children had roamed the streets or been left at home by themselves all day.

Of the first three children, Addams wrote:

''One had fallen out of a third-storey window, another had been burned, and the third had a curved spine due to the fact that for three years he had been tied all day long to the leg of the kitchen table, only released at noon by his older brother who hastily ran in from a neighboring factory to share his lunch with him.''

Two years later, in 1891, a public kitchen that provided cheap meals for housewives and laborers was added. Not content to provide Band-Aid solutions, however, they started a labor union for women who worked in the rag trade. In May, thanks to Mary Kenny's efforts, fifteen young women factory workers banded together to rent apartments and form a commune that pooled money to help out one another in times of strike. Addams furnished the building and paid the first month's rent. Prior to ''The Jane Club,'' young women had been frightened of going out on strike, despite truly deplorable conditions. If they lost their wages and their homes, they would end up on the streets as prostitutes. Many of the first women's labor unions, including the shirtmakers and cloakmakers, formed at Hull House or with the help of its radical women residents.

From Starr's creation of the first club, a reading club, ''clubs'' that combined entertainment, recreation, education, and agitation grew. A club for men, for children, for students, an improvement club for the neighborhood, a social science club, and an ''eight-hour-day'' club which encouraged women in factories to ''stand by an eight-hour day'' in the years before enforcement was a matter of routine were just a few of them.

Within several years, Hull House added an art gallery, a music school and little theater. Eventually, arts and craft classes, Sunday concerts, exhibitions, a choir, and an orchestra were added to the growing roster of activities.

As time went on, college extension classes, an employment bureau, and a savings bank were also added. In the midst of all this activity the idea of social work was born.

Mary Rozet Smith

The daughter of "the leading manufacturer in Chicago" in the 1860's through the 1890's, Mary Rozet Smith never left her home on Walton Place nor her invalid mother and elderly father, but she was at Hull House from the first asking what she could do. According to biographer Linn, Smith was the major source of comfort for Jane Addams until their deaths one year apart. He writes:

"One suspects that the real influence was from the very beginning her decision to be primarily concerned in making life easier for Jane Addams. That was her career, that was her philosophy."

Thanks in large part to Mary Rozert Smith Hull House was a place of warmth and conviviality, which resident Alice Hamilton described: for dinner there was the long paneled room of wrought-iron chandeliers in the Spanish style; for breakfast: a coffehouse like an English inn. For Hamilton, as for others, Hull House satisfied her longings for excitement, intellectual stimulation, companionship, as well as the sense of belonging to a community whose radical politics and unceasing work was changing the world.

Since Addams never turned anyone away, it could also be chaotic with constant demands. Jane turned to Mary for an escape. Hamilton wrote that Addams used Smith's large home on Walton Place as a refuge, without which she wouldn't have been able to manage. The others used it to escape and revitalize themselves also.

Jane Addams and Mary Rozet Smith spent more than forty years together. Hamilton says that "her coming was not only a joy but a sustaining help in time of trouble and perplexity."

It was a help financially, too, especially at the beginning when their influential friends laughed and told the women they could do nothing for the poor, that the poor wanted to live like animals and would not appreciate their help. To quote from a 1940 *New York Times* Magazine article by Lloyd Lewis in "Eighty Years":

"Aristocratic friends, members of the old Yankee ruling class of the city, had advised Jane Addams not to make this plunge into the slums. They said it would make her inacceptable in the homes of the 'best people.' "

But Addams always said that Hull House was a bridge for the well-to-do as well as the poor. To continue:

"But she remained socially eligible and able to hobnob with the city's rich; she went everywhere in those pioneering days, enlisting money and influence.''

It probably helped that Mary Rozet Smith, the daughter of Chicago's oldest aristocratic family, stood by her side ''sweetly dragooning donations from groaning industrialists.''

Thanks mainly to two society women, Louise deKoven Bowen (Mrs. Joseph T.) and Mary Rozet Smith, Hull House got the money it needed. According to Allen F. Davis and Mary Lynn McCree's *Eighty Years at Hull House*, ''without them, Hull House would have floundered.''

Smith was always giving major and minor sums herself, whenever needed. She also got her father to finance and build the Children's Building.

Unfortunately, past biographers have been particularly shortsighted when it came to Addams's relationship with Smith, not giving credence to either of Addams's relationships, even going so far as to say that ''life eluded her!''

But Addams had a fulfilling emotional life. For the first ten years of her adulthood, there was Ellen Gates Starr. Later, Mary Rozet Smith became her lifelong companion, the woman she would turn to until Smith's death forty-three years later.

Nonetheless heterosexual blinders have created some very odd conjectures. Ignoring Starr altogether, Margaret Tims in *Jane Addams of Hull House* says that Smith replaced Addams's beloved father. Tims even calls Smith, ''Mrs.,'' though Smith was not married.

Biographers also define the two women as ''spouse-surrogates,'' a deprecating enough term in and of itself, but worse, one which denies them the love and affection they actually had. To understand romantic friendships, however, it helps to realize that love comes in all guises.

As scholar Carol Smith-Rosenberg has written:

''Perhaps the most explicit statement concerning women's lifelong friendships appeared in the letter abolitionist and reformer Mary Grew wrote . . . referring to her own love for her dear friend and lifelong companion, Margaret Burleigh. Grew wrote, in response to a letter of condolence from another woman on Burleigh's death:

'' 'Your words respecting my beloved friend touch me deeply. Evidently . . . you comprehend and appreciate, as few persons do . . . the nature of the relation which exists, between her and myself. We know there have been other such between two men and also between two women. And why should there not be. Love is spiritual, only passion is sexual.' ''

Like any spouse, Mary Rozet Smith traveled with Jane Addams on most occasions. As early as 1896, Mary accompanied Jane on a recuperative visit abroad, during which they visited the pacifist-activist author Leo Tolstoy.

Just before the trip together, their almost daily letters changed to the simple yet obvious "dearest." Portions of Jane's poem written to Mary tell all.

"There sat upon a childish chair
A girl, both tall and fair to see,
  (To look at her gives one a thrill).
But all I thought was, would she be
  Best fitted to lead club, or drill?
You see, I had forgotten Love,
  And only thought of Hull House then . . .
So I was blind and deaf those years
  To all save one absorbing care,
And did not guess what now I know—
  Delivering love was sitting there!"

Addams' nephew Linn writes of that time:

"The friendship of Mary Smith soon became and always remained the highest and clearest note in the music of Jane Addams's personal life."

Smith accompanied Addams when she went to the Hague for the Congress of Women in 1915 and across Europe as she tried to negotiate a peaceful settlement to World War I. According to lesbian scholar Blanche Wiesen Cook, when they traveled, Addams wired ahead for a double bed.

"Jane Addams also slept in the same house, in the same room, in the same bed with Mary Rozet Smith for [more than] 40 years."

Nearly a quarter century after they met, Smith was still with Addams for the nine-month world tour of 1923.

The two women eventually bought a summer house together at Hull's Cove, which everyone assumed to be jointly owned.

Smith died of pneumonia a little more than a year before Addams who, at the time, was recovering from bronchitis and heart problems. Smith's death was particularly tragic in that the two women, though living in the same house by then, were not able to see each other, since both were bedridden.

Of Smith's death, Addams later wrote, "I could have willed my heart to stop beating but the thought of what she had been to me for so long kept me from being cowardly."

Linn, however, wrote of Smith's death:

"The illumination of Jane Addams's spirit dimmed when Mary Smith died; she walked as steadily as ever, but in the twilight."

Past biographers have dealt with the possibility of lesbianism, but most, like Davis, have dismissed it or called it irrelevant. For a complete picture of these women, however, it is essential to realize that they refused to marry, surrounded themselves with women, and had as important loves as any heterosexual has in his or her life.

Scholars are beginning to say that sexual orientation needs to be included in the historic package. If homosexuality is ever to be fully integrated into society, heterosexuals need to understand that many of the people they look up to were part of the historic gay tradition.

No matter what happened in bed, Addams lived in a world that is remarkably similar to lesbian culture today. Whatever her "sexuality," Addams turned to women for emotional and political support, for companionship, affection, and love. Because of Addams, Starr and Smith, Hull House grew until it had seventy, mostly female, residents—and, according to Dilling, became a hotbed of radicalism that spread over the entire U.S. We should be so lucky.

The Workers and the War

By 1910, nearly twenty years after the opening of Hull House, Addams was regarded as one of the most important women in America. Child labor laws had been passed in most states by then, sweat shops outlawed in some states, minimum wage secured in others. That same year, following the publication of *Twenty Years at Hull House,* Addams was given an honorary degree by Yale University, the first woman to receive one.

Despite the fact women did not yet have the vote, the Illinois Equal Suffrage Association urged her appointment to the U.S. Senate that year. By 1912, suffragists were saying she should run for President.

Hull House had turned Chicago around. It had helped create a new kind of local government—one that provided and coordinated public services instead of the mishmash of charity that characterized the past.

Two years earlier, Addams helped found the Chicago School of Civics and Philanthropy, one of the first schools of social work in the country which later became the School of Social Service Administration of the University of Chicago.

Addams wasn't just a reformer, she was also a thinker. Her 1902 book *Democracy and Social Ethics* presupposes an industrial-based worker democracy best seen today in social democracies such as Sweden and Japan.

People needed rights and power, not handouts, she believed. To her, the philanthropist was a fraud. No matter how well meaning or generous, workers needed rights, jobs, and a wage that would make charity unnecessary. In fact, Addams would have been appalled at the bureaucratic social work system today. She certainly would have thought that the well-paid, middle-class professional social worker who went to an office each day to dole out pittances to the poor was a far cry from the answer.

Her 1907 *Newer Ideals of Peace* tackles one of the major problems facing America today: how to integrate the welfare class, the working poor, and labor unions into a viable capitalist system. She wrote:

"While the State spends millions of dollars and employs thousands of servants to nurture and heal the sick and defective, it steadfastly refuses to extend its kindliness to the normal working man."

Addams eventually decided that turn-of-the-century socialism was not the answer. What was needed was a self-governing democracy at all levels of society.

Her idealism eventually got her into trouble. She saw the world as a global village which had to rise above individual national boundaries to solve problems. As the world headed toward war, she turned her back on nationalism. Addams had begun to see war as devastating—to *all* people, the men who fought as well as the women and children left behind.

Shortly after the outbreak of the war, Addams and suffragist leader Carrie Chapman Catt helped organize an American version of Women's Peace Party, a group originally founded by women in England and Hungary.

Addams was asked to preside over the First International Congress of Women. She went there with Alice Hamilton, in addition to many other important women of the day. To quote from Hamilton's biographer, Grant, Hamilton wrote to Mary Rozet Smith about Jane on the boat passage over:

"Miss Addams is really having a good time. She has made every woman on board feel that she is an intimate friend and they all adore her.''

Until the United States joined the war, Addams crisscrossed the Atlantic, meeting leaders of Europe in an effort to resolve the conflict. Addams spoke with eight prime ministers and presidents, nine foreign secretaries, as well as the Pope. Mary Rozet Smith usually traveled with Addams, helping keep up her spirits despite the frustration of endlessly polite but nonetheless futile visits to Europe's most powerful men.

Such an action today would be considered fantastically foolish by a society inured to the seeming inevitably of war, but the women were taken seriously. Even though their proposals for a permanent peace weren't instituted, their ideas laid the groundwork for the League of Nations, the precursor to the United Nations which is slowly moving closer to the kind of peace-keeping body necessary for this tiny planet.

According to a magazine article written by Addams about the mission, when asked if the Prime Minister of Hungary thought the women's task foolish, Stephen von Tisza said: ''These are the first sensible words that have been uttered in this room for ten months.''

Von Tisza explained that for nearly a year, people had come through his door asking for men, money and munitions. Addams was the first person to ask for negotiations.

Three thousand men a day died on the western front without any change in either side's military position. Addams met with President Woodrow Wilson on her return to the U.S. in 1915, but it did little good. The tide of public opinion was already against her.

When a German U-boat sunk a ship with a hundred Americans aboard, the U.S. joined the war.

As xenophobia and nationalism rose, Addams began to be reviled. In a 1915 speech at Carnegie Hall, she said that soldiers were being given alcohol before going into battle to goad them into fighting more aggressively.

It made headlines nationwide; newspapers unleashed a torrent of abuse on her for speaking ''against her country.''

Despite the viciousness of the attack, Addams knew that the hostility came from her point of view, that war was an old man's game inflicted on the young, something we in the U.S. only began to grasp in the late 1960's.

Despite the browbeating, Addams never wavered in her conviction that war led nowhere. But the aftereffects of World War I were even more horrendous than the war itself. Though she tried, she could do little against nations trying to punish the losers.

The most immediate concern for her was to get food to the conquered countries. In 1919, she attended the second Women's Congress in Zurich, Switzerland. One hundred thirty-seven female delegates from twenty-one countries met to find a way to cope with the horror of war's aftermath. Although Addams and other delegates spoke with national leaders around the world, nothing happened. It was particularly disturbing for Addams, who had seen firsthand the effects of malnutrition on a female Austrian delegate who, already skin and bones, when Addams saw her, died of starvation three months after she returned home.

Three years later, Addams published *Peace and Bread in the Time of War,* in which she wrote the woman was "so shrunken and changed that I had much difficulty in identifying her with the beautiful woman I had seen three years before. She was not only emaciated . . . but her face and artist's hands were covered with rough red blotches due to the long use of soap substitutes, giving her a cruelly scalded appearance."

The years following the war were difficult for many of the women who had been involved in peace efforts. Times were particularly hard on women like Addams and Lillian Wald who defended the immigrants of their neighborhoods. Because of the war, immigrants suddenly became suspected "aliens" overnight. Neither Addams nor Wald would have any part of it.

After a decade of triumph, Addams's name suddenly brought censure instead of applause. For the first time, the fear of communism, which was to reach its height in the McCarthy witch hunts of the 1950's, seemed a serious threat in the public eye. If the Bolsheviks could overthrow rulers in Russia, it could happen anywhere. Addams had already broken with socialism, but her denials went unheard. She was still a radical. Her efforts for world peace had been enough to put her on the wrong side of the issue.

The Daughters of the American Revolution, which had given Addams an honorary membership in 1900, now put her on a blacklist of fifty suspected individuals and organizations. The American Legion attacked her. Addams, in her inimitable style, added fuel to the fire by helping to found the Civil Liberties Union in 1920, which later became the much-reviled, but also much respected, ACLU. When Elizabeth Dilling's list came out, those listed in her exposé held an honorary dinner for themselves with Jane Addams heading the guests.

The winds of fortune are fickle, however, and quickly change. Hull

House still held a position of respect no matter what conservatives thought of Addams. By 1929, when Hull House celebrated its fortieth anniversary, it had an annual income of nearly a hundred thousand dollars. That was to change during the Depression, but it was still a far cry from the days when the original residents paid for their own way—and everything else.

In 1931, Addams was awarded the Nobel Peace Prize in conjunction with the president of Columbia University. Her own inheritance had dropped to little more than a thousand dollars a year by then, but she donated the sixteen-thousand-dollar prize money to the Women's International League, another organization which she helped found.

Honorary degrees from Swarthmore and the University of California at Berkeley followed, as well as other accolades.

But during these years, Addams's health, which had never been good, grew increasingly worse. She lost a kidney and had to have two operations for appendicitis. Her heart was failing. In 1934, she spent four months in bed with bronchitis. What was even worse, she was also losing her dearest friends and colleagues to old age and ill health. Julia Lathrop died in 1932, followed by Mary Rozet Smith in 1934.

Despite these losses, Addams still had a wide circle of friends. She spent the time after Smith's death convalescing at Hadlyme under the care of Alice Hamilton, her longtime friend and physician. Eventually, she returned to Hull House.

Addams died of cancer the next year, however, six days after entering the hospital with acute abdominal pain. She was seventy-four.

Although she was buried in the family plot in Illinois, fifteen hundred people an hour came to pay their respects as she lay in state at Hull House. Photographs of the courtyard show it filled with people wanting to say good-bye. Memorials and honors continued to follow her, even in death.

A few months after her demise, Miss Frances Perkins, the U.S. Secretary of Labor—and first woman to hold such a post—gave Addams the description that has since defined her: She invented social work.

Jane Addams

1860 Born in Cedarville, Illinois
1881 Graduates from Rockford Seminary

1883 Tours Europe for two years, returns to Baltimore
1887 Goes to Europe again with Ellen Gates Starr
1888 Visits Toynbee Hall, a settlement in London
1889 Opens Hull House with Ellen Gates Starr
      Ellen Gates Starr starts first of many "clubs"
1891 Hull House residents organize the "Jane Club," a communal residence for women factory workers who want to be able to strike
1892 Hull House publishes its report on child-labor abuse
      Hull House establishes Chicago's first public playground
1895 "Hull House Maps and Papers" published
1896 Jane Addams and Mary Rozet Smith visit Tolstoy
1910 Addams' autobiographical *Twenty Years at Hull House* published
      Addams becomes first woman to receive honorary degree from Yale University
1915 Addams helps found Woman's Peace Party and travels to the Congress of Women in The Hague
1919 Addams elected President of the Women's International League of Peace and Freedom
1920 Ellen Gates Starr converts to Catholicism and leaves Hull House
1920 Addams defends pacifists during hysteria which follows World War I; Daughters of the American Revolution calls Addams the "most dangerous woman in America"
1923 Addams goes on nine-month lecture tour of world with Mary Rozet Smith; Alice Hamilton joins them when Addams has to have an operation in Japan
1930 *The Second Twenty Years at Hull House* published
1931 Addams receives Nobel Peace Prize with Nicholas Murray Butler
1932 President Franklin D. Roosevelt asks Addams to join Public Works Administration
1935 Addams dies of cancer at age 74

Chapter Five

LILLIAN WALD

Jane Addams created Hull House as a bridge between the wealthy and the poor that each side could travel if they wanted to learn about the other. Lillian Wald created the Henry Street Settlement as a community of like-minded individuals that could replace the family itself. The founder of public health nursing, Wald believed so strongly in the idea of family that not even love affairs could pry her loyalty away from the group.

Even trivial things like nicknames show this belief. Two of the most important residents weren't even nurses: "Tante" (Aunt) Helene, Helen McDowall, the wealthy daughter of a Union Army general who bought a house behind Henry Street where art classes, musicals, theatrical events, and meetings could be held, and "Sister" Kelley, labor organizer and socialist who lived at Hull House before moving to Henry Street.

Other family members who, according to historian Blanche Wiesen Cook, were particularly beloved to Wald were Lavinia Dock, Alice Lewisohn, and Rita Wallach Morgenthau.

A compassionate and philosophical woman who took nursing in the U.S. away from its religious affiliations and into the public sector, Henry Street was nonetheless much like a convent. Since most people can't imagine celibacy even for nuns and priests, anti-Catholic propaganda has given us a picture of convents at their worst, as hotbeds of heterosexuality, nuns sleeping with priests, and aborted fetuses thrown into nearby rivers. But same-sex love and affection was much more common, whether "consummated" or not.

Despite centuries-old lectures against "particular friends," quiet female couples were often the rule. We know from books such as Judith Brown's *Immodest Acts, The Life of a Lesbian Nun in Renaissance Italy,* that at least one nun, Benedetta Carlini, the early seventeenth century abbess of the Theatine nuns of Pescia, Italy, got so out of line, she was investigated for immoral behavior. We know that religious ecstasy also led to many strange behaviors, from penitence to flagellation. In Carlini's case, it led to pretending she was a man while making love to another nun which, Brown notes, legitimized the couplings.

Monastic rules were set up specifically to guard against special friendships going too far. To quote from Brown:

"To remove temptation, the councils of Paris (1212) and Rouen (1214) prohibited nuns from sleeping together and required a lamp to burn all night in dormitories. From the thirteenth century on, monastic rules usually called for nuns to stay out of each others' cells, to leave their doors unlocked so that the abbess might check on them, and to avoid special ties of friendship within the convent."

But as we know from Rosemary Curb and Nancy Manahan's *Lesbian Nuns: Breaking Silence,* rules are sometimes more useful for pointing out "problem" behavior than doing anything about it.

At Henry Street, there were certainly no lectures against special friends. Love affairs were up front among the women living there; they had their "steadies" as well as their "crushes." The "steadies" in Wald's life were residents, including Dock and Kelley. The "crushes," were women such as Mabel Hyde Kittredge and Helen Arthur, who resided at Henry Street temporarily (or not at all) and wanted more of an exclusive relationship with Wald than Wald was willing to give. But no matter which side of the emotional fence the women were on, they remained close friends all their lives.

Nearly a decade older than Wald, roly-poly Lavinia Dock soon became Wald's mentor when she joined the other ten residents. A former superintendent at Johns Hopkins University School of Nursing who wrote *Materia Medica,* one of the first nursing textbooks, "Docky" brought a fiery temperament and a background of union organizing and suffragism to Henry Street. A reputed "manhater," Dock's radicalism probably was the wedge that drove Wald and her apart some twenty years after coming to Henry Street. During the years Dock was one of Wald's closest confidantes, she not only helped Wald write speeches and articles but also helped shape the field of public health nursing here and abroad.

According to Blanche Wiesen Cook's article, *Female Support Networks and Political Activism: Lillian Wald, Crystal Eastman and Emma Goldman,* Dock moved out of Henry Street, resigning with an "icy and formal note" in March of 1916. For ten years, there is a gap in their voluminous correspondence. Cook theorizes that politics was the straw that finally broke the camel's back, mainly Dock's involvement with Alice Paul's Congressional Union, a radical suffragist group of women willing to get arrested for their antiwar feminism.

Because Wald was trying to persuade President Woodrow Wilson not to get involved in World War I, she became one of the most outspoken critics of the group's tactics. "Docky" wrote in a 1916 letter to Wald, that war, when women were being called a national menace for advocating peace, was the perfect time to press for their rights.

It is ironic the two would break over feminism since Wald was an early militant suffragist who organized the first march for women's rights down Fifth Avenue.

Five months later, Dock resigned and left Henry Street permanently. Either their correspondence during the next decade has been lost or the break was so severe that they didn't write for ten years.

When Dock next writes, however, her tone is pointed, if loving. In 1925, they take up again and all is forgiven, if not forgotten—if there ever was any true emotional hostility. Dock writes (to quote from Cook's article):

"Dearest I would scrape together money if you need—you have done the same for me."

Dock came to the hospital when Wald became ill after a vacation to Mexico with Jane Addams and Mary Rozet Smith. When doctors found the tumor was benign, Dock wrote Wald's nurse that she was so worried:

". . . my knees wobbled as I went down the steps to go to the train."

By then, she is again signing her letters "With love, yours ever, Docky."

Though they called themselves "steadies" and saw themselves as a family, there really isn't a word in English for the relationship that Lavinia Dock and Florence Kelley had with Wald.

A graduate of Cornell whose father was a member of Congress for twenty years, "Sister" Florence Kelley enrolled at the University of Zurich after meeting M. Carey Thomas, who was studying there. Kelley didn't finish her degree but instead became such a socialist she translated Fredrich Engels into English.

During this time, she also married another socialist, but after five years, divorced him and brought her three children to Hull House to join the great social experiment there. Once at Hull House, she put her long, dark hair into braids on top her head, threw away her corsets, let the "stays" out of her dresses, and took to wearing black. Kelley stayed eight years before taking a job in New York and moving to the Henry Street Settlement.

While at Hull House, Hamilton wrote that they used to wait up for Kelley and bribe her with hot chocolate to talk to them. But that they had to be careful. She would lay into anyone who was being sentimental or foolish in their opinion.

At Hull House, Kelley fought for the workers. Her chapter in the Hull House papers on the conditions of factories and the working life of women led to the prohibition of child labor, regulation of conditions in home sweat shops, and the limiting of working hours for women at a time when minimum wage didn't exist and forty thousand children worked in New York City alone. Kelley was the force behind the "eight-hour-day" club that helped women factory workers stand up to shop stewards and factory owners who wanted to ignore the "eight-hour-day" law when it was first instituted. She also became the first woman factory inspector during these years, who helped to see that the newly implemented laws were followed.

As if that weren't enough to keep her busy, Kelley also went to law school and was admitted to the bar during the years at Hull House.

Kelley took her whole family to Henry Street when she moved there in 1899 to head the National Consumers' League, where she helped organize some sixty local and state Consumers' League branches.

Once in New York, she used her geographic position on the East Coast to fight for minimum wage legislation and passage of child-labor laws at the federal level. By the time she was through, she had seen laws against child labor enacted in forty-seven states.

Though she wasn't a nurse—and had little, if anything, to do with nursing—Kelley was one of many Henry Street women who changed the face of industry in this country.

Sister Kelley was an equal but Wald was also a mother figure to women at Henry Street such as Alice and Irene Lewisohn.

Leonard Lewisohn, one of Wald's most important financial supporters, brought his two daughters, Alice and Irene, to Henry Street in 1904 to cheer them up (and give them something to do) when their mother died. The two began teaching classes in dance and theater. They later started New York City's first street festival and in 1915, according to Clare Coss's *Lillian D. Wald, Progressive Activist,* founded the Neighborhood Playhouse Theater, "a living monument to the best and most innovative in theater, music, and dance." Ten years later, the theater premiered James Joyce's play *Exiles* after failed attempts by other theaters in Europe to put it on. A typically Joycean linguistic extravaganza, the play wasn't seen in Paris until 1954.

Alice Lewisohn described Wald in theatrical terms, to quote from Coss:

"This crisp blue figure, the gay voice, welcoming smile, cordial gesture, handsome face ovaled by dark hair. . . . She was vital, real, exuberant, and most overwhelming of all, joyous. . . .

"The Leading Lady [their name for Wald] conducted us downstairs and into the dining room, the others following. . . . Bubbling spirits sparred back and forth across the table, and, at its head, delving into a deep Chinese bowl, the Lovely Leading Lady turned, mixed and dressed crisp green lettuce leaves."

For years, Alice signed her letters to Lillian "Your Baby Alice."

Later, after a vacation the sisters took with Wald, Alice's sister Irene wrote, to quote from Cook:

"I have some memories that are holier by far than temples or graves or blossoms. A fireside romance and a moonlight night are among the treasures carefully guarded."

Because of its spiritual essence, friendship was regarded more highly than love itself in this era. For these women who created a family out of friendship, this was especially true. Many of the residents lived together, worked together, vacationed together, and fought for change together for more than fifty years.

Though "the family" didn't extend quite as far as Hull House, their lives were intertwined with the women at Hull House. Jane Addams and Lillian Wald believed in many of the same ideals and principles. They fought to see many of the same laws and programs created in their respective states and were associated in the public mind. Despite living hundreds of miles from each other on the East Coast and the Midwest, they were great friends—at a time when travel was slow and communication difficult. They were linked by letters and train at first, later by telephones and planes. They vacationed together, traveled to

foreign countries together and spent most summers together at the house
Addams owned with Smith in Bar Harbor, Maine.

While it might seem exceptional for women to form their own families, it was fairly common in an era of utopian communes. Cross-dresser
Mary Edwards Walker founded an all-woman colony called "Adamless
Eden" when she retired. By the turn of the century, there were some
hundred communes in the U.S.

In fact, our supposed "ideal," the nuclear family—mom, pop, and
two kids—didn't even exist until the 1950's. And this model deterio-
rated rapidly after that decade. So much so that sociologist Arlene Skolnick, author of *Embattled Paradise,* says that the nuclear family of the
1950's was the exception, not the rule.

Until the middle of the twentieth century, extended families of grand-
parents, parents, children, aunts, uncles, even cousins were common. In
poverty-stricken neighborhoods such as Wald's, the number of people
living together was very high. Fifteen to twenty people sometimes
shared a flat in the Henry Street neighborhood.

According to U.S. Census data, family size has steadily dwindled
since 1900. The average household was nearly five people in 1900. It
dropped to 3.3 people by 1950 and has steadily shrunk to 2.6 people
in 1990, the last year for which data is available. Though made up of
fewer people, families today are often blends of children from past
marriages, intergenerational families, and other configurations that are
only now beginning to be recognized as "family."

Throughout history, single women have formed communes—even if
they didn't call them that. From Sappho's "school" to the convents of
the Middle Ages, women who wanted to live together found ways of
doing it.

And not just Western women. Even China has a history of women's
communes. When Chinese women got economic freedom by working
in the silk factories, they, too, left behind the idea of marriage and
family to create their own families. From 1865 until the Depression put
an end to the silk industry in the 1930's, these Chinese "marriage
resistors," formed communes and, being more liberated sexually,
bonded in threesomes as well as pairs.

Wald's idea also extended to the children they served. The women
later founded a family for children that consisted of a year-round home
in the country for eight children, called the nieces and nephews. But
that came later, after Wald founded Henry Street.

The Early Years

Wald's belief in the goodness of human nature motivated many people in her life. Lavinia Dock said, to quote from the 1938 R.L. Duffus biography *Lillian Wald, Neighbor and Crusader:*

"People just naturally turned their best natures to her scrutiny and developed what she perceived in them, when it had been dormant and unseen before. I remember being greatly impressed by this inner vision that she had."

One of four children of Max and Minnie Wald, Lillian probably got her trust from her mother, a woman who prided herself on it. According to Duffus, when Minnie needed the laundry done she hired a woman off the street who was carrying a load of laundry. Lillian and her sister were horrified. Their mother was going to let a stranger take their clothes away? How could they trust someone they didn't know? The solution was simple: You asked. When the woman said she was honest the matter was settled.

" 'There! Didn't I tell you?' Minnie cried triumphantly."

Needless to say, the laundry came back intact.

Wald's mother was constantly helping people who were hard up. She gave clothing to needy people and rented a carriage so the family maid could ride in proper style to her wedding. When Minnie came to Henry Street to live after her husband's death, there were strict orders not to let her give anything away for fear she would give away the store.

The Wald family didn't just act out of kindness but out of a deep sense of compassion—a belief that probably came as much from their religion as from their heart. In Judaism, compassion is not just a concept but a concrete way of life. A custom on Sabbath is to ask a guest, a traveler or needy person, to share the evening meal. Unlike charity in many other religions, sharing the Sabbath meal is a specific way of spreading life's goodness. This simple act often creates a sense of community with others that is all too sadly lacking in many religions, no matter what their stated beliefs.

Wald's mother and father also knew what it was like to see the worst in people, to face fear, mistrust, and oppression. Wald's parents came to America to escape the anti-Semitism of Central Europe in the late 1840's. Being Jewish, Wald knew what it was like to be both "other" and "enemy." She didn't experience this as a child growing up in the midwest at a time when who you were was more important then where your parents came from or what religion you were. She did, however, come face-to-face with it in the witch hunts following World War I.

As the child of immigrants, Wald was also conscious of the rich cultural heritage immigrants like her parents brought to the U.S. Her own Polish-German-Jewish heritage was rich in history, art, music, and language. Long before "Black Pride" and other roots movements of the 1960's, Wald understood the pride that went with knowing one's heritage and keeping its customs alive.

Yet she also helped start a group later that tried to assimilate immigrants into the mainstream culture. She believed immigrants would be taken advantage of if they didn't know the language, customs, and laws of their adopted country. But Henry Street's activities—from plays and festivals to informal club activities—encouraged the children of immigrants to know and be proud of their roots.

In a sense, Wald came from an informal tradition of social work. As such, she didn't need the religious conversion that led Jane Addams or Florence Nightingale to their chosen vocations, though Wald *did* grow up in circumstances far above the slums of the Lower East Side. So different, that she always referred to her childhood as "spoiled."

Her parents *were* well off. Family legend had it that one ancestor was a friend of a Polish prince, another of a Russian czar. Her father, Max, ran a successful optical business. From eight years of age, Lillian was sent to the very posh Miss Cruttenden's English and French Boarding and Day School for Young Ladies and Little Girls.

But like Florence Nightingale, Wald was bored by the life of a young lady, by the meaninglessness of the socializing and visiting. Like Nightingale, she wanted something she could sink her teeth into; she wanted a challenge.

Wald did not have to wait years to find her calling, however. Nor did she have to fight her family when she found it. When her sister became pregnant, Lillian went to stay with her. As she watched the uniformed private nurse helping Julia, she realized that was what she, too, wanted to do. From there, it was only a short step to nursing school and her first assignment at the Juvenile Asylum, where the poverty and degradation she encountered changed her life forever.

Her parents thought their exuberant, undisciplined daughter would never make it through nursing school, but she did. In fact, she did so well she even thought of becoming a doctor and enrolled at the med school founded by Elizabeth Blackwell, the first American woman to become a doctor.

Med school was the turning point for Wald, however. While there, she joined a program for immigrant women sponsored by philanthropist Betty Loeb. During one of her first visits to a tenement on the Lower East Side, she realized that the problems of the world were more pressing than getting her degree. Faced with a woman who was still lying in the bed on which she had miscarried and hemorrhaged two days earlier because there was no one but a child to help her, Wald never returned to med school.

She and another nursing friend rented a flat on the top floor of a five-story tenement (which took them two months to find because they insisted on a bathroom). Even though they furnished the fifth floor walk-up simply, news of their arrival spread like wildfire.

According to Tommy, the boy whose family lived in the basement, "them ladies live like the Queen of England and eat off of solid gold plates," Wald wrote in her autobiography.

Years later, Wald suddenly realized to her horror where an adolescent explaining socialism got his image of wealth:

"The millionaires sit round the table eating sponge-cake and the bakers are down in the cellars baking it. But the day will come ... when the bakers will come up from their cellars and say, 'Gentleman, bake your own sponge-cake.'

"Mixed with my admiration for the impressive oratory was the guilty sense that the settlement was probably responsible for the picture of licentious living manifested by the consumption of sponge-cake—our most popular refreshment."

The house may have been in the poorest section of town but the furnishings were still middle-class. To quote from Beatrice Siegel's biography, *Lillian Wald of Henry Street* it had: "the look of a private home enriched ... by gifts of antiques from friends, a Duncan Phyfe dining table, a silver tea service, and silver candelabra on mahogany buffets."

But Wald and Mary Brewster were there to do a job. And do it they did. Two years later, Betty Loeb's son-in-law, banker Jacob Schiff, donated the house at 265 Henry Street. Like so many whose lives Wald changed, Schiff remained a lifelong friend and backer. When he died, he donated the building at 99 Park Avenue as a memorial. It became the administrative office which, after thirty years of growth, was desperately needed.

What affected Wald first and foremost—and what would always affect her most profoundly—were the conditions of the children, however. To quote from Duffus:

"There were nursing infants, many of them with the summer bowel complaint that sent infant mortality soaring during the hot months; there were children with measles, not quarantined; there were children with ophthalmia, a contagious eye disease which may destroy the sight; there were children scarred with vermin bites."

In addition, there was tuberculosis, typhoid, and pneumonia, all overshadowed by rising unemployment and breadlines, homelessness and hopelessness.

Wald and Brewster did what they could, and in the process started the field of public health nursing. Wald also realized that nursing someone to health without changing the person's life was a stop-gap measure. Their housing, their work, had to be changed. That's what Wald intended to do—start with the little things she could fix immediately and work her way up to the big ones.

Crushes and Controlled Chaos

No matter whom Wald came into contact with, she influenced their behavior for the better. That included her crushes. The daughter of a prestigious Madison Avenue minister, Mabel Hyde Kittredge was considered a Park Avenue socialite who, according to Blanche Cook, "frequently played bridge whist all night after she had played in a golf tournament all day." But, after meeting and becoming involved with Lillian Wald, Kittredge helped set up the free-lunch program in the New York City schools and helped found the Association of Practical Housekeeping Centers, an organization which taught young women "domestic science."

Kittredge even lived at Henry Street for a time, but being a fairly conservative member of her class, she had a hard time feeling comfortable with the socialist leanings of the commune.

In 1904, she wrote to Wald, apologizing for a lapse of speech that betrayed her snobbery using the phrase "your people" and "my people" to denote class differences.

Even her apology couldn't hide the class-ridden worldview of an "us" and "them."

Nonetheless, Kittredge lived at Henry Street for a few years—and Mabel and Lillian had an intense relationship during this time. Wald turned to Kittredge for comfort and even advice. Mabel wrote in a letter to Lillian, to quote from Cook's article:

"I seemed to hold you in my arms and whisper all this. . . . If you want me to stay all night tomorrow night just say so when you see me. . . . Then I can hear you say 'I love you'—and again and again I can see in your eyes the strength, and the power and the truth that I love. . . . All this I have before me—never a thought of weakness because you dared to be human."

Wald eventually asked Kittredge to leave. Whether it was because of her politics, her jealousy of the other women or what, is the sixty-four-thousand-dollar question.

After 1904, however, Lillian was pulling away. The two women still saw each other one night a week, but Lillian was busy and often broke their dates. Mabel found it harder and harder to control her jealousy, not just of the demands on Lillian's time but also of the other residents.

After being stood up, Kittredge wrote and tore up one letter, only to write and send another, again quoting from Cook:

"But what business has a great grown woman like myself to sit up in her nightclothes and write nothings. . . . I am getting altogether too close to you . . . all those doors that you have pushed open for me? Half open—dear—just half open. . . . I can feel your arms around me as you say I really must go."

She also wrote, after Lillian had promised to visit her, quoting her broken promises.

" 'Long evenings on the back porch'—it sounds fine—and improbable."

Whether Kittredge was being paranoid or justified is hard to tell, but her later letters show how difficult it was to have a love life in the fish-bowl atmosphere of a settlement.

"There are times when to know that Miss Clark is standing behind one curtain, Miss MacDowell behind another and to feel an endless lot of people forever pressing the door or presenting unsigned papers makes me lack that perfect sympathy with 'work for others' as exemplified by a settlement. No wonder I am called 'one of your crushes.' "

Kittredge eventually gave up, her emotions so strong that she couldn't even bring herself to attend the Henry Street Christmas party. Nonetheless, she represented Lillian Wald at the Hague Women's Conference where she might have found someone else. A decade later, she was accompanying Alice Hamilton on *her* travels.

It took a special kind of woman to love a strong woman like Wald yet still give her the time she needed not only for her work but for the other women who were part of her long-standing family. Though Eleanor Roosevelt's family was a biological one, journalist Lorena Hickok faced the same problem with her. And as the First Lady became more and more popular—and more and more in demand—she was able to give less and less time to Hickok. Hickok got to spend so little time with ER that she finally gave up. Though it lasted for years and was affectionate for many years after, the demands on Eleanor Roosevelt's time eventually broke the relationship. As the nation's First Lady with grown children and grandchildren, Eleanor had more pressing demands on her time than her love life.

After Wald and Kittredge broke up, however, Wald became involved with a cross-dressing lawyer named Helen Arthur who couldn't live within her means and had to have her money managed by Wald. Wald had apparently taken Arthur's bankbook and was doling out an allowance when Helen wrote after the frustration of Christmas shopping on a budget, again to quote from Cook:

"What's vacation money compared to Christmas toys—Surely it is more blessed to give than to receive interest on deposits! Couldn't you be an old dear and let me rob it for a month?"

Arthur, who played on the mother-son relationship of the two women in her letters, ran into the same problem of time that Kittredge did, but she seems to have had more understanding of what she was up against. She wrote, again quoting from Cook:

"Now that I am being severely left alone—I have much time to spend in my own room—the walls of which formerly saw me only from 2 until 7 a.m. . . . Summertime has spoiled the judge [Arthur] who longs to get back to your comfortable lap and the delights of kicking her pajamaed legs in peace and comfort instead of being solicitously hustled from your room at 10 o'clock."

Arthur seems to have understood what Wald was to others and how important her work was to the world.

"I think so often of the hundreds who remember you with affection and of the tens who openly adore you and I appreciate a little what it all means and I'm grateful to think that your arms have been close around me and that you did once upon a time, kiss me goodnight and even good morning."

And, later:

"Little by little there is being brought in upon me the presumption of my love for you—the selfishness of its demands, the triviality of its complaints—and more slowly still, is coming the realization of what it ought to bring to you and what I mean it shall.''

Eight years later, Arthur was still involved with Henry Street, now appointed to manage the finances of the theater. But by then, Helen and Lillian were no longer a couple. Helen had become involved with Agnes Morgan, artistic director of Henry Street, instead.

What makes expanding relationships like this particularly difficult to understand is that we have so few models of them in history. But gay women, like gay men, often think of their ''ex's'' as family, especially if they have been together any length of time.

The sense of sexual ownership, of possessiveness, found in heterosexuality doesn't appear to be as strong. Gay people don't have to own each other because they don't have to prove paternity. Gay friendship circles expand to include ex-lovers, who are often warmly received and even admired by new partners. Celeste West, author of the delightful book, *A Lesbian Love Advisor,* calls the phenomena ''pluralism.'' She calls ex-lovers ''alumnae,'' from the idea that we all learn valuable lessons from each other in relationships and graduate from the lover's ''school.'' Of course, many circles overlap—since every woman is the center of her own. Although many heterosexuals also remain close to their ''ex's,'' the phenomena doesn't seem to be as widespread in heterosexual culture, nor as complex as the extended families lesbians and gay men often create.

As Cook points out, if these women are to be understood, it is essential to realize that they had rich, full emotional lives. Historians tend to make them look like dried-up spinsters or martyred saints, neither of which are good role models. If we understand and give credit to these networks which were central to the women's emotional well-being, we will have a fuller, healthier picture of their lives.

What Wald said about herself bears this fullness out. She not only thought of her childhood as spoiled but thought of *herself* as spoiled even at her death. She felt surrounded by love and goodness, even though she usually worked a twenty-hour day. Volunteers gave countless hours, people gave generously, and many women loved her. Wald was the emotional center of the commune.

But despite Wald being the keystone of Henry Street, she was an able administrator who downplayed her talents.

Called the head ''worker'' or ''resident,'' she took calls for help night and day and made assignments each morning. But here, cooperation was the key. The residents once explained to a group of visiting anarchists that if Wald didn't assign a job, someone else just did it if they felt like it—which appalled the anarchists. They couldn't believe they'd get everything done with such an anarchistic system. Controlled chaos was the norm for a group that actually ran like clockwork.

While Addams was starting social work in Chicago, Wald was seeing to the beginnings of social work in New York. Having been trained as a nurse, Wald also went further to create a system of public health nursing in New York that became the model nationwide. The idea that nurses, paid for by the city who would serve the sick of the area, no matter what race, nationality, or creed, was a revolutionary concept in its day. Until then, there were no nurses for the poor except those from religious organizations which usually only served their own faith. At the time, 90 percent of the people living in the Lower East Side never saw a doctor or visited a hospital. A private nurse would have been an unthinkable luxury.

Wald wrote in her 1915 book, *The House on Henry Street:*

"... I realized that there were large numbers of people who could not, or would not, avail themselves of hospitals ... and a humanitarian civilization demanded that something of the nursing care given in hospitals should be accorded to sick people in their homes."

Like Florence Nightingale, Wald also helped set up one of the first teacher training colleges in the U.S. for nurses, helped found one of the first American public health nursing organizations, as well as setting up a nursing service for the Red Cross. She also was responsible for seeing that nurses became a part of the public school system.

Though Florence Nightingale gets most of the credit for turning nursing into an upstanding profession, she only worked as a nurse on her off time. Nightingale's first job was as an administrator. Wald, however, began as a nurse. Only later, as the Henry Street services grew, did she become an administrator.

Nurse or not, Florence Nightingale had made such a difference that by the time Wald wanted to become a nurse, it had become a suitable profession for a young lady. But Wald saw immediately that it wasn't possible to heal the sick—and keep them well—without also making changes in the working conditions of the poor and the horrible circumstances in which poor children lived.

During her first nursing assignment while still in school, Wald was confronted with the abominable treatment of society's cast-offs: institutionalized children who had had a run-in with the law or been orphaned or abandoned.

Coming from a home full of love and warmth, Wald was appalled at what she found—children who were treated without any real care whatsoever, especially when it came to such necessities as medical attention.

Wald acted on the spot, as she did throughout her life. Faced with a child about to lose a tooth which she believed could be saved, she said she'd bring in her own dentist to exam it if the presiding doctor didn't fix it.

From this seemingly minor experience, Wald learned that one person *could* make a difference. That simple belief became the philosophical underpinnings of later crusades and practical theories. By the time Wald retired, she had improved the lives of children tremendously. She helped start a system of foster care that got children out of institutions where they were treated like numbers and into homes where they could have the love that Wald herself had known as a child. She also saw the introduction of school nurses and vocational classes, of special ungraded classes for handicapped and disabled children and summer camps for ghetto kids.

But she also knew that children couldn't get an education or become good citizens without food and rest. Henry Street started out with solutions such as "milk stations" which delivered milk to the poor in the neighborhoods they served. As time went on, the settlement (with Mabel Kittredge's help) also fought for the introduction of free school lunches.

But even helping children only touched the surface, Wald realized as she visited the crowded tenements of the Lower East Side. Lack of ventilation, people living any number to a room, even using the same bed round the clock in shifts when someone else was working led to the quick spread of tuberculosis, which was rampant then. During Wald's long career, she fought for laws that required windows in each room of a house in addition to the larger issues of maximum hours and minimum wages. She also sought to outlaw cellars as living quarters.

Wald believed that each person, no matter how poor, deserved basic rights. Strangely enough for a woman of her socialist leanings, she also believed that payment for services, no matter how small the amount, allowed people to keep their dignity and be honest about their problems.

By paying for their services, "visiting nurses [were] . . . lifted out of 'charity,' " she wrote in her autobiography.

"The nurses at Henry Street always let people pay, if they possibly could, even if it was only a penny."

Unlike Hull House, where residents had to either have an independent income or a job in order to pay for its services, the nurses were paid by Henry Street.

Budding neighborhood gang members were even paid for the errands they ran in an attempt to keep them from a life of crime. If they could earn money and feel they had a stake in society, it would keep them from the seemingly "easy money" of the streets.

Like her mother, Lillian Wald brought out the best in people, trusting them to "do the right thing." Not wanting to disappoint her, they usually did. Bankers gave money; socialites helped start theaters and school-lunch programs; street urchins became upstanding citizens.

She also believed if that if people only knew the truth, they would do something. She wrote:

"Conditions such as these were allowed because people did not know. For me there was a challenge to know and to tell. . . . If people knew things . . . such horrors would cease to exist."

But telling was what later got her into trouble.

After the War

Wald saw two major economic depressions in her lifetime and each affected her profoundly. During the first, in the 1890's, she decided to quit studying to become a doctor and left Women's Medical College to work with the poor.

By the second, in the 1930's, Henry Street had more than 100 nurses on staff who made hundreds of thousands of visits annually. By then, it had seven buildings that served twenty-five thousand local people. Medical treatments had improved, and some services were even covered by the city. But the Red baiting that followed World War I hurt Henry Street's finances. People weren't willing to give to "socialists" like Wald no matter how much good they were doing.

And there was always more to be done. The Depression hit the Lower East Side first. Immigrants who had taken the lowest-paying jobs and had been struggling, even in good times, to make ends meet felt the weight of the downturn long before the actual crash sent everyone else reeling. The last hired are always the first fired. It was a terrible end to a time that had been filled with hope.

The change in attitude started with World War I. Prior to the war, liberals believed that everyone could work together to make the world a better place, that there could be a "brotherhood of man." That dream died soon after the war with Germany ended.

Massive starvation in Europe followed the war's end. In the U.S., hard times were apparent even though starvation didn't stalk the land. Money for social services had been funneled into weapons. By 1918, milk, sugar, and wheat were in short supply.

That same year, a flu epidemic swept the globe, killing more people than World War I. During the first four days of October, the nurses at Henry Street were called upon to deal with five hundred cases of flu and the resulting pneumonia. Not only had the war depleted supplies of medicine, but by November people were dying in such massive numbers that there weren't even enough left to handle the dead, much less the living.

Wald later said:

"At no time in the history of the city was it so ill-prepared. War needs had depleted available hospital beds, doctors, nurses, druggists and supplies, and later, when the need for them came, there were insufficient laundresses, grave diggers and even shroud makers."

And there was worse to come. Wald had been outspokenly critical of the war. She felt that no matter what countries or issues were involved, the principal losers were women and children. In a 1915 speech, she had said:

"The voices of free women rise above the sounds of battle in behalf of those women and children abroad, for it is against women and children that war has ever been really waged."

Wald's remark is a far cry from the usual patriotic rhetoric of men going to war *for* women and children. Wald could see early on that despite the slogans, women had no say in war. They would suffer and die, starve and be raped, no matter who lost or won.

After the war, the witch hunts began. Like the ones that followed World War II—and the ones against homosexuals now that the Cold War is over—people bent on having an enemy created a new one when the old one surrendered.

When the Allies defeated the Germans, people turned on each other, looking for the enemy within. Breadlines and looming strikes made it seem as if the country could go the way of Russia into bolshevism, socialism, and anarchy if patriots weren't vigilant. National strikes by unions—some of the first to demand the right to organize or bargain for wages and benefits—hit the country hard. Strikes by steel workers and railway workers, a threat by coal miners added to the tension. People were scared.

The Russian Revolution made everyone who had sympathized with socialism, pacifism, or union organizing suspect. Lillian Wald's name, along with that of Jane Addams and Alice Hamilton, headed a list of sixty-two subversives in a *Who's Who in Pacifism*. At first, the women joked that they were in the "best of company," but as more lists were compiled, given to the press, and presented to Senate committees which gave them even more credence—and publicity—Wald got worried.

She knew she was a patriot of the best kind, one who questioned her country and tried to make it better. But she and Addams were being held up as people who had wanted to overthrow the government and establish "a soviet government on the same lines as in Russia." Something Wald had never wanted to do.

But she couldn't retract her words. She *had* defended Russian freedom fighters in public and in her book, *The House on Henry Street* and she now paid a heavy price for it. As the public began to turn against them, Henry Street began to lose funds at a time when they were needed more than ever.

By then, nurses trained through Henry Street were healing the sick in countries as far away as Finland, Armenia, China, and the Philippines. In New York City alone, Henry Street nurses made three hundred fifty thousand calls annually. And as the decade advanced, the numbers rose. Long before the crash of 1929, the women at Henry Street knew that things were going downhill fast.

The nurses could see an oncoming disaster in their rising case loads, unemployment, and general fear among the people. An informal census found that 25 percent of the people in the area were unemployed and another 30 percent could only find part-time work. Wald wrote in letters:

"Fear has entered into the heart of the nation, and it stalks like a black beast. . . . The unemployment situation absorbs the greater part of my time. It seems disgraceful that so large and resourceful a country as ours could fail. It is a challenge to captains of finance and business. . . .

"I know that if there were some recurrent epidemic of disease the scientists would get busy to find out the real cause and to remove it."

But neither fear of fascism nor a Depression could stop her. Wald wasn't getting any younger (she was fifty-eight in 1925), but she still pushed herself.

A year earlier, she had traveled to Russia to give advice on the problem of orphaned and homeless delinquents, which had been caused by the upheavals of revolution. On her return, she was exhausted. She arranged a vacation to Mexico to celebrate her birthday with Jane Addams, Addams's intimate friend Mary Rozet Smith, and other longtime Henry Street residents.

But even though it was supposed to be a vacation, the women continued their usual frenetic pace. Wald and Addams were invited to meet with officials wherever they went, invitations they could hardly refuse. In Cuernavaca, they were visited by then-President Calles.

At the end of the trip, Wald picked up an intestinal bug. When she got home, she was forced to have an appendectomy and hysterectomy. She convalesced at the summer house she had bought earlier. By then, she also had a tingling in her right hand. She spent nearly a year recuperating. Then she picked up her superhuman schedule again.

But the days when she could sleep by the phone to answer every call were over. She had anemia and was constantly tired. Her heart was giving out.

The fortieth anniversary of Henry Street was in 1933. But Wald was so sick, she was back at her country home, "House-on-the-Pond," trying to appreciate the elms and willows and the pond itself. So ill she thought she was going to die, she nonetheless rallied. How could she miss the Henry Street's fortieth birthday reunion?

People came from all over the country; messages came from all over the world. The reunion was broadcast over the radio. President Franklin D. Roosevelt and Eleanor, both longtime friends of Henry Street, sent their congratulations. Ever humble, Wald listened to the accolades on the "wireless" and said:

"Where I was the sole subject, I tried hard to think that they were talking about a stick of wood."

The anniversary festivities went on for days, consisting of musicals, parties for the children and adolescents, and a forty-year reunion celebration for the men and women who, having been part of the Henry Street clubs, were now members of the settlement alumni association.

The anniversary was the beginning of many honors Wald received, including an LL.D. degree from Mt. Holyoke on the occasion of *its* seventy-fifth anniversary.

In 1927, Helen Hall took over as head worker though Wald remained president. And in 1934, Wald used some of her spare time to write a second book, *Windows on Henry Street.*

Wald died in 1940 of a cerebral hemorrhage. Comrade and lifelong friend Lavinia Dock, wrote:

"As I look back, I marvel at her sunniness. If there was even a tinge of melancholy or sadness it never showed. I never saw her dispirited or dejected or downcast. I never saw her show annoyance or irritation or anger toward any other person. . . . It was always marvelous to me that she came down to breakfast (and in the old days it was early) after writing letters until late in the night, as gay, vivacious, full of energy and enthusiasm, brimming with ideas, suggestions and ready for amusing anecdotes, as someone else might be in the later part of the day."

Before she died, Wald saw social security, unemployment insurance and old-age pensions added to the safety net for the poor as well as the recongition by society that there should be a minimum standard of living beyond which "no one [should] fall." She saw the poor change from an oppressed class which felt it had no rights—and no right to any rights—to one which believes in each human being's right to dignity as well as comfort. As importantly, she saw women, to quote Siegel,

"Who now went themselves . . . to demand their rights instead of having others speak for them."

Lillian Wald

1867 Born in Cincinnati, Ohio

1891 Graduates from New York Hospital School of Nursing

1892 Enrolls in Woman's Medical College, New York

1893 Founds settlement on Lower East Side with Mary Brewster

1895 Moves settlement to house on Henry Street

1904 Co-founds the National Child Labor Committee

1910 Establishes the Department of Nursing and Health at Columbia University

1913 Henry Street Visiting Nurses Services has ninety-two nurses who make 200,000 visits annually in New York City

1915 Wald's autobiography *House on Henry Street* published
Helps found the American Union Against Militancy and the Women's Peace Party
Mabel Hyde Kittredge represents Henry Street at first
Women's Peace Conference in The Hague

1917 Wald resigns from the American Union Against Militancy

1918 Chairs the Nurses Emergency Council during the flu epidemic

1919 Listed with Jane Addams as an "undesirable citizen" by the Overman Committee of Congress for pacifist activities

1934 Second book, *Windows on Henry Street*, published

1935 Fortieth anniversary celebration of Henry Street honoring Wald broadcast on radio

1940 Dies of a cerebral hemorrhage at age 73

Chapter Six

ALICE HAMILTON

Alice Hamilton's personal life is shrouded in mystery. Nowhere in her autobiography nor in the two biographies about her is a romantic attachment mentioned. Yet tantalizing clues are found throughout, the first being her family.

If there were ever a case for "gayness" being genetic, Alice Hamilton's family would have been a scientist's dream. Of the ten female cousins born in Hamilton's generation who survived to adulthood, none married. The only female cousin to marry, was born a generation after Alice. On that marriage, Alice wryly commented: "That taboo is over at last."

Historian Barbara Sicherman puts the onus on the times and the family expectations of independence and achievement. But the expectations of the family cannot have been that great, as Alice and her sisters ran into trouble from the relatives when they actually left home to pursue careers and did not return to care for her aging father. (Her mother was still alive but a daughter was thought necessary to read to them and keep them both company, if nothing else.)

None of the four sisters in her family married. Two—Edith and Margaret—seemed to have strong, even lesbian, attachments.

The eldest, Edith, was involved with Doris Fielding Reid for more than forty years, from 1919 till Edith's death in 1963. Edith also might have been involved with Lucy Donnelly prior to meeting Doris.

Edith met Lucy when they were both undergraduates at Bryn Mawr.

Donnelly later became a professor of English literature (and chair of the department). Lucy was also a lifelong friend of Carey Thomas's younger sister, Helen, whom she met at Bryn Mawr.

Alice's younger sister, Margaret, ended up living with Clara Landsberg. At one point, there was friction with Edith over Margaret and Clara's relationship—and the fact that Clara was being included in the planning of the sisters' summer home at Hadlyme. (The sisters Edith and Margaret lived together in Baltimore prior to Edith moving in with Doris. Edith and Doris eventually bought their own summer place in Maine.)

Alice wrote to Margaret about the battle with Edith—and the importance of Clara in Margaret's life. To quote from Barbara Sicherman's biography *Alice Hamilton, a Life in Letters*:

"She knows that Clara is almost more necessary to you than anybody in the world and that if you are to be happy, it can only be together with Clara, and with Clara happy."

It was a very small world, much like today's lesbian circles. Margaret met Clara through Alice, who roomed with Clara at Hull House for eighteen years.

"Clara and I have lived together, in the same room, for eighteen years more or less, and I have the tenderest affection for her, and so close a knowledge of her that nothing she could do would antagonize me for long. I could not think of a life in which Clara did not have a great part, she has become part of my life almost as if she were one of us." (All quotes from letters are from Sicherman.)

Clara taught night classes at Hull House and German at the University School for Girls before moving to Baltimore and working at Bryn Mawr School teaching Latin—where Margaret taught English and Edith was headmistress. Talk about networking!

Clara later moved in with Margaret and Alice at Hadlyme, where both Margaret and Alice deferred to her in household matters. In the same letter, Alice tried to work out the necessary financial matters for the three of them to retire together. She writes to Margaret about their prospective household:

"If you can bring yourself to feel that this is on the whole no more mixed a household than most household of grown-ups—and indeed I don't know of any less mixed one—then you can look forward quite serenely to life in Hadlyme."

Alice's unmarried female cousins also bought a house for their retirement in Deep River, Connecticut, to be near the sisters at Hadlyme.

Little is said about sister Norah's love life, if there was one. She was an artist who headed the art classes at Hull House after Ellen Gates Starr left. In 1901, Norah had a nervous breakdown in Europe and lived a somewhat bohemian life thereafter, alternating between Hull House in Chicago and Greenwich Village in New York. She never fully supported herself and relied on her sisters for financial help. Her sketches appear in both Addams's and Alice Hamilton's books.

At first glance, Alice Hamilton looks like a spinster, but glances can be deceptive, especially given the family history. Hamilton also sounds like a spinster sometimes, calling her life at Hull House "spartan" in her autobiography, *Exploring the Dangerous Trades.*

Spinsters do have a traditional, if not entirely well-thought-of, role in society. In the past, the maiden aunt stayed home with the extended family to help care for children and aging relatives.

Many women in history were, in fact, simple spinsters. Many played the traditional role of maiden aunt. Even some of Alice Hamilton's cousins did just that. But others joined convents or female professions as they became available and often waged political battles for women's rights.

If anything, Alice Hamilton's life shows that the image of history as a solid—is an illusion. History is a living, breathing entity, more like a river. Despite our stereotypes, history is not set or static, except in its most obvious form, that of textbooks. Constantly changing, it is fed by thousands of historians and their discoveries.

Alice Hamilton is an example of history in the making. On the surface, she looks like a spinster. But underneath, she, too, might have had romantic friends. To find out, we must look at the clues and read between the lines. We must become historical detectives, hoping to find the one piece that will make the puzzle complete.

Being a spinster was also a cover for many lesbians of the era. Looking at Alice Hamilton's life leads one to wonder.

Hamilton never married. Unlike Florence Nightingale, who fought a tremendous psychological battle over the issue, marriage never crossed Hamilton's mind. There were suitors, but she discouraged them all.

For her, there was no choice whatsoever between marriage and career. She would have a career. The family fortune was dwindling and she had to earn money. And, of course, the possibility of anyone ever supporting her never crossed her mind.

Hamilton was drawn to Jane Addams and Hull House the minute she heard Addams speak. Hamilton applied for a place there as soon as she finished her degree. She then lived at Hull House for twenty-two years. After she moved to Boston to take a position at Harvard, she went back to Hull House for summers until Jane Addams died in 1935. She was also Jane Addams's private physician and later became Lillian Wald's physician.

She might even have had romantic attachments. After Mabel Hyde Kittredge and Lillian Wald broke up, Mabel accompanied Alice on her holiday, conference, and work-related travels. Alice was also attached to Julia Lathrop, another Hull House resident. When Lathrop went to Washington to head the Children's Bureau, Hamilton stayed with her there.

But at this point there are only clues.

One thing is certain, however. Alice Hamilton lived a homosocial life, her personal life enmeshed with like-minded independent women. Much more so than was typical of the era. As such, she is part of a tradition that is almost entirely forgotten today.

Whether married or not, women used to live their whole lives in female-only subcultures. The world was divided into two very separate spheres, work and home, as were the ideas about those spheres. Men dominated work, governed by reason; women dominated the home, governed by emotion. Men had little contact with women, even when socializing. When they did, relations between the sexes were stiff and formal. It was like two alien creatures meeting in some no-man's land.

As Carol Smith-Rosenberg points out in *The Female World of Love and Ritual: Relations between Women in Nineteenth-Century America*:

"Indeed, from at least the late eighteenth century through the mid-nineteenth century, a female world of varied and yet highly structured relationships appears to have been an essential aspect of American society. These relationships ranged from the supportive love of sisters, through the enthusiasms of adolescent girls, to the sensual avowals of love by mature women. It was a world in which men made but a shadowy appearance. . . .

"Friends did not form isolated dyads but were normally part of highly integrated networks. . . . The ties between sisters, first cousins, aunts, and nieces provided the underlying structure upon which groups of friends and their network of female relatives clustered. . . . The emotional ties between nonresidential kin were deep and binding and provided one of the fundamental existential realities of women's lives."

Later, during the Red Scare of the 1920's, commie hunters would draw up spider-web charts to show the relationships of such radical groups as Hull House and Henry Street, both of which were part of Hamilton's personal life.

One of Hamilton's most important relationships was with her mentor, Jane Addams. Hamilton had heard Addams speak when she was in college. Addams was an inspiring speaker whose commitment to social justice also inspired Hamilton. As soon as Alice graduated, she applied for a job in Chicago as well as a position at Hull House, since there was no salary attached to Hull House work. She went for an interview, which apparently went well, but was disheartened by it. Though already a physician, she felt unworthy. She wrote that compared to the others— who could teach art or music—she felt she had little to offer.

The worry persisted and worsened when she found out there wouldn't be a vacancy as she had hoped. She went home for the summer to the family's house at Lake Mackinac with a feeling of sorrow. Then a letter arrived. Someone had left. The residents of Hull House would like her to join them.

In fact, Hamilton had a lot to offer. As a trained physician, she started their first health clinic. In 1902, during a typhoid epidemic which was particularly severe in the Hull House area, Hamilton helped put pressure on Chicago's local government to find the cause, which turned out to be drinking water that had been contaminated by a leak in the local sewer. To quote Sicherman:

"The nineteenth ward, with less than 3 percent of the city's population, had suffered more than 14 percent of the casualties. . . . Two Hull House residents visited 2,002 dwellings and found that only 48 percent had modern sanitary plumbing; their careful maps and charts graphically illustrated that the incidence of typhoid was 'greatest in those streets where removal of sewage is most imperfect.'

"It was probably the most acclaimed discovery of her career. Certainly none had more immediate impact. Hull House residents launched an attack on the Chicago Board of Health for its lax enforcement of existing sanitary regulations. A Civil Service Commission inquiry followed and found evidence to support the charge. Many of the sanitary inspectors were subsequently dismissed; five were also indicted for bribery."

Through Hull House, Hamilton also began to hear about the effects of industrial diseases, workers who got pneumonia and palsy, as well as other chronic illnesses and quiet killers from their jobs. Her interest was also sparked by the publication of *Dangerous Trades,* by Thomas Oliver, the first book about the hazards of industrial pollutants.

Hamilton began reading everything she could get her hands on about job-related diseases, all of which material came from Europe. At this time, she was also asked by John Andrews to help on the first survey of industrial disease in the U.S. of "phossy jaw," a deterioration of the jawbone. As Addams had learned, "phossy jaw" came when the women workers in match factories inhaled the phosphorus put on matches. By showing how hideously disfiguring the poison was—they found 150 cases in fifteen or sixteen factories—it was outlawed two years later. The report about it was the first one in the U.S. on industrial diseases. The survey was also the turning point in Hamilton's career.

Hamilton had been doing research at the Memorial Institute for Infectious Diseases, the leading center of bacteriological and pathological investigation at the time. But her growing interest in industrial poison led to what would eventually become a whole new concept not only in medicine but in employment—that in the long run, it was in everyone's best interest to have a healthy working environment.

Until Hamilton's studies showed that employees were becoming too sick to work, the turnover of workers in some of the most dangerous industries was as high as 50 percent *every few weeks.* Employers blamed it on alcoholism and the "shiftlessness" of immigrant workers.

Hamilton knew better. She had known immigrants at Hull House— the lowly immigrant was her neighbor and friend. She had also seen how hard immigrants worked to support themselves and their families against insurmountable odds: language barriers, social customs that were different and laws they didn't understand. She wrote in her autobiography *Exploring the Dangerous Trades*:

"The employers could, if they wished, shut their eyes to the dangers their workmen faced, for nobody held them responsible, while the workers accepted the risks with fatalistic submissiveness as part of the price one must pay for being poor."

Hamilton knew that the work itself was slowly poisoning them, giving them stomach pains and trembling hands, pneumonia and rheumatism, frightening them so much that they eventually left through fear or, if they stayed, through illness. Hamilton was young and inexperienced, but nonetheless, she set out to prove that things could change.

Addams was the one who challenged Hamilton to make her mark in the world. Years later, Hamilton said in a 1957 interview that she wouldn't change a thing about her life: She was satisfied that life for the worker was better—and that she had played a part in that.

Despite her humility, her part was not small. At a time when the budding profession of industrial medicine was "tainted with socialism or feminine sentimentality," Hamilton almost singlehandedly created and created respect for the field in the U.S. Her pioneering research, her determination to bring the insidious and even invisible injustices of the workplace to the public's attention—and to see that they were gotten rid of—may be taken for granted today. But Hamilton helped invent the concept that the working environment should be a safe place.

Studying Medicine

Alice was so close to Edith, her elder sister by two years, that they lived almost as one until separated by college. After they finished their undergraduate degrees, they went to Europe to do graduate work together, then lived in Baltimore until Alice's job took her to Chicago.

Like Florence Nightingale, both women were educated at home. Though children were educated in schools by Edith and Alice's day, their parents wanted to "home-school" them because they didn't like what they saw in public schools. Their mother didn't want them spending all day cooped up inside; their father thought mathematics and American history unimportant.

As a result, their parents taught them what they had learned. From the time they were toddlers, their mother, Gertrude, spoke French with them. They learned German from the family servants. Their father, Montgomery, who had been educated in Europe, taught them Latin. In her teens, Alice taught herself Greek and Italian.

Although their education was eccentric by modern standards, their fluency in languages became the basis of both their careers. Edith's early interest in Greek and Roman "stories" prepared her well for the pop-historian role she later assumed when she moved to New York and began to write about those early civilizations. At Hull House, Alice's fluency in German and Italian not only helped immigrant workers trust her but also enabled them to talk about medical symptoms in a language they knew. Her familiarity with *their* language allowed them to give her details of symptoms they probably wouldn't have been able to had they been forced to speak English. Her command of French and German also enabled her to give scientific papers at conferences in Europe and helped cement a worldwide reputation.

The homosocial network Alice later created with her sisters and cousins very much mirrored her early life of kinship and companionship.

When Alice was six weeks old, her parents left New York and moved in with her grandmother in Fort Wayne, Indiana. Her father then built a house on the three blocks in the city her grandmother owned. In addition to her three sisters, Alice also had eight cousins near her age. She was especially close to Agnes and Allen, who were collectively known as the "three A's."

An upper-middle class family with servants and a second home, their summers were spent at their house on the Great Lakes.

Alice got more than a love of languages from her parents. Her mother was a liberal who believed in a woman's right to privacy, a room of one's own and a career—something her own mother, Gertrude, never had. When the time came for the girls to go to college, there was very little opposition from their parents.

Alice's mother wasn't the only liberal in the house. Her grandmother was friends with both Susan B. Anthony and Frances Willard, women's rights advocates who stayed with Alice's grandmother when they were in town.

Gertrude also instilled in Alice a belief in activism that would be one of the guiding principles of her life. Alice wrote that her mother divided the world into those who said somebody should do something— and those who actually did it. Needless to say Alice became the latter.

By the time Alice left home for Miss Porter's School in Connecticut, she was planning to go into medicine. After Miss Porter's, both Edith and Alice decided to prepare themselves for a career. In a way that shows what Alice wanted out of life, she wrote that with only teaching, nursing, or doctoring available as a career to a woman, as a doctor she could travel—and be her own boss. It was, in fact, her only hope of a "wide, full life"

Alice did run into trouble with her family when she said she wanted to be a doctor, however. Though Elizabeth Blackwell had become the first woman doctor in the U.S. in 1849 and there were some forty-five-hundred women doctors by 1890, it was not exactly a respectable profession, especially for someone as "la-di-da" as Alice. Edith's desire to be a scholar was fine, but even Edith was against Alice making such a "low-class" choice. In letters, Alice wrote that they thought her a "bluggy-minded butcher" because she wanted to see an operation. Though one-third of her medical school class were women, even Alice admitted that the men were of the "roughest class" and that she was getting into some "queer society" by studying medicine. In fact, her choice of a working-class career freed her from many of the limitations she would have faced had she chosen a more middle-class profession.

When it came time for college, the deficiencies in the sisters' education showed up. Edith had to study botany and mathematics before she was eligible for admission to Bryn Mawr. Alice had to bone up on physics, chemistry and anatomy, subjects neither had bothered with.

In 1891, Alice was admitted to the University of Michigan, one of the most advanced med schools in the country, a place where lab work had recently been added to the standard lectures-only.

Women had been admitted two decades earlier but they still faced discrimination. "Hen medics" sat on the side of the room separated by a red line. They studied anatomy in a separate class from the men since it would have been too embarrassing for them to have talked about such a sensitive subject together.

While Alice was in Ann Arbor, sister Margaret joined Edith, who was making her mark at Bryn Mawr College. Norah had gone to New York City to study art.

At college Alice began to realize she didn't actually like medicine. She hated the blood and gore of surgery. The "first death" she faced as an intern—of a women who had just given birth to a child—was more than she could bear emotionally. She realized she had to find something less traumatic for her than being an actual practitioner and began to seriously question her choice. Once she realized she loved microscopes and theory, however, she found a way out. By the time she graduated in 1893, she knew she wanted to study pathology, the origin of disease.

Hamilton did her internship at the woman-run New England Hospital for Women and Children in Boston. During that time, she had two truly eye-opening experiences. The first was meeting Rachelle Slobodinskaya (Dr. "Slobo"), who had had to flee Russia for being a revolutionary during Bolshevik suppression. The second was getting lost one night in a slum. The incidents made her realize what a very sheltered and privileged life she had led. It seems amazing in this day and age that anyone could be so naive, but at the time, there were no televisions, radios, or movies—nothing but newspapers, which rarely carried stories about anyone suffering or starving until the muckraking years a few decades later.

A "cherished" friend, as biographer Madeleine Grant calls her, Rachelle Slobodinskaya would later live at Hull House with her husband Victor Yarros and become a founder of the birth control movement in this country. But at the time, she was going to school by day and doing piece work in sweat shops at night to put herself through school. Alice, who was supported by her family, was appalled. It was the first time she had actually known anyone who was struggling to make ends meet—and exhausting themselves in the process. It was also the first she had heard of the appalling conditions women in factories and home sweat shops were expected to put up with.

Not only was Dr. Slobo's life an eye-opener but Hamilton's first night on duty in the Roxbury slum was even worse. She had sat up with a sick woman until dark, and once she got outside, realized she didn't know where she was. Everything looked so different in the dark, she didn't recognize any landmarks.

Seeing nothing but ill-clad men, she got too frightened to ask directions and suddenly realized it was the first time she had ever been out alone at night—except on a college campus. She walked and walked, getting more and more confused until she saw a young woman who looked fairly frowsy but was at least female. Getting up her courage, Hamilton flagged her down. The young woman turned out to be a chorus girl who was much amused by this well-bred but obviously unsophisticated lady wandering the neighborhood lost after dark.

"Just walk along fast . . . not looking at anybody, and nobody will speak to you. Men don't want to be snubbed; they are looking for a woman who is willing," she said.

Although the advice is completely different from what we would give today, Hamilton got home safely and later wrote that that simple advice served her for years in tough neighborhoods and houses of ill repute.

Her choice of medicine separated her even further from her family. By becoming a doctor, she was thrown into the thick of life—at a time when such subjects as birth and pregnancy were totally taboo. Her mother had run into trouble with the rest of the Hamilton clan by talking about "certain subjects." And there Alice was going into whorehouses in an era where the word "prostitute" couldn't even be said in polite company.

After her internship, Alice joined Edith in Germany for further study. They became among the first women to attend graduate school. (A decade earlier, M. Carey Thomas had left Germany for Zurich after meeting with resistance and realizing she wouldn't be granted a degree, no matter how many classes she took.)

The summer before they arrived, two foreign women had been granted doctorates from a German university. At the time, women were only allowed to enroll in classes that professors would let them attend and could not actually enroll at the university itself. Needless to say, both met with considerable resistance.

In her autobiography Alice downplayed the sexism they ran into. According to Sicherman, however, she had hoped to study bacteriology with two well-known professors in Berlin but neither would let her into their classes. In Leipzig, she was barred from attending autopsies. In Munich, she wasn't allowed to perform the animal experiments necessary for the subject she wanted and had to change to another. It was a long, frustrating road.

She worked mostly in the lab on her own. When she wanted to attend a lecture, however, the professor insisted on chaperoning her to class, seating her separately—and escorting her out before the male students could leave. It was most embarrassing.

In her autobiography, Alice was gracious, calling the University of Munich, where they finally went after Leipzig didn't pan out, "gay and easy and friendly." So friendly, she compared the townspeople to Southerners for their hospitality.

Even so, she later wrote: that women were pushed into the gutter by soldiers or students walking "four abreast."

"Indeed once when I, being light and quick, had dashed up the steps to the gallery and secured a front seat, a great blond Siegfried of a student caught me under my arms from behind, lifted me out and took my seat. It was a man's world in every sense, and at the top was the army, living in a world of its own, adored and feared by the common man."

Prophetic words that would foretell a Germany decades later truly spellbound by a strongman who would challenge the world—and also challenge Hamilton's strongly held belief in pacifism.

Despite the obstacles, however, they studied until Edith got a letter offering her the post of headmistress at the Bryn Mawr School for Girls in Baltimore.

Alice went with Edith to Baltimore, enrolling for further study at Johns Hopkins. The two only separated when Alice got a job teaching pathology at Northwestern University and moved to Hull House in Chicago.

Medical Detective

At Hull House, Hamilton was thrown into the radical life of settlement work. Although she had trouble adjusting at first, she eventually

settled into the life there. She met Julia Lathrop, there, whom biographer
Sicherman terms as her "closest friend." Hamilton described Julia as:

". . . the most companionable person, with a sense of the absurd and
a way of telling absurd stories that was unique . . ."

Later, when Lathrop was appointed the first Chief of the Children's
Bureau, Hamilton felt herself lucky to be working in Washington, where
Lathrop would live.

Madeleine Grant, in *Alice Hamilton, Pioneer Doctor in Industrial
Medicine,* gives a telling anecdote of Lathrop:

"One day an old friend of Julia's gave a parrot to the day nursery,
boasting that the bird knew not a single swear word. It was like Julia
to reply:

" 'That lack in his education will soon be rectified in our nursery.' "

Lathrop had been at Hull House almost since the beginning. Less
than a year after it opened, she joined Starr and Addams to become
one of the original residents and one of the most important.

Unlike Hamilton, Lathrop threw herself into the hubbub of Hull
House, helping with the school and day-care center, even answering the
call for a midwife when an adolescent girl, alone in a tenement, began
to give birth. When Addams later asked her if they should be acting
as midwives since they hadn't had any training, Lathrop replied that if
they only did things they'd been trained to do, they'd never do anything
at all.

Hull House made a name for itself very fast, so fast that the local
and state governments were soon turning to them for information. After
three years, the governor of Illinois asked Lathrop—a Vassar graduate
who had studied law—to use her skills as a trained investigator to
survey the state poorhouses and mental institutions. The stark descriptions of the horrifying conditions of charitable institutions were one of
the more disturbing chapters of the *Hull House Maps and Papers.*

In 1895, Lathrop and others, using maps from a Hull House resident
that worked at the U.S. Bureau of Labor, surveyed the area to find out
what social conditions were really like. The resulting *Hull House Maps
and Papers* showed that there were nearly twenty different nationalities
living in deplorable squalor in their area. To paraphrase Margaret Tims
in her biography, *Jane Addams of Hull House,* people lived with agricultural animals in the courtyards and slaughtered them in basements,
sorted rags from the dumps with children playing nearby, and cooked
food on streets piled with garbage.

Lathrop relied on facts and figures rather than rhetoric. Many people contrasted her style with that of Ellen Gates Starr, who was so fiery that Hamilton once said she hoped Ellen wasn't still striking by the time she returned, as "she is so difficult when she is striking."

Hamilton learned both negotiating and diplomatic skills from watching Lathrop visit a badly run mental hospital.

"The superintendent was at first distinctly hostile, but Julia's tact gradually softened him until at last he was pouring out all his many grievances and difficulties. She listened with sympathy and I thought that would be the end ... But to Julia that was only the preparatory spade work. She then proceeded to tell him gently, but with devastating clarity, what was wrong with his administration of the asylum, for which he, after all, was the only one responsible. He took it, with startled meekness, and I learned a lesson I never forgot ... to say the unpleasant things which had to be said."

In 1899, Lathrop went further, joining Hull House resident Lucy Flower to work on the creation of a juvenile court system in Illinois— the world's first.

In 1912, she became the first woman to head a federal bureau when William Howard Taft appointed her to the Children's Bureau, which, among other things, tried to lower the high infant and maternal mortality rates in the U.S. Thanks to her work in this post, she was also at the top of the Red List some thirty years later.

During Lathrop's years in Washington, Alice used to stop at her place whenever she was in town, writing that "... as usual, I stayed with Julia Lathrop in her apartment in the Ontario. . . .

"I went there often, staying with Julia Lathrop ... and drinking in refreshment of spirit from her very presence."

Hamilton came to Hull House in 1897, nearly a decade after Lathrop arrived. Unfortunately, there is little about Lathrop in her letters of those early years, though both Addams and Lathrop were continual sources of inspiration for Alice. Despite the indecision of the first two years—and early sense of failure—she wrote that "to know Miss Addams and Miss Lathrop is gain enough to make the two years seem worthwhile." In later letters, she talks about how immature she was when she first arrived at Hull House and credits both Addams and Lathrop for educating her to life itself. Hamilton felt a bit removed from Hull House in the early years because she had been doing research instead of being out changing the world, but she soon became part of the inner circle of Addams, Lathrop, and Kelley. Though Addams and

Kelley inspired her to fight for social justice all that much harder, she turned to Julia for companionship.

Hamilton's first government assignment came in 1910, more than a decade after arriving at Hull House. By then, she had done research on typhoid, tuberculosis, and phossy jaw—and helped make changes in all those areas. Like Lathrop, she was becoming known not only in her field but also by the powers that be. Like Lathrop, she was also tapped by the Illinois governor when he wanted to survey industrial diseases in the state, the first such study in the U.S.

After years of research in European medical journals on lead poisoning in other countries, Hamilton was faced with finding out what the situation was like in Illinois. She wrote that it was like trying to find a path through the jungle that had no openings but that she would have to penetrate all the same.

She consulted thirteen industrial chemists just to find out that there was no lead in pottery glazes used in Illinois. But she found lead almost everywhere else: in enamel paint used for bathtubs, in tinfoil on cigar wrappings, in polishes for cut glass, to name just a few.

In March, she began visiting factories across the state.

"I found much dangerous work going on in all of them. One of the vice-presidents . . . was both indignant and incredulous when I told him I was sure men were being poisoned in those plants. He had never heard of such a thing; it could not be true; they were model plants."

He went to the door and shouted to a passing workman to come in, then asked the scared worker if the lead had made him sick. To which of course, the man replied no. But Hamilton was not taken in and gently stood her ground—as Lathrop had taught her.

Not only was she up against indignant foremen and owners, but the factories and hospitals of the day were much less efficient record-keepers. Tracking down statistics of men who did not speak English and whom the hospital had only identified as "Joe" or "Charlie" with no address given was particularly daunting. On the other hand, "hospital history sheets noted carefully all the facts about tobacco, alcohol, and even coffee consumed by the leaded man, though obviously he was not suffering from those poisons; but curiosity as to how he became poisoned with lead was not in the intern's mental make-up." Hamilton often as not got vital information from the wives by visiting their homes.

Nonetheless, she found cases of poisoning in every factory she visited. What was worse, she found a complete lack of understanding of how it was caused. Everyone thought it was caused by eating lead from the hands during mealtimes or from rolling tobacco. Which meant that if the workers just washed their hands, everything would be fine. Hardly anyone understood that you could be poisoned from a dust that was inhaled—or that anything could cause damage slowly by breathing it or having it seep into the skin. And lead was not only one of the most insidious but most commonly used chemicals at the time.

Most manufacturers simply didn't understand the problem. Hamilton had to convince employers that their ideas concerning how to fix the working environment were wrong. She also had to convince them that slow but long-term poisoning was important. She was not only up against a lack of concern on the part of many manufacturers but the fact that accidents, not industrial diseases, took precedence in everyone's mind.

She visited a hospital in one manufacturing town where the intake clerk had seen so many patients from the company he had a stamp made which "appropriately enough, he uses with red ink. All down the page came these red blotches, just like drops of blood."

As if hospitals weren't bad enough, at a mill she encountered a scene straight out of Dickens, a factory filled with lead dust where the men not only worked but ate lunch. Seeing her horror, the foreman said, " 'I'll show you something you will like,' he said, and he led me to a big stable where great dappled grey horses were standing on a clean brick floor, eating from clean mangers, and rubbed down till their coats shone.

" 'Mr. B. is awful proud of his dray horses,' he said. 'He thinks nothing is too good for them.' "

In the next few months, Hamilton visited every factory in Illinois—304 in total—and found 70 different processes that led to poisoning. She found nearly 600 cases of poisoning, which she knew just scraped the surface. In one instance, she found a worker's wife using powder that contained lead to scrub pans. Not only was the worker being contaminated at work but both he and his wife were being contaminated at home. By June, she had statistics for the first conference on industrial diseases held in the U.S.

Soon, Hamilton was representing the governor and the state of Illinois in speech after speech to economic associations, scientific organizations, and manufacturers themselves. From her surveys, she had an impressive array of statistics from factories to back her up.

When she spoke to manufacturers, she used what would become her

M.O. all her life. Rather than focus on the distress of the worker or the injustices she eventually decried in her autobiography, she focused on the hidden cost to the employer—of having to replace and train up to half the people every few weeks.

Although there had been much research done in Europe, what Hamilton realized from actually seeing factories in the U.S. was that factories differed greatly from place to place—and that there were no laws governing their operation in Illinois or any other state. In the back of her mind, she knew that this would eventually be her most important battle.

From the state study, she was asked by the federal government to survey dangerous trades across the U.S. She began with what she just studied in Illinois—lead poisoning. In the first six months, she covered twenty-two factories in the Midwest and Northeast. All told, she investigated every lead manufacturing factory in the U.S. but three.

Along the way, she did what she could to convince factory owners and managers to institute reforms.

From the first, she remembered Lathrop's training. Start at the top and make friends before dropping the bombshell. After years of which, she wrote that, looking back, it was astonishing how well her informal methods had worked.

Hamilton's 1911 report showed more than 350 cases of lead poisoning, with 16 deaths, found in little more than a year. A month after she completed her inspection for the federal government, the first state law governing industrial poisonings in Illinois was enacted.

It was declared unconstitutional by the Illinois courts but eventually was recognized by both the legislature and the courts.

She wrote in her autobiography that once the connection between poison and poisoning was made—the insurance companies made sure factories were up to scratch—because they didn't want to pay out claims.

From lead manufacturing, Hamilton turned to factories which used lead, places that had enameled bathtubs, sinks, and toilets. In Chicago she went to a union meeting at a saloon to examine nearly 150 workers for a "lead line" in the gums, her method of diagnosing lead poisoning. More than one-third had this early symptom.

Next came the manufacture of smaller items—pottery, vases, and tiles which used lead glaze. These factories were usually staffed by women. Here, she found an even higher degree of poisoning. In time, she was able to prove that women were more easily poisoned than men by the same chemicals.

Hamilton never felt being a woman was a handicap. And in some instances, it wasn't. At first, many captains of industry didn't take her seriously and they let her have the run of the place. Years later—when striking laborers thought she was a government spy—the workers would often tell a sympathetic woman symptoms they wouldn't tell a male doctor.

At a factory in Joplin, Missouri, being a woman came in handy when they tried to hoodwink her. She discovered that everyone in the village knew she was coming. To quote from Grant: 'We all knew you was coming,' one of the wives told her. 'They've been cleaning up for you something fierce. Why, in the room where my husband works they tore out the ceiling, because they couldn't cover up the red lead. And a doctor came and looked at all the men and them that's got lead, forty of them, has got to keep to home the day you're there.' ''

Although most of the reforms she fought for took years, two factories she inspected were quickly put in order because of contacts she had with wealthy liberals.

After visiting the Pullman Company, which made railroad cars, she mentioned to Jane Addams the appalling conditions she had found there. Addams put Hamilton in touch with the main financial backer of Hull House (next to Mary Rozet Smith). Mrs. Louise deKoven Bowen was one of the largest stockholders who had lobbied for many reforms over the years.

"Changes took place with breathtaking speed," Hamilton wrote.

By the time she finished her research in 1915, she was the leading American expert on lead toxicity and other industrial poisons. In the process of doing her research, she had also invented the field of industrial medicine in this country.

Political Activism and Mabel Kittredge

Because of Jane Addams's failing health, Hamilton accompanied her to the 1915 International Congress of Women that tried to stop World War I. Mabel Hyde Kittredge was also at the conference and on the ship, as was Florence Kelley, Emily Greene Balch, and Carrie Chapman Catt.

During this period, Hamilton spent more time with Mabel Kittredge, Lillian Wald's old flame. (They had broken up nearly ten years earlier.) Alice met Mabel either through Norah, since Mabel was Norah's landlady, or through Henry Street. While it might be stretching it, one can't help but wonder if Mabel was involved with Alice, since they traveled together off and on for at least ten years, or if perhaps, Mabel was also involved with Norah, then became friends with Alice. Unfortunately, only time (and some honest detective work) will tell.

Alice wrote to Mary Rozet Smith of the voyage over:

"But my special croney is Miss Kittredge, Norah's friend and landlady. I hope she will stick to us, for I foresee a Cinderella kind of time if we go to England. Everybody on board wants to go to England with Miss Addams and though she is lying low and not saying whether or not she will go, I know that when she does she will have annexed a lot of them and I shall be lost in the shuffle. In that case I shall break loose with Miss Kittredge."

Alice and Mabel ended up taking a side trip to Belgium, which was then occupied by Germany. She again wrote to Mary:

"Miss Kittredge and I are making a desperate and probably quite futile effort to get into Belgium. . . . We have already wasted three precious days in the pursuit of this wild plan and though today the consul was very sanguine we do not really believe we can get in."

They did get in, but it was a terribly frightening experience. In her autobiography, she wrote about the atmosphere of suspicion and fear which even she began to feel. During a border search, they confiscated her guidebook because it had maps, cut the label out of her hat, and patted her down.

To get them through, Hamilton dealt with the young German officer by talking of her school days and joking with him when he said that not all Germans were brutes. The others were dumbfounded at her duplicity and Alice wrote: "I suddenly realized another of the effects of living under tyranny—it makes liars out of decently truthful people. For I wanted our passports more than I wanted to tell the truth."

Although Kittredge has been called a socialite, she was also a political activist, though not of the caliber of Hamilton, Addams, or Wald. After the war, Kittredge went to Belgium as part of the Belgian War Relief to help feed children starving in the war's aftermath.

Like most settlement women, they were both pacifists. Hamilton wrote in her autobiography that war also means killing as well as dying and that every country expects its young men to kill for it.

The women were able to do little against the war machine, however Hamilton ended up spending the next two years investigating munitions factories for the Department of Labor, an even more dangerous trade.

Kittredge went with her on some of her wartime work. In Hopewell, Virginia, the two lone women were taken for ladies of the night when Alice had been "boldfaced" enough to talk to the owner of a Greek restaurant she recognized from her Hull House days.

Investigating munitions was not only another pioneering venture, but it was made doubly difficult by wartime secrecy. The Navy didn't agree to cooperate until Franklin Roosevelt, then assistant secretary of that branch, interceded. Hamilton was still not given information on plant locations though.

If there was anyone in Washington who knew, they weren't telling her. She was expected to find the plants by herself.

Not that that stopped her from finding and investigating them. She likened the yellow and orange clouds that escaped from the munitions factories to the pillar cloud the Israelites had followed. "I would vaguely hear of a nitrating plant in the New Jersey marshes and I would spot the orange fumes and make my way to them."

A few days into the job, Hamilton realized that one misstep at a bomb plant could blow everything sky-high. She watched with terror as workers carried thousands of crystals to and fro, expecting them to stumble and end it all any second.

Plus, some of the fumes could kill a person in twenty-four hours who didn't even realize they'd been poisoned.

In one day, at one factory, she saw eight accidents that could have killed them all, though she realized it immediately. To quote Grant: "Hundreds were made ill from breathing nitrous fumes. American physicians at that time knew almost nothing about the various symptoms— much less about their treatment."

Hamilton found nearly twenty-five hundred cases of poisoning.

But fear never stopped Hamilton. At fifty years of age, she went down eight hundred feet into a mine, wearing a safety lamp on her head and crawling on hands and knees to a ladder that led farther down into the pit. Biographer Grant writes:

"She [went] down an eighty-foot ladder, then walked on slippery rails over deep pits. Her guide never looked back to see that the rails were so far apart that she could scarcely make a step, but she knew that one false move and she would fall between the rails into the blackest pits she had ever seen."

Hamilton didn't find any long-lasting damage from the machinery she was investigating at that time, but she did wonder about the relationship between the chemicals in the dust-filled air and the high rate of tuberculosis or "miners' con" in the area. Twenty years later, she worked on a study for a federal committee which investigated silicosis and "consumption," as it was called then.

By the end of the war, Hamilton was known throughout the world for her expert knowledge of industrial medicine. In 1919, she was asked to join the faculty of Harvard University as a professor, the first woman appointed to a teaching position there. Hamilton was immensely pleased at the prospect, but she still wanted to be able to do research for the federal government. The university was more than happy to comply since it had conditions of its own. To quote Grant:

"She must never insist on her right to use the [all-male] Harvard Club, which at that time had no ladies' entrance and to which no faculty wives were never admitted; and she must never demand her quota of football tickets."

In her humility, Hamilton downplayed the significance of the achievement of breaking into the all-male bastion of Harvard, saying she was the only candidate, since industrial medicine wasn't very popular yet as a branch of medicine.

But she was not by any means the only candidate. She was, by far, however, the best.

She also downplayed the sexism. But one can guess that she could have cared less about an exclusive all-male club and even less about football. She stayed at the Women's City Club in Boston before moving in with Katy and Armory Codman and wrote in a letter to cousin Agnes that after listening to the fascism of the City Club that "the doctor and his wife are radical, thank Heaven."

Hamilton taught at Harvard for sixteen years, during which she trained doctors from all over the world to recognize industrial diseases. During these years, she studied many different forms of poisoning, including mercury poisoning in the hat industry. In fact, the term "mad hatter" comes from the bouts of insanity which used to affect hat makers. Through her efforts and those of other reformers, a different chemical was found to create felt for hats that wasn't harmful to the people making them.

But science wasn't Hamilton's only passion. From the days of her early adulthood, when four men had been convicted of throwing bombs during the Haymarket riots simply because they were anarchists, Hamilton remembered something she had been told by a friend then: Use the scientific method of inquiry when it came to political issues also. She applied this to the 1920 case of Sacco and Vanzetti, the convicted murderer-robbers whom she believed were found guilty because of their anarchist leanings. Hamilton read all six thousand pages of the court transcripts.

Through this battle, she managed to make herself even more unpopular than she had been as a pacifist during World War I.

With Katy Codman, she helped fight for the accused through seven court appeals and a last-minute stay of execution. Though it failed, Hamilton stood by to the end, even speaking at a memorial for the men two years later where she said that it is often hard for Americans to accept that immigrants can become disillusioned, more so even than the native-born whose hopes aren't as high to begin with and who haven't given up everything to travel thousands of miles in search of a better life.

Years later, when she was nearly a hundred years old, she came out against the Vietnam War early on, writing in 1963 to protest the war itself and in 1965 the use of poison gas.

In 1924, Hamilton had a chance to visit the former Soviet Union to inspect Russian factories and see how socialized medicine worked. Mabel Kittredge went with her, as did two other women.

The trip was one of her hardest, for many reasons. Russia was not yet recognized by the U.S. and fear of "Commie Bolshevism" was rampant in this country. No one in their group spoke the language and the fear in the former Soviet Union was palpable. In addition, they could not turn to anyone, not even the U.S. government. If they needed help, the only organization in Russia they could turn to were the Quakers.

Getting into trouble wasn't a superfluous thought.

The Russian Revolution had happened less than a decade earlier. Fears of counter-revolutionaries and counter-espionage were rampant. They were warned they would be followed by spies who would report their every word. Careless words even in English, could get them—and others—into trouble.

She and Mabel went off alone with a male friend. Alice was appalled to find they also had to share the train berths with him. More worldly wise, Mabel was less worried. She said she had traveled that way before—and that it was easy. Although Alice was reticent at first—having a man in their compartment—she eventually got used to it.

In Russia, Hamilton saw the world's first hospital for industrial diseases. Though she was not impressed by the fanaticism in the new Russia, nor the fear, she *was* impressed by the Russians' ability to treat tuberculosis. Antibiotics hadn't been invented yet and rest was the only cure. In Russia, unlike the U.S., people were given time off to rest.

On her return to the states when she tried to tell Americans about these and other advances, she was booed and her findings met with total disinterest. It was the beginning of two communist witch hunts Hamilton faced in her lifetime, neither of which broke her spirit, softened her words, or slowed her activism.

When she retired from Harvard in 1935, Hamilton began studying other poisons. She was hired by Frances Perkins, who in 1933 had become the first woman cabinet member in the U.S. As Secretary of Labor, Perkins asked Hamilton to study poisoning in the newly created rayon industry.

For many years, she had been writing about industrial diseases for scientific journals and mainstream magazines and in 1925 had written the first U.S. reference work on industrial poisons in the U.S. Once she retired, she added her witty 1943 autobiography *Exploring the Dangerous Trades* to the books she had published in her field.

When Alice retired, she moved to Hadlyme, the 150-year-old farmhouse in Connecticut she and her unmarried sisters bought when the family sold their home in Indiana. After Margaret retired from teaching in Baltimore, she and Clara also lived there with Alice. And Norah had a studio. They even remodeled one wing so Jane Addams could stay while she was recuperating.

They usually spent winters with Edith in Washington, D.C., or traveled to warmer climates such as Guatemala for the cold months.

During her final years, Hamilton received many honors and awards, including five honorary doctor of science degrees—one of which was given to her by President Mary Woolley of Mt. Holyoke College, the woman who had a long-term relationship with author Jeannette Marks.

Hamilton also was the first woman to receive the Lasker award for public health. It came with a one-thousand-dollar prize which was usually donated to charity. Ever the imp, Hamilton used the money to take Margaret and herself to Mexico for the winter. In later years, she would hold up the statue of the Winged Victory she also got and tell visitors about her glorious trip to Mexico.

Three months after she died at age 101, Congress passed the first law that allowed the federal government to set standards and enforce healthy working conditions in the U.S. Hamilton would have been terribly pleased at that, too.

Alice Hamilton

1869 Alice Hamilton born in New York City

1893 Receives medical degree from University of Michigan, Ann Arbor

1895 Goes to Europe with sister Edith

1897 Joins Hull House; starts a health clinic

1902 Fights city for clean up of contaminated drinking water in typhoid epidemic

1909 Helps report on "phossy jaw" in match-makers, which leads to elimination of toxin

1910 Heads Occupational Disease Commission and begins study of lead poisoning in industry

1915 Goes to International Women's Peace Conference in The Hague

1916 Buys Hadlyme

1917 Investigates illness caused by the manufacture of explosives in World War I

1919 Becomes Professor of Industrial Medicine, Harvard Medical School

1920 Begins annual guest lecture at Bryn Mawr College

1924 Visits Russia with Mabel Hyde Kittredge to study industrial reforms there

1925 *Industrial Poisons in the United States* published

1932 Friends begin to die: Julia Lathrop and Florence Kelley

1934 *Industrial Toxicology* published
    Jane Addams spends summer with Alice at Hadlyme after Mary Rozet Smith's death

1935 Retires from Harvard
    Appointed as a medical consultant to the Department of Labor

1937 Begins studying silica poisoning in the rayon industry
    Adds Women's Medical College in Pennsylvania and Tufts Medical School in Boston to annual lecture series

1946 First woman given the Lasker Public Health Award
    Given an honorary degree by Mt. Holyoke

1970 Dies at age 101

Chapter Seven

EDITH HAMILTON

Edith Hamilton spent most of her life in a relationship with one woman—Doris Fielding Reid, a student of hers. Such relationships are taboo these days—but they were common in years past. They were the model for homosexuality in ancient Greece and Japan.

As such, one of the most famous relationships in history, which biographers often take on face value, probably was gay, not familial. Heterosexual historians generally assume that Sappho and Cleis are mother and daughter because Sappho refers to her as "my daughter" in one of the fragments. But because mentor-student relationships were the gay norm in ancient Greece, "my daughter" was probably the most beloved student, not an actual relative.

Mentor-student relationships have a long and respected history in gay culture. Intergenerational relationships have much to offer, though most lesbians tend to want to pair only with women their own ages. Among other things, older women sometimes bring sophistication, wisdom, calm, and even a healthy degree of cynicism to the relationship, while younger women often add trust, enthusiasm, energy, and necessary idealism to the mix.

The problem comes when teachers seduce students. Though 90 to 95 percent of such seduction-rapes involve heterosexual male teachers and female students, gays take the rap because the majority segment of society always projects its dark side on to the minority. Hispanics are lazy; Jews are money-grubbing; blacks are hostile; and homosexuals are sex fiends. Homosexuals get blamed for sexual problems heterosexuals don't want to face.

But it goes both ways. Adolescents are often at the peak of their interest in sex and sexual exploration. The stories even today of a woman's sexual awakening, courtesy of a lesbian teacher who is either too head over heels in love to worry about the consequences of getting caught or is really stupid, abound in the lesbian community, downplayed though they are.

We don't know how or when Edith and Doris met. Doris, who wrote the Hamilton biography, *An Intimate Portrait,* doesn't say. But from what she does say about Hamilton the headmistress, we can easily imagine how Doris felt about this being who was like a goddess to the girls:

"Edith had the ability to make the life of the school interesting.

" 'Nothing was ever dull with Miss Hamilton around,' one of my classmates wrote me. . . . Was the extraordinary vitality of mind and body of our headmistress partly responsible?' "

"Grace Branham wrote in *A Tribute,*

" 'Miss Hamilton—even to those younger children, before we had entered the lighted circle of her classes—was a figure of high, mysterious power. . . . She brought with her the air of having come from some high center of civilization, where the skies were loftier, the views more spacious, the atmosphere more free and open.' "

It is easy to see how Doris would fall in love with Edith. Probably all the girls in the school, especially the lesbian ones, were in love with her. We don't know when Edith began to notice Doris, whether it was while Doris was still a student or not. We can tell from different biographies that Edith lived with her sister Margaret in Baltimore until she retired. But she was spending summers with Doris's family. When she retired as headmistress, she and Doris—and Doris's parents—bought a house in Maine. We know that she, at age fifty-four, and Doris had moved into the house together. Like many women in this book, Anna Freud for instance, living openly with a romantic friend (or lover) was not in the cards until middle age.

It's easy to understand Doris' (and other girls') enthusiasm for Edith. Not only was she older and more worldly-wise but she lived on a much more "lofty plane" than most mortals. Edith lived in the world of the gods.

For Hamilton, the gods were as real as the people she knew and loved. They not only peopled her world but created a level of reality for her that was stunning, even magical. That magic she conveyed first to her students and then years later to the world-at-large.

Not only were the gods themselves real to Hamilton but the Greek philosophers, the *gay* Greek philosophers—Socrates, Plato, Aristotle—were so real that their ideas were like breath to Hamilton, as important as the air itself. Freedom, equality, fraternity, the ideas that Western civilization is founded on grew out of a gay civilization centuries ago.

Hamilton wrote eight books but never kept a diary. As if that weren't problem enough for biographers, her letters were lost in the 1938 Connecticut River flood at Hadlyme, the summer house the Hamilton sisters shared. Edith said her sister Alice's autobiography, *Exploring the Dangerous Trades,* however, covered them both. We can only hope it does since it's all we have to go on.

Born less than two years apart, Edith and Alice were like two peas in a pod. Edith never minded relying on Alice, her younger sister. Alice never minded being led; she even followed her eldest sister to Germany when Edith went to graduate school. They were so intertwined that neither used the word ''I'' when referring to themselves as children. Actually, all four girls—none of whom married—referred to themselves as ''we'' into adulthood.

Reading ran in the family's blood. Her father's mother would be found ''crouched over the fireplace where the soft coal fire had gone out without her knowing it, so deeply involved had she been in her book.

Edith's father, Montgomery, opened the classical world to her by teaching her Latin. A bookworm himself, he inadvertently taught her how to do research at an early age by telling her to look up the answer in the encyclopedia whenever she asked a question—about Latin, Greek, or anything else.

That system probably would have stymied most, but it taught Edith the true secret of knowledge: the joy of discovery. As a result of loving her early education, Edith read Greek and Roman literature, philosophy, and drama in the original languages all her life. And though Hamilton is best known as a writer, she didn't begin writing until she retired. To her students—and even the rest of the world—she was one of the great teachers.

Possibly because she was the eldest, Edith was the teacher of the family. She loved the classics, unlike Alice, who preferred children's books. Edith tricked Alice into reading ''great literature'' by telling the story up to a particularly dramatic point, then stopping. She would give an action-packed version of the *Iliad* or *Le Morte d'Arthur* then stop at a crucial moment and tell Alice to read the rest if she wanted to find out what happened. Alice's biographer, Madeleine P. Grant wrote: "It was Edith who taught Alice the real love of reading. She would dramatically tell her about some episode from Scott or De Quincey. She might stop at the most exciting spot, such as Amy Robsaut's death in *Kenilworth,* and say, 'Now, Alice, you've got to finish it yourself.' "

As a child, Edith was already known for a prodigious memory. She recited works such as Macaulay's *Lays of Ancient Rome* so often that Alice apparently learned them by heart from hearing Edith do them.

Edith realized early on that reading was the key not just to knowledge but to life itself. Years after, she was appalled to find that Reid's nephew, whom she adopted and raised, couldn't read. Doris wrote:

"Dorian would be six years old in the middle of November and early in October Edith took me aside and said,

" 'You know, Doris, the boy can't read!'

Her face registered as much astonishment as if he were about to be sixteen!"

Edith and Doris set up a teaching plan and in six months' time, when they moved to New York, Dorian was promoted a grade above his age.

Like her father and his mother before him, Edith was never without a book. Even when combing her hair she would often be caught reading at the same time.

Edith also had a sense of drama that not only pervaded her books but her life.

As a child, Edith always came up with the games. The eldest of four girls until a brother was born nearly twenty years later, she would entertain them—and myriad cousins—with dramas created from books she was reading. In childhood, they were cowboys and Indians, but they also played Robin Hood, the Knights of the Round Table, and the Siege of Troy.

She once told De Quincey's tale of horror, *The Avenger,* with such realism that it haunted her sister Margaret for years. Margaret later said she never opened a closet door without fearing "a man's boots coming out from behind the dresses," wrote Reid.

With her flair for drama, it was not surprising that Edith was considered the emotional one in the family. Alice wrote that along with "her times of gaiety over the beauties of the outside world or a new book or some amusing family episode, she had sudden and deep depressions that mystified me."

Edith hid her depressions well, though. Reid was particularly surprised when Edith said, years later, how worried she'd been about her future—and what she would do with herself—the winter she retired.

" 'That was a hard winter for me. I had been a very busy headmistress and suddenly I had nothing to do. As you know I never thought of writing and I somehow had a wretched feeling of futility.''

That was before Hamilton discovered writing, before she began turning the world on to Greece—and before she began raising four of Reid's nieces and nephews.

The Woman Question

Edith attended Miss Porter's Girls School in Farmington, Connecticut. The family thought Edith bright, but once she got to Miss Porter's, Alice wrote that she was struck that everyone *else* thought Edith was, too. In fact, Edith said she never actually learned anything at Miss Porter's. And after a classical education usually reserved for aristocratic men headed for Oxford and Cambridge or Harvard and Yale, it was probably true.

Girls' schools were very different in those days. In the late 1800's, girls were allowed to study whatever they liked. If they didn't like a subject, or were doing badly, they simply dropped it and took an easier one. Miss Porter's was known for concerts by famous musicians, but that was about it. The idea that girls should be required to study—and pass—the same subjects as boys wouldn't come into vogue until later. And Hamilton was one of the women who saw to it. When she became headmistress of the girls' school Carey Thomas's companion, Mary Garrett, founded, Edith would see that classical subjects as well as math and science were added to the curriculum.

Hamilton might have had a better education than most men, but before she could show it, she had to get into college, not an easy task given the limited focus of her education. She might have been learned beyond her years in the classics, but she knew nothing about math, a requirement of Bryn Mawr College, the school she wanted to attend. But that didn't stop her from teaching herself—the way she had learned everything else. According to Reid, Edith "bought a book, taught herself the subject, and passed the examination.''

Having mastered mathematics in a few months, she whizzed through college in two years and won the Mary E. Garrett Fellowship for a year's study in Europe besides. Because a woman could not travel alone, Alice, who had her medical degree by then, joined her.

M. Carey Thomas had gotten a doctorate from the University in Zurich more than a decade earlier, but that was the exception, not the rule. At most European universities, women were only admitted to graduate classes if a liberal-minded professor would let them in. The two Hamiltons set out for Germany, the center of classical learning at the time.

At the University at Leipzig, they were told they could attend classes but must remain invisible. They could *not* participate in discussion—and would not be given degrees. They decided to try elsewhere and began negotiating with other German universities for better conditions. In 1895, they left for Munich after being told that Edith might be allowed to take the exam for a degree but that she could only attend lectures if she were willing to sit behind a curtain. For Edith, it was enough. Given her intelligence and understanding of the classics, she probably only needed to take the exam anyway.

According to Alice's autobiography, Edith only got in because of a fluke. There was a split on the classics faculty already between the Catholics and the Protestants—and the Protestants took up her cause.

The first day of classes there was nearly a riot, however.

A professor had offered to escort Edith to class, which she thought ridiculous. But since women usually had a chaperone everywhere they went, she agreed. To her surprise, the quad was packed with men waiting to see the first women bold enough to try to get an advanced degree.

Edith ran the gauntlet with the men ogling her and making comments as if she were some kind of circus animal. Completely taken aback by the attention, she held on to the professor's arm for dear life.

When she got to class, she found another surprise. The idea of a screen had been discarded. Instead, she was forced to sit on a platform in the front of the room facing the male students. That way, she wouldn't "disturb" them. (There had also been a question of whether she might have to sit next to a man and *touch* him if there weren't enough books to go around. Horror of horrors!) Alice commented that what was so ironic about the whole arrangement was that most of the graduate students were married men with wives.

Neither Edith nor Alice wore their politics on their sleeve. Though there was great political struggle for women's rights going on at the time—the first wave of feminism was in full swing—Alice and Edith pushed the boundaries quietly by action rather than words. The only known instance of Edith getting on a soap box for anything was at Bryn Mawr where she successfully fought a rule against student smoking and other women enforcing it by turning each other in. She felt that spying on fellow students was "beneath contempt."

Both Edith and Alice Hamilton broke barriers without statement or fanfare. At the time, Edith said she thought the incidents in Germany "amusing." She later wrote:

"The head of the University used to stare at me, then shake his head and say sadly to a colleague, 'There, now you see what's happened? We're right in the midst of the woman question.'"

Edith probably would have finished her doctorate had she stayed. But the Fates had other plans. At the end of the academic year, a letter arrived from M. Carey Thomas asking Hamilton to take over the Bryn Mawr prep school. Thomas's second partner and life-time friend, Mary Garrett, had just built a beautiful new school for girls in Baltimore. Thomas was the acting headmistress for the first few years, even though she was 125 miles down the road at Bryn Mawr College outside Philadelphia.

Edith was brought to Bryn Mawr prep precisely because of "the woman question."

Thomas and Garrett hoped to create a real school for girls, a school with standards where students—even females—were expected to excel. Even by the time Hamilton took over, girls were not expected to study Latin or prepare for college like their male counterparts. Thomas had planned a two-pronged attack by requiring the highest entrance standards of any university at Bryn Mawr College, and instituting those same requirements at Bryn Mawr prep school.

It was particularly difficult for a girls' school in what was still considered the Old South. In fact, it would take nearly twenty years—until around 1910—for the idea that education made women infertile to die out. And as headmistress of Bryn Mawr School, Edith Hamilton was one of the people directly responsible for the destruction of that ridiculous notion.

But that was more than a decade away. When she took the job in 1896, she had her work cut out for her. Luckily, Hamilton had street smarts as well as intellect. She knew enough to downplay her bluestocking roots—and her love life.

According to Reid, she didn't harangue the parents about educational requirements or curriculum; she inspired by example. With her obvious love of learning, she managed to assuage fears of daughters getting too smart and dumping marriage and children for higher goals. Before she was through, she was able to create advances which would have been unacceptable if suggested by a more superficially radical woman.

Hamilton also believed that anyone could succeed, if they found what interested them and worked hard enough. Although this may seem obvious today, it was an heretical notion at the time, especially when applied to women.

Being self-taught, Hamilton had been allowed to find what she loved and had excelled as a result. The secret was in the excitement of discovering new and unknown worlds. Years later she wrote:

"Again and again I saw that delightful thing, an awakening to the joys of knowledge. I became convinced that the real education was a matter of individual conversion."

Against the furor of destroying woman's bodies by taxing their minds, Hamilton pressed on, charming the parents while she pushed the girls to find what they loved.

"It is not hard work which is dreary; it is superficial work. That is always boring in the long run, and it has always seemed strange to me that in our endless discussions about education so little stress is ever laid on the pleasure of becoming an educated person, the enormous interest it adds to life."

Before she retired twenty-six years later, Hamilton had shown by example that education was a delightful thing, for women and men both. And for more than a quarter century, she inspired women to find their highest calling, whatever that would be.

If parents thought education was pushing their daughters toward lesbianism and worse, sports was even more beyond the pale. In its day, even the clothing—bloomers and a loose blouse—was considered a radical fashion statement, one with obvious political overtones. The Hull House basketball team was known city wide for its bloomers and all-female team. Looking back, it's obvious that some things have a long historic tradition, including the equation of lesbianism and sports. At the time, people thought that exercise caused infertility. (Everything caused infertility in those days!) But Hamilton managed to start a girls' basketball league between Bryn Mawr and other girls' schools.

Hamilton not only overcame parental objections but convinced the press not to cover the game, even though it was newsworthy, given the fact it was a first. At the time, "getting one's name in the paper" was tantamount to scandal. Unless one of three things happened—birth, marriage, or death—it was considered improper for a Bryn Mawr lady to have her name in the paper.

But that didn't stop Hamilton or her students. Fear of the press, fear of parental disapproval, only added to the excitement. Millicent Carey McIntosh, Carey Thomas's niece who later became president of Barnard College, described the first game:

"I think the greatest excitement I ever had in my life was at the St. Timothy's game. Nothing could ever equal the atmosphere that surrounded this one great event of the year. We were dressed in brown serge bloomers. When we acquired the bloomers, it was really like receiving a knighthood from the Queen."

An Intimate Portrait

Once Hamilton retired, she and Doris (and Doris's parents) bought ten acres on the ocean in Maine and moved another house to the site. Originally planned as a summer escape, the two women decided to live there year round and hired a contractor to make major changes. When it was supposed to be ready nine months later, they came up to the site only to discover that the work wasn't finished. They had three new bathrooms with fixtures but no walls. The fixtures were sitting in the open air! Still, they moved in that night. Doris and her father, a professor of geological physics at Johns Hopkins, set about building partitions and bookshelves. That is, until Doris overheard Edith and her mother, who published a play about Florence Nightingale, talking. Edith's comment about the "endless shelves" was that "the more she saw of hand carpentering, the better she liked the machine product!"

After twenty-five years in Baltimore, they thought they wanted to live in a more rural environment. Hamilton already owned a summer home in Connecticut with Alice and Margaret, but the weather in the summer was too humid for Edith. She preferred being on the ocean at Sea Wall.

Edith and Alice Hamilton spent most of their life in cities, but they both loved the outdoors.

But Sea Wall was a summer house, hardly fit for stormy Maine winters. The outer walls had no insulation. Running water came from a well. The pipes were expected to freeze. Reid's father caked them with wax and hoped for the best. When Reid's parents left in September, Edith, Doris, and Doris's nephew, Dorian, stayed.

Despite the lack of running water and insulation, Edith loved the coast. No amount of inconvenience bothered her. Reid wrote:

"A road had been made from the so-called highway down to the house. It was a road, that is, if one's idea of a road is elastic enough— no car could possibly go up or down it during the winter snows and rains. The grocer would leave our supplies on the main road and Edith would walk up with Dorian's sled and fetch them down. She loved these walks, which she usually took alone, and she would come back looking radiant."

Edith didn't just love the outdoors, she reveled in its wildness.

"Huge cakes of ice, some as big as our house, floated in the ocean. Green and blue and sometimes greenish blue colors radiated from them as the light and sun shifted. As the tide went out the salt water froze white on the rocks and looked like snow. When the temperature suddenly dropped and the water became warmer than the air, the ocean steamed, Edith said, like a supernatural, giant teakettle.

" 'It looks positively wicked.' "

Hamilton had a spiritual sense toward nature that was inhabited not just by trees and flowers, birds and bees, but also by the spirits which gave them life: nymphs and naiads, dryads and oreads. The trees, streams, flowers—each had stories about them that were as real to her as the characters in television sitcoms and soap operas are to people today.

They planned to stay at Sea Wall permanently but one winter was enough.

Despite the detail of Reid's biography, it leaves gaps and much of the emotional side unanswered. After Hamilton retired, Reid got her first real job. Until then, Reid had studied music in New York and had hoped to be a pianist. In what would seem to be a move to keep their lives independent, Reid took a job teaching in New York. She would move into finance later, becoming a stockbroker and later the vice-president of an investment firm. Reid later admitted she saw her career as a "rest cure" from the never-ending demands of family life that Edith took over.

Edith was old enough to retire at the point Doris was becoming serious about a career. Perhaps it was the age difference that accounted for the fact the two women took turns having professional careers. Once Hamilton finished hers, Reid started hers. First they lived in Baltimore for Edith's career, then they moved to New York for Reid's. In her late seventies, Hamilton followed Reid to Washington, D.C., when Reid's career led them there.

Once Hamilton retired, they took in a string of Reid's nieces and nephews, four in total by the time they were through. Reid doesn't really say "why," except that it was better for them to be with two dykes than with their parents. Not that Hamilton was ever much of a wife in the usual sense. She did cook and became a mother to Doris's nieces and nephews, but once they got to New York, her life turned around, too.

People they met—magazine editors and theater people—were immediately impressed by Hamilton's love of Greece. The way Hamilton talked, the stories she told, made people "feel as if she must have just had lunch with" Aeschylus. She once told a friend who dropped by that she had had such good company that day. When asked who it was, she replied "Plato."

Friends were so enthralled by her closeness to the Greeks that a group began meeting weekly at the apartment just to talk to her about Sophocles, Euripides, and Aristophanes. Rosamond Gilder, editor of *Theatre Arts Monthly,* was in the group. She soon asked Hamilton to write something—anything—for the magazine.

Hamilton said no. She *had* lectured at Bryn Mawr—one class in Virgil—but she wasn't used to writing. And she didn't see the point. In fact, she was loath to join the academic scholars on Greece, people who had no real feel for the subject. She thought ancient Greece had been "softly dimmed by the dust of centuries of scholarly elucidation."

She also knew her limitations. She didn't have a graduate degree and wasn't a classics scholar in the traditional sense of the term. Just because she loved the subject and knew it backward and forward was hardly reason to think her an expert.

But Gilder prevailed, talking her into writing a piece on Greek tragedy. That article led to another—and another.

Seeing the articles, an editor at W. W. Norton asked her to write a book.

Again, Hamilton said no, repeating that Greece had been written to death. But the editor persisted. He even dangled a contract in front of her. She refused to sign, but she was tempted. When she finally decided to give it a try, she found she not only had a real talent for writing but something to say.

From then on, Hamilton juggled writing and family life. Though supposedly retired, she was now writing books on top of raising adolescents. She would often say dinner was going to be a few minutes late, dash into her study and work out a new idea while everyone waited. Luckily, Hamilton had the ability to work in snatches, no matter where she was. Whenever she had a thought, she jotted it down on scraps of paper.

Probably because Greece was as alive, as real to her as the table she wrote on or the chair she sat on, the writing came easily, naturally. It was probably like Mozart, already hearing the music in his head, complete, orchestrated, masterful. Writing it down was like taking dictation, "scribbling and bibbling."

By the time Hamilton began writing about Greece, she had been living the classics for nearly sixty years. To her, the foundation of modern Western civilization, the ideals Greek society gave the world, were part of her everyday thoughts. Perhaps because they were so real to her, she explained them in a way that was so simple yet compelling it has rarely been equaled since.

In 1930, her first book, *The Greek Way,* came out. Almost overnight, it became a bestseller. Today, it is still a classic.

The Glory That Was Greece

Reid never mentioned the word "homosexual" or "couple" in her biography of Hamilton but their life was obviously a lesbian one. It is also an undercurrent which runs through her work. Whether she knew it consciously or not, the gay woman writing about the world's most important gay culture was the intertwining link between the two, a call that drew Hamilton toward the ancient world like a sailor toward the sea. As Lillian Faderman argues, it is only in the twentieth century that the conditions have been right for gay culture to re-emerge in the world as an entity. And only since Stonewall, have we begun to define it as such.

The big question about gay culture is: How is it different from mainstream, heterosexual culture? Though Hamilton was writing specifically about a pre-Christian culture which had not yet split body and soul, her descriptions of ancient Greek philosophy could almost be used to explain that indefinable entity, "gay sensibility." In *Mythology,* she writes:

"On earth, too, the deities were exceedingly and humanly attractive. In the form of lovely youths and maidens they people the woodland, the forest, the rivers, the sea, in harmony with the fair earth and the bright waters.

"That is the miracle of Greek mythology—a humanized world, freed from the paralyzing fear of an omnipotent Unknown. The terrifying incomprehensibilities which were worshipped elsewhere, and the fearsome spirits with which earth, air and sea swarmed, were banned from Greece. It may seem odd to say that the men who made the myths disliked the irrational and had a love for facts; but it is true, no matter how wildly fantastic some of the stories are. Anyone who reads them with attention discovers that even the most nonsensical take place in a world which is essentially rational and matter-of-fact. . . . The exact spot where Aphrodite was born of the foam could be visited by any ancient tourist; it was just offshore from the island of Cythera. The winged steed Pegasus, after skimming the air all day, went every night to a comfortable stable in Corinth.

"The terrifying irrational has no place in classical mythology. Magic, so powerful in the world before Greece, is almost nonexistent. There are no men and only two women with dreadful, supernatural powers. The demoniac wizards and the hideous old witches who haunted Europe and America, too, up to quite recent years, play no part at all in the stories. Circe and Medea are the only witches and they are young and of surpassing beauty—delightful, not horrible.''

Gays are currently under siege for their hedonism. But perhaps the flaw lies in people who cannot see the wisdom of pleasure, the wisdom of living life as it is given to us. In the same introduction, Hamilton brings up these values. If gay culture values anything, it is beauty and its attendant art, above most else—even religion. For most gays, beauty has a mythic, almost supernatural, quality. In Greece, Hamilton writes:

"The priest is rarely seen and is never of importance. In the *Odyssey* when a priest and a poet fall on their knees before Odysseus, praying him to spare their lives, the hero kills the priest without a thought, but saves the poet. Homer says he felt awe to slay a man who had been taught his divine art by the gods. Not the priest, but the poet.''

In *The Echo of Greece,* she continues:

"It is difficult if not impossible for us to realize how very serious a matter beauty was. Epaminondas, the greatest leader Thebes produced, told the Thebans they would never be equal in war to the Athenians unless they brought the Parthenon and the Propylaea to Thebes. No Greek would wonder at the remark. Of course if the Thebans lived with incomparable beauty before them they would become better men and better fighters. Beautiful art produced beautiful characters. That was in the Greek creed.''

To the Greeks, outer beauty showed inner beauty. The earth was the god, life the only world they knew. And they made the most of it.

In *The Greek Way,* Hamilton points out another area of similarity between early Greek culture and modern gay culture which is especially relevant in the age of AIDS, an age where gays have had to form their own networks to get decent medical care, to get emotional and even physical help in the face of a crisis of immense proportions, a crisis that is killing gay men at an alarming rate.

''They were not tempted to evade facts . . . The Greeks look straight at it. It was a Roman who said it was sweet to die for one's country. The Greeks never said it was sweet to die for anything. They had no vital lies.''

And Hamilton also wrote prophetically in *The Echo of Greece*:

''Socrates told them that the citizens of a democracy could be slaves. Men were free not when freed from outside rule but when they were masters of themselves.

''What he taught he lived. He was himself the example of the life of self-controlled freedom. His death was voluntary. He could have escaped if he had chosen. He chose to die.''

Prophetic words in the age of AIDS and the right-to-die issue.

To Hamilton, Greek artists, philosophers, and statesmen were as real as the people next door. Once Hamilton started writing, she turned out books very quickly, given the breadth and depth of the subject she tackled. But she knew the culture not just because she had been immersed in it since childhood but because she had a gut-level feeling for it. She knew it instinctually, in her bones.

She also had been questioning and conversing with the Greek philosophers for more than half a century. When she finally decided to write it down, all she had to do was put down her discussions on paper. Her second book, *The Roman Way,* came out two years after *The Greek Way.*

Impressed with her ability to make difficult and complex ideas understandable, another publisher asked her to update Bulfinch's *Mythology* with one of her own. He wanted an outline, but, of course, Hamilton refused. How could she produce an outline if she didn't know what she was going to write?

Since her previous books were selling well, the publisher took a chance.

To write her most enduring book, Hamilton read every original and every translation of Greek, Roman, and Norse myths. She only spent three years working on it, but she pored over the myths, pulling together bits and pieces from three different cultures and twelve hundred years of weaving and reweaving the same episodes. To put what she did in perspective, she said in the introduction:

"To bring them all together in one volume is really somewhat comparable to doing the same for the stories of English literature from Chaucer to the ballads, through Shakespeare and Marlowe . . . and so on, ending with, say, Tennyson and Browning."

A decidedly difficult task but one she relished. She decided not to unify the tales by making them sound alike but rather leave them in the language of the original author, whether simple or polished, naïve or skeptical.

Mythology came out when Hamilton was in her early seventies. Although that might seem elderly by most standards, Hamilton still thought of herself as young. She didn't start touring or giving formal lectures on ancient Greece until she was in her eighties. In her nineties, when asked to translate some work, she said she'd save that for her "old age." Needless to say, she never got round to translating.

By the time they moved to Washington, D.C., in 1943, all the Reid children were grown and the child-rearing days over. But Hamilton and Reid were still very much tied to Reid's family. After Doris's father's death, her mother came to live with them and stayed until her own death a decade later. (Hamilton's mother lived with her daughters at Hadlyme after her husband died.)

But Hamilton wasn't just interested in ancient Greece, she was also interested in the origin of religion. *Prophets of Israel* became her third book. In Washington, she began work on the 1948 *Witness to the Truth*. During these years, she also wrote *Spokesmen for God* as well as *The Echo of Greece*. All garnered laurels and high praise.

Famous by the time they moved to the District of Columbia, Hamilton began entertaining such well-known guests as author Isak Dinesen, historian Arnold Toynbee, poets Robert Lowell and Ezra Pound. Nonetheless, Hamilton still "disappeared" during these evenings. Reid wrote:

"When she had had enough, it seemed she would vanish. We would look up and she just was not there."

Though the years continued to add up, Hamilton never seemed to age and never thought of herself as "old." When she was eighty-nine, they took a second trip to Greece. When Alice urged her to stay longer because she wouldn't "be going abroad again," Edith said to Doris:

"Can you imagine why Alice thinks I won't be taking another trip?"

To prove her point, Edith took *three* more trips to Europe before she died.

Being a "tough old bird" probably helped her live to nearly a hundred years of age. Hamilton was physically active almost to the end and only broke her pelvis in her nineties when she "went out shopping in the pouring rain [and] attempted to jump over a gutter flooded with water."

Six weeks of traction later, she got up to give the keynote speech at the fiftieth anniversary of the Classical Association of the Atlantic States.

Like most of the women in this book, Hamilton received many honors in her life but the most cherished was that of being made a citizen of Athens. In Greece, she was presented with the award at a performance of her translation of *Prometheus.*

Hard of hearing but still vibrant, Hamilton said in her address:

"For Athens, truly the mother of beauty and of thought, is also the mother of freedom. Freedom was a Greek discovery. . . .

"Greece rose to the very height not because she was big, she was very small; not because she was rich, she was very poor; not even because there was in the Greeks the greatest spirit that moves in humanity, the spirit that makes men free."

Not everyone would agree with Hamilton's assessment that the Greeks were the first to discover freedom. Those who believe that the goddess-worshipping culture of Old Europe—a civilization which many believe couldn't be bothered to invent weapons—would undoubtedly say that a society without weapons is much more free than anything we've had since.

Hamilton knew, however, and was quick to point out that the Greek ideal of freedom did not include women or slaves. In *The Echo of Greece,* she wrote:

"At this point slavery, universal in the world then, confronts the readers. Many men in Athens had no share in the rights of man. . . . Solon's new idea of political and legal rights for every man was not disturbed by any revolutionary notion cropping up about slaves being men. Solon believed with complete conviction that the poorest and lowliest citizens in Attica had the right of and the capacity for self-rule, but slaves never entered his brilliantly daring and constructive mind. When the Greek achievement is considered, what must be remembered is that the Greeks were the first who thought about slavery. To think about it was to condemn it, and by the end of the second century, two thousand years before our Civil War, the great school of the Stoics, most widely spread of Greek philosophies, was denouncing it as an intolerable wrong.''

Before Hamilton died in 1963, she had a stroke and went into a coma. The doctor told Reid that Edith would never walk or talk again. To which "Edith opened her eyes, looked up, and [said] '' 'Pooh' ''— the closest most women ever got to swearing in those pre-"free speech" days.

Hamilton walked—and talked—again. She also lived two more years to the ripe old age of ninety-seven. Before she died, the woman who initially refused to write because she didn't have a graduate degree was honored with a doctor of letters from Yale, one of the most prestigious in the country.

Edith Hamilton

1867 Born in Dresden, Germany
1894 Awarded Master of Arts from Bryn Mawr College
     Granted Mary E. Garrett Fellowship to study in Europe
1895 Becomes first woman admitted to the University of Munich
1896 Becomes headmistress of Bryn Mawr School for Girls
1920 Tries to resign from Bryn Mawr for health reasons
1921 Goes to England with Doris Fielding Reid, does not return until two months into fall term
1922 Retires as headmistress of Bryn Mawr after 25 years
1924 Moves to New York City with Doris Fielding Reid
1930 *The Green Way* published
1931 *The Roman Way* published
1940 *Mythology* published
1943 Moves to Washington, D.C., with Doris Fielding Reid

1949 *Spokesmen for God* published

1950 Wins the National Achievement Award

1957 *Echo of Greece* published

Hamilton made an honorary citizen of Athens and given the Golden Cross of the Order of the Benefaction by King Paul of Greece

1962 Awarded the Jane Addams Medal for Distinguished Service by Rockford College

1963 Dies at age 95

Chapter Eight

NATALIE BARNEY

Natalie Barney was a sexual outlaw. Like JoAnn Loulan today or Pat Califia (minus the S/M), Barney didn't buy into the myth of monogamy nor did she bow to the prevailing sexual mores. She was a seductress who wasn't afraid to admit it. In later years, she calculated that she'd had hundreds, if not thousands, of lovers. Maybe she'd succumbed to the myth of the seductress herself. Maybe she'd really had that many over the years. After all, when you live ninety-five years, it's not that hard for the numbers to add up. Whatever the actual figure, she was proud of every one of them.

But beyond the one-night stands, two-week affairs, and three-month liaisons, she also had women who were great loves, women who became a permanent part of her life: women like Liane de Pougy, Renée Vivien, Romaine Brooks, Elisabeth de Gramont (Lily Duchesse de Clermont-Tonnerre), Dolly Wilde, Nadine Wong, and the last, met in her eighties, Janine Lahovary.

Luckily for Barney, she was immensely wealthy, having inherited three and a half million dollars. Not having to work, she had enough time to live life to the fullest. Luckily for us, she also had time for literature. In this regard, her accomplishments were many. She ran a salon that premiered the works of Europe's best and brightest for more than fifty years. The writer Colette read chapters of a novel in progress; the musician Wanda Landowski played the harpsichord; the composer Darius Milhaud played Debussy. The dancer-cum-spy Mata Hari rode

through the courtyard naked on a white horse as the climax to Pierre
Loüys' play about Daphnis and Chlóë.

She was also farsighted; in the early part of the century, she began
writing for women rather than men. She understood that women would
eventually constitute an audience for their own writing and would eventually create a literary style out of their unique experience. To further
this end, she was the first woman who, according to Karla Jay's *The
Amazon and the Page*, organized women writers. The evening her Academy of Women (*Académie des Femmes*) dedicated to Gertrude Stein,
they had a reading from Stein's novel *The Making of Americans* (in
French, translated by Barney) and songs Virgil Thomson composed
from her work. Not until the 1970's would women, as a group, begin
to see their literary contributions in this light and try to create, consciously and deliberately, a literature of their own.

Barney also started a foundation to help raise money for struggling
writers such as poet T. S. Eliot and founded a prize in honor of the
lesbian poet (and ex-lover), Renée Vivien.

And Barney wrote—and wrote and wrote. Despite the disclaimer that
her life was her art, by the time she died, she had twenty volumes,
poetry, plays, essays and aphorisms as well as a novel, to her credit.
Though she is dismissed as a writer today, at the time she was considered one of the four great contemporary women writers of France.

Jay also points out that Barney and Vivien helped reclaim Sappho
as a *lesbian* poet. Though there seems to be agreement about Sappho's
lesbianism now, there was little then. Sappho's poetry was bowdlerized;
her life used as the setting for heterosexual fantasies of suicide over a
young man, a marriage to a man from afar, and a daughter—scenarios
that completely ignored the pederastic, mentor-student model of ancient
Greek homosexuality and the content of Sappho's poems.

By using Sappho as a model, the two writers were not only able to
show her lesbianism in a brighter light but also able to give credence
to their own belief that lesbianism was a separate and distinct cultural
entity from heterosexuality. As such, Barney was one of the foremothers
of modern lesbian culture, a feminist of the highest order who, despite
her seemingly apolitical nature, shed light on the oppressive nature of
heterosexuality.

Passion was the driving force in her life. God was not love; Love was
god. But her way of loving was the opposite of the typical Casanova. As
Jay states, Barney held up Aphrodite against Eros, what could be
deemed lesbian versus heterosexual love. In the heterosexual Don Juan

model, Eros "loves 'em and leaves 'em." Aphrodite on the other hand, loves them, serves them, incorporates them into her life, and often helps them with their career.

In her first serious affair, Barney and her lover, Liane de Pougy, collaborated on a novel. As Jay points out, Barney and Vivien did their best, if not also their most, work as a result of their time together.

Though Barney was a terrible snob, when it came to love she was a true democrat. Her first great love was a courtesan.

Barney was in Paris studying French verse when she came into contact with the *demi-monde,* the free-floating world of highly paid courtesans who were so much a part of French society that they attended the theater more often than respectable wives did. Driving in the Bois de Boulogne in a glass coach, Barney saw the most celebrated courtesan of the day, Liane de Pougy, a woman who would later marry a prince and, on his death, retire to a convent.

Liane was a beauty of great repute with dark hair, dark eyes and lips (in an era before lipstick). Natalie fell instantly in love with this mysterious woman, ignoring the young man with her who tried to tell her that Liane was just a highly paid call girl. Natalie didn't care. She had found the love of her life. She would do anything for her. Her only worry was whether Liane would have her or not.

Though she was a young, unknown woman, she did have her wealth in her favor. And Natalie, too, was a great beauty with a seductive quality. Radclyffe Hall described her later in the *Well of Loneliness*:

"She was dressed all in white, a large white fox skin was clasped round her slender and shapely shoulders. For the rest she had masses of thick fair hair, which was busily ridding itself of its hairpins; one could see at a glance that it hated restraint."

Just like Natalie.

Never shy or at a loss for words, Barney sent flowers to Liane with the note:

"From a stranger who would like to cease being one."

When she saw one of her irises in the belt of Liane's jacket, Natalie was ecstatic. She donned a page's costume she had had made for the occasion and presented herself at Madame's door early the next morning. Madame was not awake. A servant answered the door and informed Natalie that Madame never rose before eleven. Natalie left with her tail between her legs, her calling card the only evidence of her visit.

Intrigued by this audacious admirer, Liane agreed to meet her. But what if she didn't like this new woman? What if Natalie was not up to her usual exacting standards? (Despite being a courtesan, Liane only had the best.)

With the help of a confidante, Liane hatched a plan. A friend would pose for her while she watched from behind a curtain. If this bold woman seemed worthwhile, Liane would appear.

Barney was not taken in by the ruse for a second. She immediately recognized the ploy and, angry and frustrated at being so close to her idol yet so far, burst into tears. Seeing her distress, Liane came forward to meet her. Apologizing, she promised to meet tomorrow—when they could be alone. . . .

Barney left, confident that all would go well. Liane had used *tu,* the intimate form of the French *you,* to address her. Natalie knew they would at least become friends, if not lovers.

Always the adventurer, Barney delighted in saying she had spent the money her mother left her for a portrait of herself or flowers for women.

So began, in her early twenties, Barney's first major adventure—and first literary affair.

According to George Wickes's biography, *The Amazon of Letters, The Life and Loves of Natalie Barney,* Barney later helped Pougy write *Sapphic Idyll (Idylle saphique).* The novel, which traced their lesbian love, became an overnight sensation and made Natalie almost as infamous as Liane.

Natalie didn't care. What society thought never bothered her. Only when her father found out and ordered her home did she wish she had been a bit more discreet in courting a courtesan.

But discretion was never her strong suit. She later wrote, that discretion did not mean the better part of valor but oblivion, pure and simple.

Even at an early age, she never had doubts about honesty or the "perilous advantage," as she called it, of her sexual orientation.

She and Liane ordered blue enamel rings from Lalique and spent idyllic afternoons together—until Pougy's patron called her to Italy. Barney blithely followed Liane to Italy, then England.

During this time she dreamt of being the white knight in shining armor who rescued Liane from the "perils of prostitution." Barney even planned to marry a rich young suitor for his money—if he promised a "Boston marriage" for them while the two women lived in wedded bliss.

What Barney didn't realize was that Pougy was wedded to her profession—to the freedom, the wealth, even the prestige it brought. Offered five hundred thousand francs for her company, she sped back to Paris to be with a young man willing to pay such a price. Barney eventually tired of waiting. And though she didn't care how many men Pougy slept with, she threw Liane's ring away when she heard Liane had also slept with the wife of a client. Despite her theoretical stance, Natalie, too, was prey to jealousy though she rarely suffered from it. She was usually too busy.

Even jealousy did not stop her loving Liane, though, nor pining for her when she was forced to return to America after her father heard about the escapade. In America, she could do nothing but read about Pougy's success at such dubious venues as the Folies-Bergère—while attending the round of debutante balls Natalie's position in society demanded.

Until her father's death, she successfully fought all attempts to marry her off. At a point of particular exasperation with the proceedings, she suggested marrying Oscar Wilde's ex, Lord Alfred Douglas—which made her father realize that there might be a fate worse than her remaining single, particularly if she *married* a scandal. In fact, a friend and later lover, the poet Olive Custance, ended up marrying Bosie, the man who, on his deathbed, said he had only loved Oscar.

Barney was absolutely certain of what she wanted at a remarkably young age—and what she didn't want. She wrote, to quote from Anna Livia's recent translation of Barney's selected writings, *A Perilous Advantage, the Best of Natalie Clifford Barney*:

"After those two years of society life, in which I played my role as a debutante very successfully throughout the series of parties, balls, cotillions, luncheons for young ladies and Embassy dinners, I was eager to resume my exploration of other worlds and, particularly, to pursue the kind of adventures which excited me, in contrast to the rigid protocol of high society."

No matter *what* she wanted, Barney was smart enough to play the game. She participated but held out.

Barney was opposed to marriage physically, intellectually, and politically. In her mind, marriage was another form of prostitution. The woman gave up her freedom by selling herself to one man. In return, she was respected by society. The prostitute, on the other hand, sold herself to many but was owned by no one. She might lose her place in society but she kept something much more valuable—her freedom.

In the epigrams that later made Barney famous, she commented about marriage:

"What makes marriage a double defeat is the fact that it works on the lowest common denominator: neither of the ill-assorted pair gets what they want.''

''To be married is to be neither alone nor together.''

''He had the three signs of the non-entity: a receding chin, the Légion d'Honneur, a wedding ring.'' (Unless otherwise noted, all aphorisms are translated by Anna Livia.)

Though adept at keeping up appearances when necessary, Barney was not to be tamed. Neither her father, nor society itself could make her into something she didn't want to be.

''The world is a distorting mirror which makes us appear unrecognizable,'' she wrote in one of the *pensées* quoted by biographer Jean Chalon.

She would not let herself be distorted, no matter how hard her father or anyone else tried. In 1902, when her father died in Monte Carlo, she inherited half of what was known as the ''fabulous Barney fortune.''

She was finally free to become what she most wanted:

''That most difficult of accomplishments—oneself.''

Sappho Moderne

Gertrude Stein might have said of Barney that she was famous before she was famous. Her wealth, her Bohemianism, her affair with France's most beautiful courtesan, paved the way for the interest that greeted her first book, *A Few Sonnet-Portraits of Women* (*Quelques portraits-sonnets de femmes*). If Barney already had a slight reputation by 1900, her lesbian sonnets, illustrated by her allegedly unsuspecting mother, made her infamous overnight. The French took the book seriously, but the papers in Washington, D.C., tore it apart, beginning with the blaring headline ''Sappho Sings in Washington.''

A year later, in 1901, Pougy's *Sapphic Idyll* (*Idylle saphique*) added to Barney's infamy even more.

That was a good year for love—and a good year for turn-of-the-century lesbian literature. The same year, another of Barney's great loves, the dry goods heiress London-born Pauline Tarn, published another book inspired by Barney, *Studies and Preludes* (*Études et Préludes*). For it, Pauline became Renée Vivien, the pseudonym she used the rest of her life.

No one has inspired as many portrayals in fiction as Natalie Barney. Over the years, Barney appeared in at least six books as: Florence Temple Bradfford in *Sapphic Idyll* by Pougy; Flossie in Colette's *Clau-*

dine series; Evangeline Musset in Djuna Barnes's *Ladies Almanack,* Laurette in Lucie Delarue-Mardrus' *The Angel and the Depraved* (*L'Ange et les pervers*); and Valerie Seymour in Radclyffe Hall's well-known *Well of Loneliness.*

Some of her lovers even wrote about her twice. Pougy's second book also followed Flossie through trials and tribulations and a later version of Vivien's 1904 novel *A Woman Appeared to Me* (*Une femme m'apparut*), had a Lorely whose description only added to Barney's growing legend from Chalon):

"Lorely is the pagan priestess of a resurrected cult, the priestess of love without husband or lover ... who is known by the layman as Sappho. She will teach you the immortal love of women.... Lorely has eyes of icy water and hair like the moonlight. You will love her and shall suffer from this love. But you will never regret having loved her." (From Chalon's biography.)

Natalie returned the favor by writing books of poetry and portraits, memoirs—*I Remember* (*Je me souviens*) and *Indiscreet Memories* (*Memoirs Indiscrete*)—and a 1930 novel, *The One Who Is Legion, or A.D.'s After-Life,* the only book of Barney's published in English, about her lovers.

Born in Dayton, Ohio, raised in Cincinnati and the District of Columbia, the "wild girl from Cincinnati" took Paris by storm when she arrived at the turn of the century. One of the wealthiest women of her day, she also had other desirable attributes: wit, intelligence, playfulness, and nerves of steel. A writer, hostess of renown, and seductress, Barney courted and became friends with some of the most famous men of her day but only took women lovers. Men were granted her mind, her respect, and the right to hold her hands; women were given everything else.

Appropriately enough for the sensuous pagan she turned out to be, Barney was born on Halloween, 1876. Her mother was also a matron of the arts, an heiress to a whiskey fortune who, after she separated from her husband, became a well-respected portrait painter. Her father sold the family railroad business, the Barney Car Works, in order to follow his true calling in life, that of *bon vivant.* Both Alice Pike and Albert Clifford Barney were bombshells whose eldest daughter would first be known for her silver-blond locks in an era when extraordinarily beautiful tresses were commonplace.

Rather than going to school, Natalie and her sister, Laura, had governesses. Her great-aunt also spoke French to Natalie. *She* had refused to learn English, even though she lived in Louisiana. Years later, when Barney chose to write in French rather than English, she would say her bilingual education was rather like having a mistress and a wife: you could never be sure of either.

In fact, Barney was sure of both. Though her first book had made her infamous, her 1910 collection of witty but wise epigrams, put her in the ranks of serious artistic contenders. The 1920 *Thoughts of an Amazon* (*Pensées d'une amazone*) put her up there with the stars.

It hardly mattered that Barney had little formal education or that her childhood was spent riding, fencing and dancing. Even when she went to Les Ruches, the girls' boarding school in Fontainebleau, her course of study was hardly academic. She studied "deportment and how to curtsey," singing and drawing, handwriting, and almost as an afterthought, composition and French poetry. Barney summed up her education:

"My only books were women's looks."

Les Ruches was later made infamous for its schoolgirl crushes when used as the setting for *Olivia,* the anonymous lesbian novel eventually acknowledged by Dolly Bussy, gay historian Lytton Strachey's sister. While Barney claims that the "atmosphere of feverish passion which permeate[d] [the] little book no longer existed" when she was there, she was already well aware of what often went on among friends at private school, if they knew what they wanted. And Barney definitely knew what she wanted.

When her family moved to Washington, D.C., in her early teens, she was already attracted to women, particularly those whose portraits her mother painted. In an excerpt from Livia's *A Perilous Advantage,* she writes:

"My mother hired a studio not far from our schoolroom where the most interesting, or the most beautiful, women of Washington society would sit for her. I would sometimes be present at these sessions, perched at the edge of the platform on which the models sat. One day one of these beauties, still tense from the ball the previous night, posed so badly that she begged me to soothe her nerves by softly stroking the palms of her hands. . . . Using the art of touch in this way, I learned not only to sooth my mother's headaches, but also to calm my classmates' nerves. How many hands were held out toward my fingers, especially at exam time."

Hands would play an important part in Barney's erotic repertoire. The only part of her body she allowed men, the first she gave women.

Barney certainly could have afforded to go to college—and women's education was more acceptable by then. But she chose to continue with a tutor in Paris studying French verse and classical Greek. After being whisked back to America by her father during the scandal of Liane de Pougy, she attended the lectures of M. Carey Thomas' lover Mamie Gwinn at Bryn Mawr, where another early love (of Barney's) Evalina Palmer, the biscuit heiress, was enrolled. Such a small world.

By then, Barney had met another great love of her life—Renée Vivien. Natalie was still in love with Liane when she met Renée but that changed quickly.

A letter from Liane arrived just as Renée and their mutual friends picked her up for the afternoon matinee. All during the performance, the letter was burning in Natalie's hands. Though she was in Paris, she had not seen or heard from Liane and feared the worst. Finally, she excused herself to read it. As she feared, Liane had written to say goodbye.

Until then, Natalie had only had eyes for Liane. Her thoughts were on Liane the rest of the afternoon. But when they went for a drive in the Bois, Violette Shilleto, an earlier love of Renée's who died young and haunted Renée ever after, asked Renée to recite one of her poems. On hearing her words, Natalie suddenly woke up.

Renée had already read Natalie's sonnets and was interested in meeting her. But for Natalie, Renée's writing was completely new. When she heard the poem about death, Natalie became fascinated. How could anyone be in love with death when life was so beautiful?

Natalie also said she saw the spark of genius in Renée immediately and was drawn to that like a moth to a flame. But their affair was doomed from the start.

There couldn't have been two women more temperamentally unsuited—in their response to life and in that age-old question of monogamy versus non-monogamy. As a result, their affair was almost as tempestuous as Vivien's life—which revolved around death and eventually led to suicide from alcoholism, drugs, and starvation—what we now term anorexia.

But they did have one burning desire—to bring an understanding of Sappho and ancient lesbian culture to the modern world.

On a visit to London, Vivien found Henry Wharton's new edition of Sappho. Vivien's version was published a decade later and they dreamed of establishing a colony of women writers on Lesbos.

They never did realize that dream, but Barney did establish something very similar in Paris some twenty years later—a salon specifically for women.

Barney saw herself as a modern-day Sappho. Had she been born today, she probably would have said she was the reincarnation of the Tenth Muse. Barney wanted to re-create the pagan world of "the early Greeks," a world that esteemed beauty and art above all else, a world that did not hate the body and denigrate it but loved and worshipped it. Of Sappho, she wrote:

"When she speaks, she seems to exist only for art; when she loves, one knows that she lives only for love." (From Wickes.)

Like Sappho, Barney believed in the power of love to create tribal families which could include current and past loves as well as permanent partners and close friends. She wanted to see a world where possessiveness was not the governing factor in a relationship. In this sense, Barney was so far ahead of her time that few people today can appreciate her stance.

Like other women in this book, Barney was part of what seems to be a gay cultural tradition of ex-lovers becoming family, much closer and more important than blood relations. In her case, ex-lovers became so close that biographers such as Wickes even admit the word "friendship" does not capture a relationship which he says "transcended love."

In fact, this relationship is closer to the meaning of the "Platonic" ideal espoused by the Greeks than the modern conception of friendship without lust. Unlike the Christians who were to create the mind-body duality centuries later, the Greeks had no such split. Casual sex and "sleeping buddies" were probably the norm, not the exception, easily incorporated into a larger tribal unit if the person's character and aesthetic fit seemed compatible.

Barney tried to fix this false dichotomy by upholding the importance of friends. With typical Wildean flair that downplays the importance of the subject and creates a witty contradiction in terms, she said:

"I am very lazy when it comes to friendship. Once I give it, I never take it away." (From Chalon.)

Despite the flippancy, there *was* a theoretical base to Barney's belief in the power of sexual love. No matter what her other intellectual or political accomplishments, her role as a sexual pioneer cannot be overemphasized. Unlike Victoria Woodhull, who advocated free love but eventually married, Barney never settled down to one person and continued throughout her life to expand her circle of intimates. Throughout the fifty years with Romaine Brooks, she took lovers, "passing fancies," as Brooks dubbed them, but also had serious, long-term relationships with Dolly Wilde and Elisabeth de Gramont, the Duchesse de Clermont-Tonnerre.

Sexual freedom is still one of the biggest taboos of American society. Some sexual freedom was gained in the 1960's but that step forward has been overshadowed by the AIDS crisis. Unfortunately for gays, they will never be fully accepted by a society that can't come to terms with sexuality. As long as sexual pleasure is as guilt-ridden as it is, even happily married gay couples will remain suspect. No matter how hard they try to be "like everyone else," gays will never be able to hide behind the smoke screen of propagation. They will always be together only because they want to be together. Intimacy, affection, companionship, may be the glue that binds them, but lust will always be seen as the draw. No matter how asexual they might actually be, homosexuals will be seen as sexual beings first and foremost. As such, sexual freedom is a crucial component of gay civil rights as well as human rights. As long as society itself disdains the body, it will never be free.

Barney understood this necessity and fought for sexual freedom—in her writing and in the way she lived her life—until her death. Her greatest accomplishment may be that, in the face of overwhelming odds not just from society but also from the women she loved most, she succeeded at all.

The Amazon of Letters

Barney understood that love could be a cruel, as well as a delightful, mistress. In the Greek dialogues, she showed how truly seductive she could be:

"And then the unknown woman—persuasive and fearsome, sweet and terrible, turned to me and said, 'If you love me, you will leave everything you cherish, both the places you remember and the places you long to go; and your memories and your hopes will be nothing but desire for me. If you love me, you will look neither forward nor backward, you will know me only, and your destiny will carry my footprint alone. If you love me, infinity will be my lips, you will have no prison but my arms and all your desires will be for my body.'

"And sobbing, I replied, 'I love you.'" (From Livia.)

Barney and Vivien called themselves Sappho and Attis. But when Barney brought the poet Olive Custance into the ever-expanding Sapphic fold, it drove Vivien into the arms of another, Helene, the Baroness von Zuylen de Nievelt.

Suddenly, Natalie was faced with a richer and even more powerful rival. (The Baroness usually set up her lovers with a house and a trust fund.) Though thwarted, Natalie did not give up. Renée was still her primary love and she wanted her back.

Natalie began to court Renée all over again. She enticed the opera star Emma Calvé to sing an aria under Renée's window. Standing admiringly to the side, Natalie picked up the coins people tossed when they opened their windows. When Renée came out to listen, Natalie threw a bouquet of flowers with a note—which unfortunately was intercepted by Renée's maid, a woman probably in the pay of the Baroness.

When that ploy didn't work, Natalie attempted to meet Renée incognito, following her to Monte Carlo and then Bavaria for the Wagner festival in Bayreuth. There, she disguised herself and slipped into Renée's box at the theater. Renée, who had gone to the festival alone, was overjoyed to see her and agreed to go to Constantinople.

During that trip, they finally got to Lesbos where they had planned to start the school. After the initial shock of finding Mytilene more modern (and ugly) than they expected, they forgot and forgave—and settled into a short-lived dream. To quote Jean Chalon, who in *Portrait of a Seductress* mixes Barney's autobiography with later reminiscences:

"Everything in Lesbos delighted them: the rustic hotel, the old servant, a moulting dog. They swam, stretched out on bed of dry seaweed, fed on peaches and figs and breathed in roses and stars. Renée was at last aroused by the caresses of Natalie, who could barely suppress the urge to shout: 'Nuptials! nuptials!' "

According to biographers, Renée had her first orgasm (at least with Natalie) on Lesbos, which probably helped the relationship immensely.

But their ecstasy was short-lived. When the Baroness beckoned, Renée followed. Always flirting with death, Vivien died five years later. There is some controversy over how much Barney's behavior contributed to Vivien's slow suicide, with biographers taking sides like jilted lovers. Whether Barney contributed or not, for she probably was honest about her free-wheeling love life, it must have been heartbreaking for anyone to lose the early intensity Barney brought to a love affair. To watch it being transferred to another was more than most could bear.

Barney might have been a sucker for limerance, the physiological state people usually go into when they "fall in love." During the six months (or so) it lasts, the person doesn't have to eat or sleep and can have sex seemingly endlessly. As an evolutionary device, it is a perfect way to ensure the survival of the species. The real test of love comes when limerance wears off, when people wake up and wonder if they even *like* the person. For many, Barney's butterflylike flitting between lovers might have been one blow too many.

Natalie returned to Paris alone. *There,* as she told Chalon, she "married 20 rue Jacob," a two-storey house at the end of a wooded courtyard that, in the middle of metropolitan Paris, had a Greek temple dedicated to friendship in it. Seeing the Temple des Amies, she knew she had found her spiritual home. Although Barney had the money to buy it ten times over, she never did. According to her lifelong housekeeper and friend, Berthe Cleyrergue, she cared little about possessing people or things.

By the time she found the rue Jacob house she had published the 1910 book of aphorisms that began her serious literary reputation. *Scatterings (Eparpillements)* followed the French literary tradition of *pensées,* or thoughts. Unfortunately, English literature doesn't really have an equivalent—at least in book form. Oscar Wilde came the closest by using the witty aphorisms in plays. It was the perfect vehicle for showing off his quick-witted, sarcastic repartée as it was for Barney. In fact, Barney is closest in English literature—and in life—to Wilde, who also used contradiction and reversal to stunning effect. Barney was known for such sayings as:

"The only way to get rid of temptation is to yield to it."

"Literature is becoming quite unlivable."

And, for someone who harked back to the mores and philosophy of ancient Greece:

"The epigrams of today are the truths of tomorrow. The epigrammist has replaced the Oracle." (From Jay's introduction to Livia.)

Barney always went for the wit, even if it contradicted logic or life. As such, her sayings often contradict *each other*. And some don't hold up to close scrutiny. But most are usually perceptive and often brilliant.

It's unfortunate for the English reader that Barney wrote almost exclusively in French. As a result, her work and thoughts have essentially been lost to us. And although her work is beginning to be translated, she will never hold the place in the English pantheon of writers that she did in France. During her lifetime, Barney was regarded as one of the four great women authors of the twentieth century, on a par with Colette, Anna de Noailles, and Marthe Bibesco.

Critics and scholars often ask why Barney wrote in French though the answer seems fairly obvious. Had she written in English, she never would have been published. Take *Fernhurst,* Gertrude Stein's 1904 novel about lesbians, not published until decades later. Or E. M. For-ster's *Maurice,* embargoed until his death. Even from the safety of France, Barney was lambasted by American critics and derided for her love of women. Her first book confirmed the wisdom of the choice.

Barney also felt she belonged in France. She not only fit intellectually and emotionally, but as a writer, and a woman, she felt she could achieve more respect than she ever would have in the United States. In that, she was undoubtedly right. She was very highly regarded in her day—as a wit, a writer, and philosopher.

There were other reasons, too. The French not only regard their art-ists, musicians, and writers as minor gods in a way that is unheard of in English-speaking countries, but they also have a tradition of lesbians in fiction. Even if the books, usually written by men, often border on the erotic, the tradition is there—in a culture which makes less distinc-tion between literature and erotica, or even pornography.

Perhaps most importantly, homosexuality was legal in France, one of the few places in Europe or the U.S. at the time.

It may be hard for Americans to understand that their compatriots are sometimes more comfortable in another country because we are so used to people immigrating here, but Barney was just one of many Americans who found their cultural home elsewhere.

Barney used her seductive powers on men, too, if their minds inter-ested her. After the publication of her first book of aphorisms, she became great friends with one of the most distinguished French writers of the day, critic Remy de Gourmont. Barney made no bones about courting him. She sent him flowers and copies of her books, as she did most of her conquests.

At the time, Gourmont was badly disfigured by lupus and rarely left his house. Although he had weekly "at-homes," few people came to visit. Barney never did persuade France's leading critic to grace her salon but she did entice him to attend the dinners afterward with three or four select guests, usually close lesbian friends. For some months, she also visited him Sundays.

To the elderly, isolated Gourmont, Barney meant much more than he ever did to her. From the inspiration, pleasure, and heartache of their friendship, he wrote two books. The first charted their philosophical discussions; the second, the emotions he had hidden from her. When they came out, *Letters to the Amazon* (*Lettres à l'Amazone*) and *Intimate Letters to the Amazon* added even more to her legend. Not only was Barney a lesbian who had affairs with the most famous women of her day, but now she was loved by one of the most highly respected men in France!

Critics have posited that Barney must have slept with Gourmont to have exercised such a fascination over him. Certainly Gourmont's words, "You came and you brought me back to life" might make it appear so. But biographer Chalon, who also had a deep and lasting friendship with Barney toward the end of her life, denies it. He quotes Barney, who had an acute understanding of the predatory nature of heterosexuality, on the subject:

"When you want to make someone crazy, you must not give in."

Gourmont called Barney his "Amazon," which also referred, in French, to her riding habit. (Barney rode even into her later years.) Gourmont's book was such a hit that a number of women tried to claim the title. Not to be outdone, Barney called her next book of maxims, *Thoughts of an Amazon* (*Pensées d'une Amazone*). Nearly a decade after her literary liaison with Gourmont, she published another book of witticisms, aptly entitled *New Thoughts of an Amazon,* (*Nouvelles pensées de l'amazone*).

Despite a fairly decent literary output, Barney said she didn't care if she was remembered after her death. Maybe she was just covering her bases in case she didn't make it into the Literary Hall of Fame when she said she was only interested in the here and now. Tomorrow was too far away, she said. "Forever . . . far too long."

Like Wilde, she prided herself on the richness of her life.

"My life is my work," she wrote. "My writings are but the result." (From Klaich.)

The Salon

Like most of the women in this book, Barney was a scathing pacifist during World War I, who thought men played war games at the expense of women and, more importantly, culture. While most of her friends drove ambulances or visited the front, she refused to participate, staying at home instead to keep the altar of culture alive. One evening, poet

Milosz read a translation of *Faust* by candlelight in the Temple of Friendship while bombs dropped overhead.

Her salon came to be regarded as an oasis of peace during this dark era. Wickes said:

"Several of her friends remembered with gratitude those moments of respite from the anguish and anxiety outside when tensions relaxed and hardships were forgotten in a civilized atmosphere of intelligence, calm, and beauty.

"André Germain remembers that in the bomb-shattered winter of 1918 it was still possible to escape from the war in the peaceful, poetic climate of the Rue Jacob. From these testimonials it could be argued that Natalie kept alive the civilized values for which the Great War was supposed to be fought."

Although people had come to Barney's salon in the early days because of its bohemianism, her salon was one of France's most highly regarded by the end of the war. Hundreds of people passed through her house each Friday. In fact, the guest list reads like a Who's Who of Twentieth-century Art. To paraphrase, Dolores Klaich's "Woman Plus Woman":

". . . Writers Colette, Gertrude Stein, Edna St. Vincent Millay, Radclyffe Hall, Ezra Pound, Rainer Maria Rilke, Gabriele d'Annunzio, André Gide, Guillaume Apollinaire and the Nobel prize-winning Bengali poet, Rabindranath Tagore; composer Virgil Thomson; pianist Renata Borgatti; actress Marguerite Moreno; painter Marie Laurencin; journalist Janet "Genet" Flanner; critic Rachilde; publisher Caresse Crosby; historian Bernard Berenson; and the Singer Sewing Machine heiress, the Princess de Polignac."

It is sometimes difficult for us to understand the importance of the salon in France, for the tradition is not as strong, in the English-speaking countries, if it exists at all. Here again, Barney's life points up the sometimes surprising differences between cultures. Salons are invariably held by women and are another example of the intellectual respect accorded to women in France.

Unlike a gallery opening, salons were strictly invitation only. Guests were usually treated to a literary or artistic premiere; witty conversation marked the best salons, as did the excellent food. Originally found by Djuna Barnes, housekeeper and cook Berthe Cleyrergue was known for her chocolate cakes and other exquisite cuisine.

In France, salons have a history going back to the late 1600's, at least. In the mid-1800's, Florence Nightingale's friend and mentor, the

Englishwoman Mary Clarke, held a popular salon in Paris. "Clarkey" had learned the ropes from an earlier salon hostess, Julie Récamier, whose close friendship with Madame de Staël still keeps historians guessing.

Arman de Caillavert's salon was probably the most famous salon immediately prior to Barney's, with author Anatole France as the literary draw. Other Frenchwomen of letters also held salons during this era; Barney's closest rival, Mme. Aurel held salons on Thursdays. These, luckily, did not conflict with Barney's Fridays.

Following the war, another lesbian American, Gertrude Stein, also held a famous salon whose devotees were artists and ex-patriate American writers.

Barney's salon lasted the longest, however, more than half a century. Chalon states that her salon was still going strong in the 1950's. They, along with Marie-Louise Bousquet's Thursdays and Marie-Blanche de Polignac's Sundays were cited in a French magazine as being the best of the literary circuit. In its later years, such writers as Truman Capote and Marquerite Yourcenar visited Natalie's.

In the early years, the salon was considered quite bohemian. There were always lesbians present, few of whom hid their attraction for one another—so much so that a distraught embassy official once pulled out his penis, waved it around, and asked if anyone had ever seen one! Maybe the men in the room . . . A close look at the guest list shows that Barney's salons were très gay.

Called the "Pope of Lesbos," Barney was the most outspoken lesbian of her era. At a time when Radclyffe Hall was trying to show "the girl couldn't help it"—and that it made her miserable—Barney was proud of her lesbianism and publicly flaunting her love of women. While Gertrude and Alice were copying the heterosexual idea of two women living happily ever after, Barney was taking lovers by the armful, some forty at one count, liaisons and "demi-liaisons," two and three meaningful relationships at a time, running concurrently with countless others, hardly worth remembering, hardly worth mentioning, hardly worth using the word "affair."

Barney's affairs were usually very civilized, though they did have their moments. Berthe Cleyrergue remembered one evening when jealousy got the upper hand, voices were raised, and an all-night battle ensued. The next morning, a large porcelain urn was shattered, but the women were on speaking terms again and had apparently "worked out" whatever it was they were working out.

After the war, Barney came into her own. By the 1920's, people attended her salon to hear the latest in literature *and* to meet Barney herself, the philosopher who was then known as "La Rochefoucauld in skirts." To borrow from Chalon:

"With the appearance of *Reflections of an Amazon,* the plaudits came thick and fast:

"One pauses at every page to meditate;

"She enriches our French literature;

"We do not lack thinkers, some padding Pascal, others pirating Montaigne; but not in all their bombastic passages is there a quarter of the real observation that I find in the formulas of Natalie Clifford Barney, so succinct and almost always elliptical."

Over the years, many premieres took place at her Fridays. Colette's play *La Vagabonde* was first seen there, Paul Valéry's *La Jeune Parque* first heard. George Antheil's First String Quartet debuted at Barney's on New Year's Day, 1926.

Over the years, Isadora Duncan danced. Marguerite Moreno read the poetry of Renée Vivien and other, less time-worn luminaries. Historians and philosophers gave lectures.

At age eighty-eight, Barney was still going strong, though her taste was a little outmoded and she sometimes confused the past with the present, the daughter with the mother. In 1965, at age eighty-nine, artists were still trying out their work for small audiences at her salons however. She was still holding publication parties, including the party for Philippe Jullian's biography of Montesquiou, the most notorious homosexual in Paris and the model for Proust's Baron de Charlus. For the record, Jullian also wrote biographies of Oscar Wilde and Violet Trefusis.

During the 1920's, Barney was very busy. She helped found Bel Esprit, a group of regular contributors, who tried to make it possible for writers such as Paul Valéry to live without doing anything but writing. She also worked with Ezra Pound to raise money for T. S. Eliot, when Pound was trying to extricate Eliot from his job at the bank.

And in 1927, she became one of the first women to organize women writers. Her Academy of Women (Académie des Femmes) was a play on the all-male Académie Française which did not admit women until 1980. To quote Karla Jay:

"In the Academy, Barney gathered around her, as had her model Sappho, the elite writers of her era, tried to create an atmosphere of sororal cooperation and support, and gave women writers a place to try out their unpublished works before their peers.''

The Academie held evenings honoring the writer Colette, the poets Lucie Delarue-Mardrus and Mina Loy, the critic Rachilde and author Djuna Barnes, whose book *The Ladies Almanack* was published with the financial backing of Barney's Académie. They also had retrospectives of the works of Renée Vivien and Marie Lénéru.

By this time, too, Natalie had become involved with Romaine Brooks, the woman she would love for fifty years. Oddly enough, according to Chalon, neither Natalie nor Romaine could remember exactly when or where they met. All they knew was that they were in their forties and both old enough to know what they wanted. As with most of Barney's serious loves, there was an intellectual attraction that went well beyond the physical passion.

They had completely opposite personalities which complemented each other. Brooks was a recluse who loved being alone and only wanted to paint. Barney liked to party and only wanted to live life. But they were equals in the eyes of the world and each other.

Brooks had had a number of successful exhibitions of her paintings by then, and was equated in France with Mary Cassat and Cecilia Beaux of the ''non-Europeans worth remembering.'' She had already formed a distinct style and was called ''the thief of the soul'' for her ability to capture the inner essence of the person. Her portraits were not flattering, or superficial. Luckily for her, she, too, was rich and didn't have to rely on commissions. In fact, her portraits were so unusual that many people refused to pay when they saw the finished product. Brooks didn't care. She hated parting with paintings and even bought back ones already sold. By the time she met Barney, she had already painted such luminaries as Jean Cocteau. Her most famous painting today is probably her self-portrait. In it, she faces the viewer, eyes staring straight ahead. She wears a top hat and tails.

Both women were very independent. Except for the World War II years, they never even lived together. The closest they got was a two-house villa connected by a dining room, *Villa Trait d'Union,* in Beauvallon. They could be as separate as they liked yet still see each other at meals. During their years together, Barney followed the aristocratic tradition of seasonal wanderings—summers on the Riviera with Colette and Somerset Maugham, in the provinces with Elisabeth de Gramont, her Duchesse or Beauvallon with Romaine; winters for ''the season'' in Paris.

During World War II, however, Barney and Brooks, a close friend of the well-known Fascist Ezra Pound, "took refuge" in Italy. Barney was part Jewish and proud of her heritage but thought they would be safe under the protection of poet Gabriele d'Annunzio, an early love of Brooks and close friend of Mussolini, who gave Mussolini the name Il Duce.

It would be tempting to think that Barney was daring going to Italy, a Jew (at least in Hitler's eyes) spending the war under the enemy's nose. In fact, when her housekeeper in Paris was questioned by the Nazis if Barney was Jewish, Berthe put them off the track by asking how Barney could be Jewish when she was a friend of Mussolini. In Florence, they waited out the war, being frivolously aristocratic in the face of the horror surrounding them. But during these years, Barney was her most backward, trapped by her Victorian birth and upbringing, even going so far as to write Berthe to send her hairnets from Paris when the French were being carted off to the camps and trying to organize the Resistance.

Though such literary figures as T. S. Eliot, W. B. Yeats, D. H. Lawrence and Wyndham Lewis were also Fascists, they are not held to the same standards by the heterosexual community. Being part of a more liberal community, Barney's reputation has since paid the price in accusations of anti-Semitism. Unfortunately, according to Anna Livia, Barney's unpublished memoir of the war years shows that she did side with the Nazis—until they began blowing up priceless architecture such as bridges in Florence. In fact, Barney was fiercely anti-communist, one of the major draws of National Socialism. And she had never respected England or America, thinking both countries backward barbarians whose only concern was commerce. France, Italy, Germany were the true keepers of culture—Barney's god, second only to love.

Then again, when asked to help a young Jewish couple escape, Barney gave away the two tickets to New York she and her sister planned to go back to America on. She also handled the travel arrangements so there wouldn't be any problem. But one good deed doesn't wipe the slate clean.

There are few things that can be said in her defense, but unlike most Americans, she did not "go home" for the war. And during a period when the few Jews who could afford to leave Germany were being denied entry visas by the English and American governments, Barney was probably fairly typical. She was a racist in a racist era.

As farsighted as Barney was when it came to feminism, she was very shortsighted when it came to racism. It is not possible to excuse her. Even to judge her in the context of the era makes her behavior only slightly less reprehensible.

After the war, Barney and Brooks returned to France, but life was never the same again. Florence had been an idyll of love, a time when Natalie controlled her amorous adventures. Back in Paris, they spent winters at Brooks's home in Nice, summers at Barney's apartment in Paris.

But the times were changing.

By the 1950's, old loves, old friends, were dying. Renée was long dead, as was Dolly Wilde. Liane died during these years as did other women Barney had known and loved: Colette, Lucie Delarue-Mardrus, Elisabeth de Gramont, Duchesse de Clermont-Tonnerre. Natalie especially mourned the death of Lily Duchesse de Clermont-Tonnerre, a woman she had loved for decades.

Tired of a world that seemed more like the door to death than life, Barney turned her attention to posterity and her place in it, writing three books in quick succession. But though she said she had forgotten love, love had not forgotten her.

Toward the end of the decade, when Barney was in her eighties, she met a woman on a park bench who turned her life upside down.

They saw each other secretly for seven years. Then, Janine Lahovary, a married woman of sixty-five, left her husband and family to be with Natalie.

For Romaine, it was the last straw. Until Janine left her husband, they had double-dated and spent time together—so much time, Lahovary had rooms for them at her villa in Switzerland, separate ones of course, adjoining hers.

"One is unfaithful to those one loves so that their charm will not become mere habit," said Natalie.

Romaine wanted habit and comfort, not upheaval. Once Janine moved in, Romaine refused to have anything more to do with her. After nearly fifty years, she cut Natalie off completely. Romaine had had enough.

Stunned at her behavior, Natalie tried to win her back, sending emissaries on her behalf, but it was no use. Romaine refused to see her, answer her letters or messages. Brooks wanted to live the rest of her life in peace. Whether she lived peacefully or not, she did live nearly two years before she died at age ninety-six.

Although Janine was a good nurse to Natalie in her old age, she couldn't live up to Natalie's expectations. The loss of Romaine weighed heavily on Natalie. The year of Romaine's death, Barney was also evicted from her home at the rue Jacob. At ninety-three years of age, she took a suite at the Hotel Meurice.

Barney lived two more years before she, too, followed the women she had loved into the arms of death. She was buried in the cemetery at Passy, not far from the place Renée Vivien lies.

Natalie Clifford Barney

1874 Beatrice Romaine Brooks (nee Goddard) born in Rome
1876 Natalie Clifford Barney born in Dayton, Ohio
1877 Renée Vivien (nee Pauline Tarn) born in London
1894 Pierre Loüys "The Songs of Bilitis" published
1899 Barney becomes involved with courtesan Liane de Pougy
     Barney also meets and becomes involved with Renée Vivien
1900 Barney's *Quelques portraits-sonnets des femmes* published
1901 De Pougy's *L'Idylle saphique* published
     Vivien's *Etudes et Preludes* published
     Barney invites poet Olive Custance to join her and Vivien in Paris to help them found the school of women poets on Lesbos
1902 Barney's *Cinq petits dialogues grecs* published
1904 Vivien's *Une femme m'apparut* published
     Barney and Vivien go to Lesbos to unsuccessfully start school
1905 Romaine Brooks settles in Paris
1909 Renée Vivien dies; Barney establishes a literary prize in her honor
     Barney moves to the rue Jacob; officially starts her salon
1910 Barney publishes her book of aphorisms *Eparpillements*
1914 Rémy de Gourmont publishes *Lettres à l'amazone*
1919 Barney becomes involved with Romaine Brooks
1920 Barney's *Pensées d'une amazone* published
1922 Barney helps found Bel Esprit literary foundation
1926 Barney's *Adventures de l'esprit* published
1927 Gourmont publishes *Letters intimes à l'amazone*
1939 Barney publishes *Nouvelles pensées de l'amazone*
1958 Barney becomes involved with Janine Lahovary

1962 Barney's *Traits et portraits* published
1968 Brooks leaves after 50 years together
1970 Romaine Brooks dies at age 96
1972 Natalie Barney dies at age 95

Chapter Nine

SYLVIA BEACH

"Beside every great woman, there's—another woman" describes Sylvia Beach perfectly. Without Adrienne Monnier, Sylvia Beach would have never become the woman she did. Adrienne Monnier was not only Beach's lover but her mentor, the woman who encouraged her to dream and helped make those dreams come true.

Without Adrienne, Sylvia Beach might not even have settled in Paris. Once she decided to open a bookstore, she first thought of London and New York. There she would carry the latest French authors, like Adrienne. Only when the plans didn't pan out did it dawn on her to open a shop in Paris that stocked American authors.

Sylvia met Adrienne on March 14, 1917, the day before Sylvia's thirtieth birthday. By then, Adrienne was an old hand at bookselling, having opened her shop two years earlier. *La Maison des Amis des Livres,* translated loosely as "The Book Lovers' Home," was the first lending library in Paris. Cheap paperbacks didn't yet exist for the starving artist and masses. People who couldn't afford to buy hardbacks paid a subscription fee and borrowed books from the store itself.

The women felt an instant attraction to each other, not just physically but because they were each enamored of the other's culture. Adrienne loved everything American, Sylvia everything French. That day, Sylvia paid the fee and joined Monnier's library.

In *The Very Rich Hours of Adrienne Monnier,* Monnier wrote about that special moment when a customer walked into the shop for the first time for what she called "the private fixing of the soul":

". . . that instant when the passer-by crosses the threshold of the door
. . . nothing disguises the look of his face, the tone of his words. . ."

That moment was even more special for Adrienne and Sylvia. Sylvia
described Adrienne in her autobiography, *Shakespeare and Company*:

"Her dress [was] a cross between a nun's and a peasant's: a long,
full skirt down to her feet, and a sort of tight-fitting velvet waistcoat
over a white silk blouse. She was in gray and white like her bookshop."

Though Sylvia was wearing a Spanish cape and hat that day, she had
already taken to having her skirts made short (for ease of walking) and
pockets added. Working people need pockets, she used to say since she
refused to carry a purse. With bobbed hair, velvet jacket, and silk bow
tie, Sylvia looked like an effete pre-Raphaelite boy compared to the
earthy, even matronly, Adrienne.

Adrienne accompanied her to the door of the shop to say good-bye.
The wind caught Sylvia's hat and blew it into the street. Adrienne
rushed after it to retrieve it. Handing it to Sylvia, their eyes met, a look
passed between them, a moment of electricity, of knowing, for both.
They burst out laughing.

Sylvia went back often after that to talk about books, about the future.
Already, Sylvia was being drawn into the land of Odeonia, Adrienne's
name for the imaginary country that existed around her shop, a world
of spirit that revolved around art and literature rather than commerce.
In getting to know Adrienne, Sylvia began to realize that what she
wanted for herself was a "home" for American books in France.

Adrienne thought it a great idea, a perfect complement to her own
shop. She loved American authors and owned most of the few that had
been translated. But even her collection was far from complete. There
were no modern American authors, nor many nineteenth century. Even
Melville's classic *Moby Dick* hadn't been translated into French yet.
But before their deaths, both women would help introduce the French
to such American greats as Melville and Hawthorne.

The problem was money. Adrienne had been able to open her shop
because her father got a settlement for a job-related injury, which he
turned over to her. Calling herself "a deserter from the literary front,"
Sylvia decided to make money by joining her sister, Holly, who was
working with the Red Cross in Serbia.

When the war ended, Sylvia returned to Paris disillusioned forever
with the horrible waste of war. After a flurry of letters, Sylvia's mother
dipped into her savings, and soon after Sylvia's return, Adrienne found
an empty shop. Adrienne persuaded the landlady to rent to a foreigner,

helped Sylvia get the necessary papers, and served as a role model of a businesswoman for the next few years. (Not that Beach was ever much of a businesswoman. She was always more interested in the art and the artist than the money and always on the brink of bankruptcy.)

Sylvia was five years older than Adrienne but Sylvia seemed the younger of the two. Sylvia later wrote of them in the description of the shop—which had formerly been a laundry:

"Adrienne [pointed] to the words *'gros'* and *'fin'* on either side of the door, meaning they did both sheets and fine linen. Adrienne, who was rather plump, placed herself under the *'gros'* and told me to stand under the *'fin.'*

" 'That's you and me,' she said."

So began one of the most important literary partnerships of the twentieth century.

By then, 1919, the clarion call of writers was *"À Paris, à Paris, à Paris,"* "To Paris, to Paris, to Paris." Following the war, Paris became the epicenter of Western art, music, and literature. Called the City of Light since the Enlightenment, Paris was everything modern. Europeans, British, and Americans flocked to it. In Paris, they had the freedom to be who they wanted to be and do what they wanted to do. As Gertrude Stein said, Paris was where the twentieth century was.

By the time Beach opened her bookstore, two other Americans had already taken up residence in La Belle France. Natalie Barney, whose first brush with fame had already come from her affair with the courtesan Liane de Pougy, and Gertrude Stein, who had not yet become famous as a writer.

Barney, who was rumored to have a bed hanging from the ceiling but didn't, already held weekly salons at the rue Jacob where the intellectuals and the literati, the artistocrats and Bohemians of France, met to exchange ideas, gossip, and wit—and see early versions of each other's plays, poems, and novels.

At the time, Stein was best known for her collection of Cubist paintings stacked row on row, vertically as well as horizontally, across the walls, filling up the sitting room where she held her weekly "at-homes." She was also known as a theorist, even though she had not yet struck pay dirt as a writer.

Beach added to the excitement by holding readings at her shop. For American writers who wanted to breathe a more intellectual air, revel in a more intellectual atmosphere than they found at home, Sylvia's shop was the place to read the latest literary experiments in little magazines, borrow the latest books, or discuss Dadaism, Surrealism, and Modernism. Over the years, Beach helped the new ones get published in literary magazines and touted their fledgling genius to agents, editors, and publishers. In a few years, she would also, against all odds, publish *Ulysses,* the Bible of modernism, the book by which all the others would be judged for years to come. During the two decades Beach ran Shakespeare and Company, as her bookshop was called, artists as diverse as Ernest Hemingway, F. Scott Fitzgerald, and Archibald MacLeish, lesbian writers such as Djuna Barnes, Janet Flanner, and Bryher would call it a home away from home. In it, French luminaries such as André Gide, Paul Valéry, and Valery Larbaud, Anaïs Nin and Simone de Beauvoir would find a quiet, comfortable place to curl up with an American book. Eventually, Shakespeare and Company got in the Paris guidebooks with busloads of tourists coming to see it.

Born in Baltimore, reared in New Jersey, Beach did not have a conventional upbringing, despite her father being a Presbyterian minister. Dubbed the "parson to the President," her father's parishioners were wealthy, urban collegiates who included such presidents as Woodrow Wilson, Grover Cleveland, and James Garfield over the years.

When Beach was in her teens, her father, Sylvester, took a job as a minister to the American students in the Quartier Latin, the bohemian section of Paris. There, Sylvia saw the cellist Pablo Casals and the Moulin Rouge dancer (and courtesan) Loie Fuller at her father's weekly Sunday evenings. Unfortunately, Fuller only talked instead of dancing with the light and special effects that had made her famous.

Beach wrote, after actually seeing Fuller perform some years later that while dancing with:

". . . two outstretched sticks, she manipulated five hundred meters of swirling stuff, flames enveloped her, and she was consumed. Finally, all that remained were a few ashes."

After shepherding three daughters to adulthood, Beach's mother, Eleanor, decided that she, too, could leave the nest to spend most of the rest of her life away from her husband. Their "marriage" was so unconventional that, some years later, Reverend Beach was asked formally by his offended parishoners to explain why his wife was gone and he had taken up with another woman.

According to biographer Noel Riley Fitch who wrote *Sylvia Beach and the Lost Generation,* the only trait Beach inherited from the parsonage atmosphere of her youth was her "missionary zeal" for the arts and her lifelong rejection of worldly goods. For Beach, clothes didn't matter, nor did having a kitchen or bath. All that mattered was art. For many years, she lived above her shop and was still riding a bicycle when everyone else had gone over to cars.

Her schooling, as well as her upbringing, really was bohemian. She was allowed to stay home from school because of migraine headaches that plagued her all her life. With no tutor guiding her, she read what she wanted when she wanted. Ignoring the more difficult subjects—the math, Latin, and Greek—she concentrated on poetry, literature, and languages. Rather than hire a proper tutor, her father borrowed money for travel and art. Sylvia studied the violin, French, Italian, and Spanish. Years later, she would tell an editor that she "never went to school and wouldn't have learned anything" if she had. Just put down "the colleges T. S. Eliot went to" for her alleged degrees, she said.

Although eccentric, Beach's education worked for her. Instead of being put off by studying subjects she hated, she read and read and loved every moment of it. In 1916, she went to Paris to study French literature. Before she could complete her studies, however, World War I intervened. Caught up in the patriotism of the moment, Beach volunteered to be an agricultural worker on a farm, picking crops while the men went off to war. With her bobbed hair and olive-drab pants, she must have made quite a sight in the rural French countryside whose peasants were still lingering in the nineteenth century with long flowing skirts and hair to the waist. Already Sylvia Beach was everything *moderne.*

The Joyce Years

Beach and Joyce met at a dinner party in 1920. Beach already thought James Joyce a genius from reading his first book and was enthralled at meeting him. With her usual aplomb, however, she writes of the first meeting:

"He put his limp, boneless hand in my tough little paw—if you can call that a handshake."

After an exchange of formalities, Joyce found out that she owned Shakespeare and Company. His eyes lit up and he promised to visit. In so doing a few days later, he changed both their lives.

On the second visit, Beach offered to help Joyce with his travails, which included the money to finish his seven-year odyssey in language, *Ulysses,* while he supported his family. Beach immediately began to

stock copies of his *Portrait of the Artist As a Young Man* to familiarize
Left Bank readers with Joyce's work. She also began introducing Joyce
to the French critics she knew, who would later write reviews not
only touting *Ulysses*'s monumental importance but defending it against
charges that it was obscene trash. Before she was through, Beach would
smuggle copies of *Ulysses* into the U.S., negotiate for the publication
of it in Germany, Poland, Hungary, and what used to be Czechoslova-
kia—and also mediate between a group of typically egotistical translator-
authors to see that all seven hundred pages of *Ulysses* were accurately
rendered into French. Adrienne published the French version.

By the time Beach met Joyce, *Ulysses had* been published in excerpts
in magazines. Both Harriet Weaver in London and lesbian editors Margaret Anderson and Jane Heap in the U.S. had printed parts of it in
their literary magazines. But when it was declared obscene in both the
U.S. and England, they were forced to stop serializing it. When asked
by Joyce if she would publish the book he had been working on for
nearly a decade, Beach saw an opportunity not just to publish a man
she considered one of the geniuses of the modern world but to truly
serve literature. She quickly said yes. Monnier, whom Beach considered
a "sort of partner in the firm," also agreed. It was the beginning of a
decade-long voyage that would take them round the world.

Beach helped Monnier on the literary magazines Monnier published,
but *Ulysses* was Beach's first and only venture as a publisher, work
that would not only bring her literary respectability but also notoriety.
As a result of *Ulysses,* she was constantly being offered erotica, which
she steadfastly refused. Over time, she rejected books by Henry Miller,
Frank Harris, and D. H. Lawrence, as well as the infamous Aleicester
Crowley. Though she realized *Lady Chatterly's Lover* would be a bestseller, she thought the writing "overwrought." The only person whose
memoirs she was interested in publishing were Tallulah Bankhead's,
but the story of that bisexual bombshell never materialized.

To pay for the costs of publishing, Beach began collecting advance
payments. Joyce and she compiled a list of possible subscribers that
would eventually include nearly every famous name in letters and then
some—such as Winston Churchill. She expected the book to be published in the autumn of that year, 1921, but owing to the massive length
of the manuscript, the complexity of the language itself, and the fact
that the French printers were working in English, the book did not
come out until February. Beach also let Joyce revise endless galley
proofs, which was almost unheard of, then or now. She writes that she:

"... let him have as many proofs as he wanted and [he] crowded them with as many additions as he could get onto the page. The final proofs contained more handwriting than print. ... As for me I was mad over *Ulysses* and would never have dreamed of controlling its great author—so 'gave him his head.' It seemed natural to me that the efforts and sacrifices on my part would be proportionate to the greatness of the work I was publishing."

According to Fitch, the *Guardian* said on Beach's death that:

" 'Ulysses' became the sort of book it is largely due to her, for it was she who decided to allow Joyce an *indefinite* [my emphasis added] right to correct his proof. It was in the exercise of this right that the peculiarities of Joyce's prose style reached their novel flowering."

When October came and went and no book was seen, people began demanding copies. Because Joyce added another third to the novel while it was being typeset and proofed, they would wait four extra months to see the finished version.

Until recently, there had been a question of who got the most out of the partnership, Beach or Joyce.

During Joyce's later years, his paranoia and increased need of financial and emotional support led him to become more and more isolated. It also made him think that Beach was withholding royalties. And being a woman working in a man's world, Beach realistically might not have been able to get the deals Joyce deserved. But when *Ulysses* was finally sold to publishers in America and England, Beach got almost nothing. Joyce complained to friends, but Beach never really defended herself against these charges even in her memoirs. She comes closest to explaining in her autobiography:

"Little sums went to and fro between the Shakespearean cashbox and Joyce's pocket. Scraps informing me that 'J.J.'s coffers' were empty again still turn up among my papers. The sums were usually small.

"This went on for a while, and as long as it was on a basis of 'vaet-vient' it worked. Then, as Joyce's expenses increased, I noticed with alarm that our routine was changing, and that the sums were going to but not fro."

"Joyce's labors and sacrifices far exceeded his earnings—a sad thing with genius. Joyce's expenses always exceed his income. ... People imagined, perhaps, that I was making a lot of money from *Ulysses.* Well, Joyce must have kept a magnet in his pocket that attracted all the cash Joycewards."

Their relationship started out warmly enough. They both loved puns, which Beach characterized as Joyce's "favorite sport," and witty nuances were also one of *her* favorite pastimes. When they met, Joyce had been teaching English and working for seven years on the book that would make him world famous. In addition to endless experiments in linguistics (Joyce spoke eleven languages), Joyce used working-class idioms and slang rarely heard in "proper literature." Joyce also invented "stream of consciousness," the literary device that separates modern fiction from the chronological, external approach of the past. He also claimed to have invented the interior monologue, but whether that is the case or not, his emphasis on the *thoughts* of the character changed our expectations of literature forever. Today, we expect to "really get inside" the character's head.

Joyce incorporated anything and everything into his art, including Beach and her whole family. Playing on Beach and beech, Joyce added a whole forest of Beaches to his book. Sylvia's two sisters were Mrs. Holly Hazeleyes and Liana Forrest (Sylvia's lesbian sister, Cyprian). Her mother was Lady Sylvester Elmshade (a play on her name, Eleanor). Joyce even added a Gladys Beach, the name Sylvia's parents had almost chosen for her. Her name was actually Nancy; she took Sylvia from her father's Sylvester.

The love of language drew Beach and Joyce together in much the same way it had Beach and Monnier. But with Joyce, the friendship faded and the resentment, at least on Joyce's part, lasted.

Fitch's recent biography puts to rest the question of money once and for all. In meticulously painstaking detail, Fitch records all advances on royalties and royalty payments made to Joyce. In doing so, Fitch makes it clear that Joyce got all his royalties—and then some.

No matter how much money Joyce had, however, it was never enough. Even his main benefactor, Harriet Weaver, neared her wit's end time and again trying to keep up with Joyce's unbounded extravagance. Fitch estimates that Beach herself never made more than a few hundred dollars off the venture. Beach also borrowed money from her family to publish *Ulysses* and pay for Joyce's expenses.

After a decade of being Joyce's publisher, during which Beach assumed she was making some profit, Beach found just the opposite. When Beach gave away the publication rights so Joyce could be published in the U.S. and England, her profits went up. Without having Joyce's hands in the till, without having to pay expenses for the massive publicity campaign *Ulysses* entailed, her costs went down enormously. If it hadn't been for the Depression which made the dollar next to worthless and forced the ex-patriate colony home, Beach probably would have made a profit for the first time in years.

But what Beach didn't gain in money, she made up for in publicity for Shakespeare and Company. According to Fitch, the European edition of the *Chicago Tribune* had an article about Beach and her book shop in the first of the Joyce years. If she went ahead with the publication of *Ulysses,* the reporter said, Beach would probably not be allowed back into the U.S. Needless to say, the article added enormous drama to an already dramatic publication event.

While she is best known for the publication of *Ulysses,* she was also instrumental in the creation of modern literature. She helped Monnier publish a series of magazines that introduced such budding writers as T. S. Eliot, William Carlos Williams, and e.e. cummings to the world. She is also credited with introducing Walt Whitman and Ralph Waldo Emerson to French readers and in the process, to Americans themselves who had thought them old-fashioned "fuddy-duddies."

The literary agent for Joyce, she also acted as an informal one for others. She introduced Hemingway to Jonathan Cape and acted as a go-between, taking such nervous, newly arrived writers as Sherwood Anderson to meet Gertrude Stein.

In 1926, Beach held a Walt Whitman exhibit in her shop. To go with it, Monnier published an all-American issue of her magazine, *Le Navire de'Argent (The Silver Ship)* with an essay by Whitman. The exhibit included a first-edition *Leaves of Grass,* a portrait plus several notes and verses of Whitman scribbled on backs of envelopes that had belonged to her aunt—who during a visit to the poet, had asked permission to take them from the trashbasket. Although Beach was ostensibly introducing Whitman to the French, she was also introducing the gay poet to Americans.

But Beach wasn't just a publisher, working with words and paper. Her main love was people. For a friend, she would do anything. She helped many writers, artists, and musicians including Erik Satie and George Antheil, whose Ballet Mécanique caused a riot when it was first performed and who, for many years, lived in the apartment above her shop. Gays such as Virgil Thomson and Aaron Copland also turned to her for advice and help with networking.

From the day it opened, Beach held salons at the shop. Joyce read portions of *Ulysses* before it came out. Even a drunk Hemingway, who hated doing readings of any sort, was persuaded to share his work. Afterwards, he said he would never read again, "not even for Sylvia."

The lesbian writer Bryher (quoted by Fitch) later wrote of the shop:
"Has there ever been another bookshop like Shakespeare and Company? It was not just the crowded shelves, the little bust of Shakespeare nor the many informal photographs of her friends, it was Sylvia herself, standing like a passenger from the *Mayflower* with the wind still blowing through her hair and a thorough command of French slang, waiting to help us and be our guide. . . . If there could be such a thing, she was the perfect Ambassador and I doubt if a citizen has ever done more to spread knowledge of America abroad."

Joyce's work was her first love. Banned in the U.S. and England prior to publication, Beach had to smuggle *Ulysses* into England-language countries. Hemingway had a journalist friend who helped get the "dirty" book into the U.S., someone who lived in Detroit but had a job in Canada. Excited by the venture, the man rented a room to receive the books, then smuggled them, copy by copy, on his person, as he took the ferry back to the States after work. After a while, the man's conscience started to get the better of him. As if smuggling charges weren't bad enough if he got caught, he began to worry that the authorities might also realize he hadn't paid any taxes on the contraband for commercial use and would levy an even greater fine.

Sending copies all over the world, Beach hid them under covers of such innocent books as *Merry Tales for Little Folks,* or "other volumes of the right size."

From the safety of France, Beach published the only English edition of *Ulysses* available for ten years. During that time, she went through eleven editions. Her separation from the book, when publishers in the U.S. and England were finally able to fight off obscenity charges and bring it out there, led to the closing of a chapter in her life and the opening of a new one. Beach always said the three loves of her life were Adrienne Monnier, James Joyce, and Shakespeare and Company. Now she turned to Shakespeare and Company.

After J. J.

Beach expected financial ruin after she turned *Ulysses* over to Random House, which sold thirty-five thousand copies in just ten weeks— more than she had sold in ten years. But just the opposite happened. Without Joyce's hand in the till, her expenses went down drastically. For the first few years, profits went up. It would have been smooth sailing if the economic crisis of the Depression and the threat of another war in Europe hadn't forced the Americans who were her main customers home. Monnier's customers had always been French but ex-patriate Americans and English were the bulk of Beach's. By the middle of the decade, French friends such as her first customer, André Gide, began raising money to keep Shakespeare and Company afloat. Bryher decided to add Beach to the long list of people she had begun to support after she received her inheritance, one of the largest in England.

Those years not only saw a split between Beach and Joyce but also a much more important one between Sylvia and Adrienne, who had been living together in Adrienne's apartment since the death of her first love, Suzanne Bonnierre. Adrienne had followed Bonnierre to England in their first few years; they later opened the shop together. Then Bonnierre married. The two women remained close until Suzanne's premature death a few years later, at which time Adrienne became involved with Sylvia. By the time Sylvia left for America, they had lived together for seventeen years.

They vacationed together every summer at Les Deserts, a hamlet on the plateau of La Feclaz. Paris closes down during August and everyone but tourists leave. Sylvia and Adrienne, whose ancestors came from the mountains, stayed with Adrienne's family and slept in a hayloft in the barn until they could afford to buy their own place. Until her own death, Sylvia was considered part of Monnier's family, and was included in Christmas celebrations and other holidays.

On the visit to America, Beach began to bleed badly, and discovered she needed a hysterectomy. During the months it took to recuperate, Gisèle Freund, a young photographer whom Sylvia and Adrienne had befriended, moved in with Adrienne. When Sylvia returned, Gisèle stayed. Sylvia moved into the rooms above her shop where George Antheil had lived and climbed to his flat when he forgot his key by using the Shakespeare and Company sign as a hoist. True to lesbian form, Gisèle added a color photograph of Sylvia to her collection and the series of well-known women was projected onto a large screen during an "evening" at Sylvia's shop.

Because her own flat didn't have a kitchen, Sylvia continued to eat meals at Adrienne's. Gisèle, of course, joined them. Gisèle stayed with Adrienne until the war. Being Jewish and having previously fled Germany, Gisèle left. But even with her gone, Sylvia did not return to her old abode.

Sylvia and Adrienne remained companions, however, until Monnier's suicide in 1955, more than ten years later. After suffering from the maddening effects of Ménière's syndrome, Adrienne called it quits. Beach would eventually find comfort with Camilla Steinbrugge, a friend of both Beach and Monnier, who, in another typically "incestuous" lesbian way, had often vacationed with them before Monnier's death.

With help from its friends, Shakespeare and Company struggled through the Depression. But what the Depression didn't do to the shop, the war did. Beach's family and nearly all of her American friends urged her to leave Europe. But Sylvia stayed.

Day after day, people came to the shop to say "goodbye." Even Gertrude and Alice left Paris for the safety of the countryside. The writer Arthur Koestler, who had been interned in Spain for several months, went into hiding at Adrienne's apartment. Then he, too, escaped.

Fearing the worst but not wanting to leave Adrienne, Sylvia became very depressed. Bryher, who had been at her home on Lake Geneva and was by then giving one-third of her fortune to help Jews, artists, and homosexuals escape the Nazis, came to be with Sylvia. Even when it became apparent that the Germans were going to assume control of the city, Beach remained. War was declared on September 2, 1939, one day after the Germans took over Poland. While she waited for the worst, Beach wrote:

"A lovely June day in 1940. Sunny with blue skies. Only about 25,000 people were left in Paris. Adrienne and I went over to the Boulevard Sebastopol and through our tears, watched the refugees moving through the city. . . . Cattle-drawn carts piled with household goods; on top of them children, old people and sick people, pregnant women with babies, poultry in coops, and dogs and cats. Sometimes they stopped at the Luxembourg Gardens to let the cows graze there."

Adrienne wanted to flee, then changed her mind. Sylvia went to the Embassy to see about leaving but also changed her mind. To quote from Fitch, they:

". . . watched the last of the refugees pouring in. Close on their heels came the Germans. An endless procession of motorized forces: tanks and armored cars and helmeted men seated with arms folded. The men and the machines were all a cold gray, and they moved to a steady deafening roar."

On June 14, 1940, German tanks rolled into Paris.

Beach and Monnier did not leave even though they worried because they had helped Jewish friends escape. Friends were disappearing daily, some such as Paul Léon, never to be seen again. One friend caught trying to flee was shot and interned. But Paris was their home; they could not leave her in her hour of need.

Beach fought to have Jewish friends who had been arrested released, spending hours at Nazi headquarters giving character references. It did little good. The American Embassy told her to forget her friends and leave. When she refused, they could do little but put a red embassy stamp on the door of her shop in an attempt to protect her.

Once the Nazis occupied Paris, business ground to a halt. Beach only opened the store for half a day. Because she was a foreigner, she had to report to the occupation government once a week, unlike Jews who had to report daily. Being American, her status changed to that of enemy in December 1941, when the U.S. declared war. Beach was arrested and interned at Vittel (a resort still known for its mineral water) with other British and American women who had remained behind enemy lines. She was released six months later by an old friend who was then working with the collaboration government. Shaken to the core even at being interned at a resort, she went into hiding after her arrest and stayed with a friend until the war was over.

Although Beach tried to keep going prior to her arrest, it was almost impossible. When Germans started coming into the shop, the few customers left began asking to have their books delivered. Fear was so rampant that Beach eventually closed her bookstore rather than lose it.

A Nazi came in one day and wanted to buy a copy of Joyce's *Finnegans Wake*. It was her last copy, and Beach refused to sell it, saying it was personal. Thinking she was lying, the Gestapo agent threatened her.

When he came a second time and asked again to buy the book, Beach refused. This time, he threatened to close the store and confiscate all the books if she didn't sell it to him. Still, Beach refused. He turned on his heel and left, furious at being treated so cavalierly by a woman.

As soon as he left the shop, Beach went to work moving every single book, paper, and piece of furniture up three flights of stairs into storage to protect them. In two hours time, some five thousand books disappeared. She then had a carpenter take down the bookshelves and paint over the name on the front door. In an instant, Beach removed Shakespeare and Company's existence from the world. But she saved a priceless collection of manuscripts, first editions, and a library that was invaluable, as well as the collection of photographs of ''the Crowd,'' portraits by Man Ray and gay photographer Bernice Abbot that had grown over the years to include most of the writers and artists of the period.

By the end of the war, Beach was fifty-eight years old. Friends urged her to reopen Shakespeare and Company, but she felt that that era was over, and she couldn't see starting again. She remained part of the literary scene until her death, however, and became friends with the next generation of Americans in Paris, writers such as Richard Wright.

Over the years, different publishers asked her to write her memoirs and she had tried without success during her bookstore days. Now she had the time to settle down to the task. She began writing in earnest, bringing back memories of Paris in the Twenties. The result was a very readable autobiography, *Shakespeare and Company,* published in 1959.

She also continued to translate French essays and stories into English, including Monnier's essay on *Ulysses.*

Before her death from a heart attack in 1962, after years of fudging about her education, she was honored with a doctor of letters from the University of New York at Buffalo. She already was one of the few Americans ever bestowed France's highest accolade, the French Legion of Honor. Fittingly enough, Beach's award came a year after Monnier received hers.

Sylvia Beach

1887 Sylvia Beach born in Baltimore, Maryland
1892 Adrienne Monnier born in Paris
1902 Beach lives in Quartier Latin in Paris with family
1915 Monnier opens Les Amies des Livres in Paris
     Beach goes back to Europe with her mother
1918 Beach works with Allies in France and Serbia
1919 Beach opens Shakespeare and Company
1920 Beach moves in with Monnier
1921 Beach meets James Joyce, moves Shakespeare and Company to rue de l'Odeon
1922 Beach publishes *Ulysses*
1925 Monnier starts *Le Navire d'Argent* literary magazine
1929 Monnier publishes *Ulysses* in French
1937 Monnier awarded the Legion d'Honneur

Beach moves back into apartment over Shakespeare and Company after Gisèle Freund moves in with Monnier

1938 Beach awarded the French Legion of Honor

1941 Shakespeare and Company closes after Nazi threatens to confiscate the store

1942 Beach interned by Nazis

1955 Monnier commits suicide after a long illness

1959 Beach autobiography, *Shakespeare and Company,* published

1962 Sylvia Beach dies at age 75

Chapter Ten

A'LELIA WALKER

Paris in the 1920's, a moveable feast. People often say there's been nothing like it before or since. But there was. Somewhat similar yet very different and, in some ways, even more revolutionary and influential: the Harlem Renaissance of the Roaring Twenties.

The years after World War I brought the world into the twentieth century. While women like Lillian Wald mourned the loss of innocence—the belief in one world that would see the "brotherhood of man"—the younger generation reveled in a newfound freedom. Sigmund Freud and the work of the sexologists had finally filtered through to the public. Everyone now knew that people had "urges"—sexual urges. Not only were they natural but it was unhealthy not to satisfy them. Suddenly, the Western world changed drastically, rejecting the stiff Victorian mores of the past and embracing a loose new world.

Women rid themselves of their Victorian accoutrements. They bobbed their hair, threw away their corsets, and shortened their skirts so they would have freedom of movement. To show they were New Women, they smoked cigarettes and, horror of horrors, began to wear makeup, two signs at the time of a feminist—and a lesbian. In the process, the Flapper was born. To quote from Lewis A. Erenberg's article, "Everybody's Doin' It: The Pre-World War I Dance Craze, the Castles, and the Modern American Girl":

"As mayors, vice commissioners, and social reformers decried the degeneration of American womanhood, urban America's best people

217

flocked to public cabarets. The emergence of public dancing indicated not only changes in dancing; it also symbolized broader transformations in the culture as a whole. The best people were now breaking the formal Victorian boundaries that separated men from women, blacks from whites, and upper- from lower-class culture.''

Unlike the Victorians, who had ''separate but equal'' signs on every aspect of their life, men and women were suddenly allowed to socialize with each other and get to know-and understand-each other for the first time in centuries. Everything that had been forbidden in the past was suddenly good. Dancing the tango, the foxtrot, the turkey trot, and the bunny hug was the rage—dances that were loose and sexual, innovative and free.

Amazingly enough, dancing wasn't added to the social repertoire without a fight. To quote from Lloyd Morris's *Incredible New York*:

''The scandalous 'modern dances' set off a hurricane of protest. Outraged conservatives, clergymen, educators, social workers, editors of newspapers joined in a massive attack. They were stirred to wrath by 'vice,' by 'immorality,' openly condoned and participated in by New York's 'best people.' ''

Before dancing finally won respectability, however, people even got arrested for doing it. To quote from Jervis Anderson's *"This Was Harlem, A Cultural Portrait, 1900–1950"*:

''Just two years before [1911], a girl had been brought into court in New Jersey for turkey-trotting home while singing 'Everybody's Doing It Now.' By 1914, everybody did it and laughed about old-fashioned ordinances. People who believed that the new dancing was connected with the slow, dreaded rise of black culture now found themselves on the defensive, and when *The Ladies' Home Journal* at last gave the Castles [America's premiere dance teachers, who were white but toured and did exhibition dancing to Big Jim Europe's largely black orchestra] a flattering spread, Irene knew they had won: 'The bitter outcry against dancing began to come to an end.' ''

Despite the laws of Prohibition, getting riproaring drunk was the way to show how hip and carefree you were. To quote from Sir Osbert Sitwell, the gay brother of lesbian poet Edith Sitwell (from *"When Harlem was in Vogue"*):

'' 'Love of liberty' made it almost a duty to drink more than was wise,' he noted, and remarked that at some of the best addresses it was not unusual after a party to see young men 'stacked in the hall ready for delivery at home by taxicab.'

"No one was sober."

Sex took on whole new dimensions, too. Suddenly, male and female couples were rubbing up against each other on the dance floor and smooching (unchaperoned!) in quiet corners. Though lesbianism was seen in a whole new light once sex had been added to the equation, even that kind of forbidden fruit was looked on with relish. Being staid and steady was out; experimentation was "in." It was like the sixties and the seventies combined. To quote Lillian Faderman's study of lesbianism in the twentieth century *Odd Girls and Twilight Lovers*:

"The decade of the 1920's witnessed a permissiveness among the more sophisticated to experiment not only with heterosexuality but with bisexuality as well—with erotic relationships that were more specifically genital then the romantic relationships of the Victorian era usually appear to have been. Such sexual liberation had been building in America since the previous decade. . . . Even readers of tame domestic magazines such as *Good Housekeeping* were being informed that the sex drive led one to desire various sensory gratifications and the individual had no control over its demands: 'If it gets its yearning it is as contented as a nursing infant. If it does not, beware! It will never be stopped except with satisfaction.' "

One woman more than any other epitomized the era. A millionaire who married and discarded three husbands in rapid succession, who always had an inner circle of "masculine women" who doted on her and "effete men" who did her bidding, A'Lelia Walker was the "hostess with the mostess" during an era where parties were the biggest thing going. But not only did she throw the best (and longest and wildest) parties in town, she also supported the artistic Renaissance that would put Harlem on the literary map. What's perhaps even more important, she began to see that African-American music as much as African-American art was going to change the face of culture itself.

While the Anglos headed for Paris with their hopes and dreams, African-Americans headed for Harlem, the area of New York City extending from 125th Street to 145th, Fifth Avenue to Eighth. And what they did in Harlem in little more than a decade was truly astounding. From Harlem came a new sense of self. To quote Edmund Barry Gaither in *Black Art, Ancestral Legacy: The African Impulse in African-American Art*:

"Southern blacks, northern blacks, West Indians and even a few Africans crowded into newly created urban communities, shed their often rural, parochial nineteenth-century selves, and embraced a more aggressive and assertive, more urban and comprehensive identity. At the center of this new identity was the acceptance of African heritage as a shared legacy.''

Harlem was the New World. It embodied the Roaring Twenties in a way that would make *it,* and not Paris, the true mother of the modern world. In all its wildness, its pop glory, it changed the *form* as well as the content, something Paris never could claim.

Unfortunately, because of institutionalized racism, historians are still catching up with the Harlem Renaissance. The number of books published about this time and place is probably a tenth of what has been written about Paris in these years, if that. Yet what went on in Harlem during this decade was the basis for modern culture worldwide in a way that the literature and art of Paris, no matter how important it was at the time, never became. Harlem had its authors and writers. But it also had something else, something more important. It had musicians—popular musicians who created jazz, the roots of rock 'n' roll, the *lingua franca* of today's global village.

While intellectuals mourn the death of literature at the end of the twentieth century, ask almost anyone in the world if they've heard of pop icon Michael Jackson and they'll say yes. If anything has sold American culture (and capitalism) to the rest of the world, it hasn't just been the consumer goods or the economic opportunity but the freedom of expression seen in the most concrete example of all—that sleaziest, down-and-dirtiest of all art forms, rock 'n' roll.

Paris, too, had its musicians but they stayed within the classical tradition. Despite the use of folk rhythms and atonal melody lines, they wrote symphonies and concertos, ballets and operas. Nonetheless, musicians of the time were aware of the importance of Harlem. Darius Milhaud, one of the modern music's greatest exponents, came to Harlem to learn more about the breakaway rhythms and improvised melodies that jazz composers relied on. "To the New World" incorporates some of these themes. America's own classical genius, George Gershwin, probably spent more years uptown soaking in the beat than he did in the downtown conservatories.

Despite its much-publicized break with tradition, Paris remained part of the Old World. Despite the hoopla, the writers and artists in Europe kept to the basic format—even if they changed everything inside the outline. Look at worldwide pop culture today and it's obvious what succeeded—not Paris but Harlem.

Yet even in Harlem, songs like Duke Ellington's "Black and Tan

Fantasy'' helped loosen the boundaries between the symphonic ideal and jazz. Musicians such as Fletcher Henderson and Louis Armstrong, Cab Calloway and Fats Waller changed the face of music itself, creating forms that would eventually lead, through Fletcher Henderson's swing sound, to the Big Bands of the 1940's and finally to the smaller combos of the then-happening sound, the rock 'n' roll of the 1950's.

Jazz stretched the syncopated rhythms of Scott Joplin's ragtime into a new sinuousness, into unexplored territory. Even before jazz became the rage, in the 1920's, American music had relied on African-American composers. Ragtime orchestras such as James Reese Europe's Clef Club 150-instrument orchestra which played Carnegie Hall in 1913 relied on new and different instruments to create an amazingly different sound. As Europe admitted, he had to replace oboes with clarinets and sax because hardly any blacks played the oboe. Ditto the violin, an effete "white" instrument if there ever was one. To get the sound of strings— any strings—into his orchestra, he added nearly fifty mandolins, nearly thirty harp guitars, and eleven banjos to the eight violins he was able to find. To quote from David Levering Lewis' *When Harlem Was In Vogue*:

"Europe blandly explained to the *New York Sun*'s critic that the sound of balalaikas was intentional, and that he had made a number of inspired substitutions:

" 'Other peculiarities are our use of two clarinets instead of an oboe. As a substitute for the French horn we use two baritone horns, and in place of the bassoon we employ the trombone. We have no less than eight trombones and seven cornets. The result, of course, is that we have developed a kind of symphony music that is different and distinctive.' "

The substitutions Europe made forever changed the "coloration" of the modern orchestra and the sound of music not only in the popular world but in the concert hall itself. Composers began to add more brass to their symphonies, orchestras began to beef up their percussion section. The twentieth century had dawned.

Jazz wasn't the only child of the New World. Mamie and Bessie Smith took the rural blues to the urban centers and created their own sounds while Ma Rainey, Alberta Hunter, and Bessie Jackson added their own woman-loving slant. All four hundred pounds of Gladys Bentley's cross-dressing outrageousness added even more spice to this roiling, broiling stew that would bring the black gospel tradition of call-and-response spirituals to a secular audience—as well as the juba dance and other forms of hitherto ignored black culture.

The Jazz Age wasn't just confined to Harlem. Dancer Josephine Baker took Paris by storm when she shimmied into the starring role of the 1925 *Révue Nègre* at the Champs-Elysées. After being turned down for Harlem's black revue *Shuffle Along* for being too dark, Baker got sweet revenge by becoming the hit of Europe. In Europe, Baker became the epitome of all that was moderne, all that was "le jazz hot." Even today, anyone lucky enough to have seen one of the few clips of her stage act knows that there was good reason for her success. Baker's creativity and wit on the dance floor has rarely been equaled.

While Baker danced half naked in Paris, intellectual African-Americans such as magazine editors Alain Locke were embarrassed by Baker's kind of musical nonsense. To them, it smacked too much of "Mammy-ism." But German theater and film director Max Reinhardt, famed for his version of *Midsummer's Night's Dream* with a youthful Mickey Rooney as Puck, knew better. Quoted in Lewis, he said:

" 'Ah yes,' Reinhardt persisted, catching the interview's mood change, 'I see—you view these plays for what they are, and you are right. I view them for what they will become, and I am more than right. I see their future.' "

The future was Harlem, the future was music. The revues might not have survived but their influence did—and helped create modern music video culture.

And Baker wasn't the only black American female to achieve world-wide popularity. Dancer and singer Florence Mills made her name in the show Baker didn't get into—Eubie Blake and Noble Sissle's *Shuffle Along*. Once records started being made, blues singers like Ada "Brick-top" Smith were as well known in London and Paris as they were in New York.

Musicians weren't the only black artists using their roots to change the face of culture. Gay authors Langston Hughes and Countee Cullen redefined poetry while James Weldon Johnson did the same to prose, adding rhythms not only from Southern spirituals and Northern jazz but also from an inner vision that was different from anything that had been voiced in America before. Countee Cullen asked the quintessential question of black artists: "What is Africa to me?" And the answers helped tell the story of the black experience in America for the first time. And for the first time ever, whites began to realize that there were astute minds in the bodies of people they had generally viewed only as domestics and servants.

Poet Georgia Douglas Johnson, whose letters to women suggest love affairs with them, held a literary club, the Saturday Nighters, which helped define "Negro Art." Cross-dressing feminist, Zora Neale Hurston, wrote novels about being a black woman in America and spent years as an anthropologist collecting black folk stories, legends, and myths before the oral traditions of the past were lost.

African-American actors were also taken seriously for the first time. Paul Robeson, Charles Gilpin, and one of A'Lelia Walker's bisexual lady friends, Edna Thomas, showed that blacks, too, could play the classics in works by Eugene O'Neill and other white playwrights. Not only did Thomas act in Shakespeare's *Comedy of Errors* but she later played Lady Macbeth in Orson Welles's 1936 adaptation of the all-black "voodoo *Macbeth*," as it was called.

Though black theater took more time to emerge from the roots of musical comedy, black playwrights were beginning to blossom. Plays such as *Dahomey* spoke to the African-American experience in a political way while Paul Green's *In Abraham's Bosom,* with an all-black cast and a more "literary bent" won the 1926 Pulitzer. *Porgy* and *Green Pastures* were also popular successes. In time, black playwrights showed that they, too, could meet a bottom line and bring in the bucks.

While Picasso and the Cubists worked the African heritage into their paintings, American artists such as muralist Aaron Douglas, Malvin Gray Johnson, and Lois Mailou Jones celebrated their African roots by adding Southern "folk" themes to the African images that were becoming the basis of a unique, non-European aesthetic. If anything, the birth of European modern art owes much to an African heritage rarely given credit then or now. As black activist Alain Locke said of African art at the time: It was "a mine of fresh motifs . . . a lesson in simplicity and originality of expression."

Even cartoonists like E. Simms Campbell and Mexican artist Miguel Covarrubias (who migrated to the "happening place" of Harlem like many other hipsters of the day) played their part in the development of an aesthetic that can be seen today in everything from the art-world canvases to murals, advertising, and clothing.

For all the successes, there was still discrimination, however. Sculptor Augusta Savage, who mentored so many young artists during her long career, was one of the few who spoke out about it.

Because of her color, Savage was rejected by the American committee in charge of sending one hundred American women to a summer art school in France. Savage went to the press, bringing the issue of discrimination in the arts to light for the first time, but even so, she wasn't included. Worse, her activism got her tagged as a troublemaker, which did nothing to help her career.

Even though the white world had trouble hearing that their Lady Bountiful liberalism wasn't enough, politics was as important to Harlem as art. In its day, Harlem was the hub of black political activity in the country. In fact, the years of the Harlem Renaissance are generally defined by two political events, two marches:

The 1917 silent Protest Parade down Fifth Avenue by some ten thousand to fifteen thousand black Americans protesting the still common practice of lynching. The protest followed a number of riots by whites against blacks with hundreds injured and driven from their homes around the country; and

The 1935 riot in Harlem that destroyed much of the property owned by white merchants in the area. By then, the Depression was in full force, hitting hardest on minority communities like Harlem.

The Depression and Politics

The Depression of the 1930's brought an end to the Harlem Renaissance in the same way that the eighties, an era of the money-grubbing, me-only Yuppiedom, brought an end to the expansiveness of the sixties and the seventies.

During the Depression, black unemployment was estimated to be five times that of white unemployment in New York. Blacks spent more than twice as much of their income on rent as whites, evictions ran as high as ten to twenty per day.

According to Bruce Kellner's *Dictionary of the Harlem Renaissance,* ten thousand people in Harlem lived in cellars without plumbing or toilets. Harlem General Hospital, which was responsible for three hundred fifty thousand people, had less than three hundred beds. Crimes like numbers-running and gambling, hootch and drugs—always the only ways of making "good money" open to black entrepreneurs—grew even more rampant.

Despite the Depression dashing their hopes, there had been a political push for three decades to include blacks in the American dream. Though Harlem flowered during the 1920's, blacks had been migrating to New York in large numbers looking for work and freedom since the turn of the century. By 1905, the New York *Herald* announced the start of "white flight" from Harlem by playing up a murder in an apartment on West 133rd Street.

Sociologist W.E.B. DuBois, the most prominent black intellectual of the day and founder of the National Association for the Advancement of Colored People, called for the right to vote and get an education for black people even before the war. Forty years before the Black Pride movement of the 1960's, Marcus Garvey founded a "Back to Africa" movement.

Although World War I didn't have nearly the impact on America that it did on Europe, since America was only involved for two years, it still helped the African-American political cause. After the war, reformers like Dubois and A. Philip Randolph had another card to play: Black Americans had shown their fierce loyalty to the country in World War I. Like their white comrades, they had fought and died alongside everyone else and had distinguished themselves in exceptional ways.

In fact, a black troop was the only American unit given the highly prestigious Croix de Guerre by the French. Because of their record 191 days in the trenches, the 369th Infantry—nicknamed the Hell Fighters by their French compatriots—was chosen to lead the Allied Forces on their march to the Rhine.

Music played its part here, too. Even for military marches, black musicians had created their own sound. For its triumphant march celebrating the Armistice in 1919, drum major Bill "Bojangles" Robinson led Big Jim Europe's band through the Harlem streets. Famed for its "talking trumpets," the musicians had a "Wa-Wa" sound already so unique in the musical world that French musicians thought American trumpets must have a secret, invisible valve.

" 'Swinging up the Avenue,' *The New York Times* front page reported," to quote from Lewis, 'thirteen hundred black men and eighteen white officers moved in metronome step behind Colonel William Hayward, still limping from a wound suffered at Belleau wood. They marched in the tight formation preferred by the French Army, a solid thirty-five-foot square of massed men, sergeants two paces in front of their platoons, lieutenants three paces ahead of sergeants, captains five paces ahead.

"High ranking dignitaries were present and most New Yorkers gave themselves the day off."

The Harlem Renaissance lasted just over a decade and was brought down, like Paris and everything else, by lack of jobs and lack of money. But in that short period of time, it changed forever the way America would see itself as a country.

"Jim Crow" laws, one of the barriers to equality until Martin Luther

King finally began leading marches to stop them in the early 1960's, kept the races apart socially. Whites and blacks could not share schools, restaurants, drinking fountains, or restrooms—if they existed at all for blacks. The thought of socializing together was unheard of—until people like A'Lelia Walker and white Harlemite Carl Van Vechten began opening their homes to both blacks and whites at the same time. Journalist George S. Schuyler said in *This Was Harlem*:

"Such salons in the early twenties were rare to the point of being revolutionary. At the time it was most difficult for Negroes to purchase a ticket for an orchestra seat in a theatre, even in Harlem, [blacks were not even admitted to the Cotton Club where the best black entertainment was—unless they could pass for white] and it was with the greatest difficulty that a colored American in New York could get service in a downtown restaurant. Except at Coney Island, beaches were closed to Negroes and few were the other places that would tolerate their patronage.

"Most of the white people of Van Vechten's circle knew Negroes [sic] only as domestics and had never had them as associates. It was extremely daring for a white person to dine publicly with a Negro ... but if this upper crust could be weaned over to such social acceptance, it was likely that a trend would be started which would eventually embrace the majority of those whites who shaped public opinion and set the social pace.

"To this laudable endeavor Carl Van Vechten and his famous actress wife, Fania Marinoff, devoted themselves as assiduously as any revolutionists since could."

Whether they were held at A'Lelia's apartment at Edgecombe Avenue, adjoining brownstones at West 136th Street, or the mansion at Villa Lewaro, at their most political, her salons were a gathering place that blacks and whites came to equally for the first time in U.S. history. And whether it was for formal salon or the constantly changing ebb and flow of people who dropped by and practically lived at her houses, they talked into the night to plan parties, literary events, political strategy.

"Black and white, all the swells were at A'Lelia's that night. [Writers/politicians] James Weldon Johnson had just returned and Charles Johnson was up from Fisk," Harold Jackman, Countee Cullen's boyfriend, said of one evening at Walker's in *When Harlem Was In Vogue*.

For the first time, whites began to let people of color not only into their homes but into the melting pot itself. For the first time, white magazines like the fledgling *Vanity Fair* opened its pages to black as well as white writers. And for the first time, white critics began to talk about the unique value of black art—not just the differing subjects and concerns black artists brought to the differing media but the unique point of view that each individual offered. For the first time, America began to take black art—and black artists—seriously.

The output of the Harlem Renaissance—in terms of fine art at least—may seem slight. To quote Lewis:

". . . twenty-six novels, ten volumes of poetry, five Broadway plays, innumerable essays and short stories, two or three performed ballets and concerti, and the large output of canvas and sculpture."

But that "slim" output must be weighed against the social conditions it grew out of. In the decade between a world war and a worldwide depression, an immense amount of art was created by people who half a century earlier had been slaves, people who had lived for the most part in abject poverty, with little education and no formal training. Though there had been some black intellectuals, poets, and writers before the Civil War, in a mere fifty years, black Americans had lifted themselves out of poverty to educate and train themselves for professions in large numbers. In that time, African-Americans had also risen above a self-esteem so beaten down as to be almost nonexistent. And they also began to think of the higher things in life, the finest goals an individual can aspire to, the highest society can create: Art.

One of the women at the center of this truly revolutionary world was also one of the richest women in the U.S., certainly the richest *black* woman in America, if not the world. For a decade, A'Lelia Walker's Wednesday "at-homes," Thursday salons, and weekend parties would be the talk of the town, her invitations the most sought after, her liquor the best at a time when liquor was king. Walker still needs to be reclaimed from the back burner of history but as Langston Hughes said, the dates of her emergence and demise practically define the Harlem Renaissance.

Walker's Roots

Walker was the only daughter of the richest black woman in the nation, the first black woman millionaire, Madam C.J. Walker, an inventor of a line of black beauty products.

Born in 1867, orphaned in childhood, wed at fourteen, Madam

Walker was widowed at twenty and left with a child to support. For eighteen years, A'Lelia's mother worked as a washerwoman and wondered how she was ever going to have enough money for herself and a child when she got too old and exhausted to scrub other people's clothes. Then, working on her own hair that was falling out from malnutrition, she got the idea of how to make hair grow back.

Working at night, she perfected a process that allegedly made hair grow but probably also straightened it. To quote from *Notable American Women*:

" 'The Walker Method,' or 'The Walker System' [consisted of] a shampoo, a pomade 'hair-grower,' vigorous brushing and the application of heated iron combs to the hair. The 'method' transformed stubborn, lusterless hair into shining smoothness."

From 1905 to 1910, Madam Walker pushed and expanded her ideas and inventions, moving from St. Louis to Denver, then adding offices in Pittsburgh and a laboratory in Indianapolis, which eventually became the headquarters of her empire. Walker eventually built the business from a sales force of one to some twenty thousand agents. Her sales force spanned the U.S., the West Indies, and parts of central America. And the company grossed more than fifty thousand dollars annually.

At first Walker sold the products door-to-door herself but was soon, like The Avon Lady, adding other saleswomen to her staff. By 1907, she was giving demonstrations on the technique in homes, clubs, and churches. She was also lecturing on middle-class cleanliness, and the self-esteem her beauty products could bring.

By her mid-forties, the company manufactured a complete line of black beauty products sold through beauty salons and mail order. She had nearly twenty products whose tins all bore a "before and after" picture of her shining locks.

She also trained beauticians in the art of black beauty care. Her agents wore a uniform of a white blouse and long black skirt. Like doctors, they carried their products in a black satchel.

Though "conking," as it was then called, is frowned upon now, it was the rage in its day. In Harlem, there were many black women of wealth and prominence who had made their money through hair straightening and beauty products.

In fact, the mass marketing of *any* beauty products, whether for black *or* white women, was in its infancy. For white entrepreneurs, such as Helena Rubinstein, and black women alike, there were empires to be built. Mme. Annie M. Turnbo Malone had a "Poro System," complete with "Poro Colleges" in St. Louis and Chicago; Mme. Sarah Spencer Washington had her "Apex System" in Atlanta. In addition, Mme. J.L. Crawford and Mme. Estella also had black beauty systems and products that made them rich and famous.

Later dubbed "the Queen of de-kink" by gay English author Osbert Sitwell, Walker's system allegedly had two distinctions that set it apart:

Her system supposedly "used no curling irons or straightening tongs;" and it emphasized hair-growing rather than processing or dressing.

She also was one of the first cosmetologists to emphasize hygienic work conditions in her laboratories—conditions which were later required of laboratories by state laws throughout the country.

With beauty parlors in Central America and the West Indies as well as the U.S., Walker had a third distinction: She was the wealthiest of them all.

By the time Madam Walker joined her daughter in New York in 1916, she was already famous. In 1918, she built a ninety-thousand-dollar limestone mansion, Villa Lewaro, an estate in one of the most exclusive areas of New York, Irvington-on-the-Hudson, named after the first syllables in her daughter A'Lelia's name. (Her full name by the time she married the third time was A'Lelia Walker Robinson Wilson Kennedy. She eventually dropped everything but Walker after adding an "A" to Lelia at college.)

The mansion was one of the most lavish seen in Westchester County, an area where lavish mansions were the norm. According to a 1917 *New York Times* article, the unfinished three-storey mansion had thirty-four rooms, a chapel, a large garden pool bordered by statuary and a fifteen-thousand-dollar, ten-volume limited set of operas with an introduction by Verdi. It also had the requisite retinue of butlers in white livery.

It also had a 24-karat gold-inlaid piano and a pipe organ whose programs were used each weekend morning to "awaken her guests gently," wrote Hughes.

On her mother's death in 1919, A'Lelia inherited an estate of at least $2 million. By then, A'Lelia was thirty-three years old and had been a partner in the business since she graduated from college more than a decade earlier. She had not only helped her mother start the original training center in Pittsburgh for Walker agents, called Lelia College, the year she graduated but had convinced her mother to open a showroom in Harlem, the center of black culture, after A'Lelia moved there in 1913. Until she moved to New York, A'Lelia ran the Pittsburgh college and factory.

In the Big Apple, Walker set up another training college which graduated twenty agents every six weeks. She also set up the Walker Hair
Parlor, a hairdressing establishment so glamorous it rivaled any salon
on Park Avenue. A'Lelia was in Panama on a business trip through
Central America when her mother died and she had to rush back for
the funeral.

A'Lelia was also a well-known society figure in Harlem, who threw
a series of parties at her apartment when she wasn't out at theaters,
restaurants, and clubs so much so, one suspects that if Walker hadn't been
black, she might have come to represent the epitome of the Roaring Twenties, that era of champagne, flamboyance, and "dancing till dawn."

When A'Lelia moved to Harlem in 1913, she was nearly thirty. By
then, she was already married and divorced. Though she married three
times, the marriages were short-lived. The second lasted four years;
Walker never lived with the third.

Lesbian historian Lillian Faderman has added a new perspective,
however, to the usual heterosexual assumption:

"Some believed that her various marriages were 'fronts' and her
husbands were themselves homosexuals, but like many of the sophisticated bisexual Harlemites, she felt it desirable to be married, regardless
of what this did in her affectional life."

Though sexual experimentation was in, pure homosexuality was out.
To quote from Faderman about another lesbian's experience in Greenwich Village, Edna St. Vincent Millay, "Vincent" to her friends:

"Although Millay's erotic life had been exclusively with women,
once out of that all-female [college] environment and in Greenwich
Village, there was pressure on her to become at least bisexual. . . . Millay eventually bowed to the pressure to give up exclusive lesbianism,
as many women's college graduates must have in the heterosexual
1920's, when companionate marriage was seen as the 'advanced' woman's highest goal."

Over the years, Walker was linked with three women: Mayme White,
Edna Thomas, and Mae Fane.

Originally from Philadelphia, Mayme White was the daughter of the
last black Congress member of the nineteenth century who came in on
the wave of elections that followed Reconstruction. Called by gossip
columnist Geraldyn Dismond "one of the wittiest" people she knew,
Mayme White lived with Walker for a number of years. An example
of the "handsome women" Walker surrounded herself with, White
presided over the nightclub Walker later opened.

Born in 1886, Edna Thomas was a successful stage actress who later went to Hollywood for the 1951 film version of *A Streetcar Named Desire* with Marlon Brando. Because of her beauty, she had early invitations to work in the theater but did not actually debut until she was in her mid-thirties. Her first production was in 1920, a play called *Turn to the Right*. When she appeared again with the Lafayette Players in the 1923 production of *Comedy of Errors,* she was taken for an ingenue, not because of the quality of her acting but because she seemed so young. Nonetheless, she was already thirty-seven years old. She also worked in vaudeville, singing at the Palace during the height of her career, which coincided with the Harlem Renaissance.

As with all other arts, theater was hit hard during the Depression. Between 1927 and the advent of the Works Progress Administration (WPA) money which helped to pick up the economy, Thomas had no work. It didn't help that she was also so light-skinned that she could almost pass for white. Her skin color, so useful in many ways, was a burden, however, when it came to the theater. She was too light for many black parts and not light enough for white ones. Because she was involved in politics and in plays with "communist leanings," such as *Stevedore,* which was about dock workers trying to start a union, she also ran into trouble with the House Un-American Activities Committee when it began searching for communists in the theater in the late 1930's and rescinded grants which had helped such black art organizations as the Federal Theatre keep going.

During World war II, Thomas worked with Helen Hayes in *Harriet,* a play about Harriet Beecher Stowe and she was the one shining light in the dramatization of the Lillian Smith novel, *Strange Fruit.* Thomas later said that her life had been rich and full.

Certainly, if she was talking about her private life, Edna must have felt triply blessed since threesomes are notoriously short-lived and she maintained a successful ménage à trois. Married to Lloyd Thomas, Edna lived with Olivia Wyndham-the brightest young thing of London's highly competitive "scene" before she met Edna and settled in Harlem. Husband Lloyd and Olivia, known as a permanent "house-guest," seemed to have survived for some time.

Like Walker, although not on as grand a scale, Thomas did her part for the arts and the Harlem theater. Her apartment was often the retreat of actors and playwrights for political as well as dramatic discussions, which helped create the African-American theater of the day. When Thomas died, she was called a "grand dame in every sense of the word."

Nothing could be found about the third woman, Mae Fane.

Though Walker herself wasn't known for her activism, her politics were ahead of her time in one area: gay rights. According to Lewis, whose attitude to Walker's sexuality is extremely ambivalent:

"In one subtle respect, though, her immediate influence was significant. She was especially fond of homosexuals, and those Harlemites who might otherwise have voiced disapproval of manners and pursuits considered strange or decadent learned to guard their tongues if they desired A'Lelia's good will."

Walker's inner circle was gay, including not only the "handsome women" such as White but also "effete" men, as Lewis dubs them. As we know from Langston Hughes, who claims *he* was Walker's guest, Walker also went to drag shows on occasion. In his autobiography, *The Big Sea,* the gay author describes a drag ball they went to:

"There is a fashion parade. Prizes are given to the most gorgeously gowned of the whites and Negroes, who, powdered, wigged, and rouged, mingle and compete for the awards. From the boxes these men look for all the world like very pretty chorus girls parading across the raised platform in the center of the floor.

"The pathetic touch about the show is given by the presence there of many former 'queens' of the ball, prize winners of years gone by, for this dance has been going on a long time, and it is very famous among the male masqueraders of the eastern seaboard, who come from Boston and Philadelphia, Pittsburgh and Atlantic City to attend. These former queens of the ball, some of them aged men, still wearing the costumes that won for them a fleeting fame in years gone by, stand on the sidelines now in their same old clothes—wide picture hats with plumes, and out-of-style dresses with sweeping velvet trains. And nobody pays them any mind—for the spotlights are focused on the stage, where today's younger competitors, in their smart creations, bid for applause."

Despite her contributions, Walker's life has been the fuel of gossip and titillation and her part in the Harlem Renaissance has not been given nearly enough serious consideration. She has had little written about her; only recently has there been a short biography of her mother.

We do know, however, that Walker contributed to Harlem's flowering in substantial ways. Her mother set the stage for a continued patronage of the arts even though their outlook on charitable contributions was very different.

After her business took off, Madam Walker gave money to political causes of all sorts but especially what was known in those days as "the Negro cause." She even gave money to what would now be called black nationalists, or separatists, like Marcus Garvey—at a time when such sentiments were considered radical and highly controversial.

She also gave large contributions to organizations such as the NAACP, considered a radical group in its day, in addition to giving money to homes for the aged and the YMCA and to scholarships for young women at both Tuskegee Institute and Palmer Memorial Institute, a private secondary school.

Literary awards were also given in Madam Walker's name.

She was such an important member of the African-American community that she would have attended William Monroe Trotter's National Race Congress at the Versailles Peace Conference in 1919 had it been held and had she not died in May of that year.

Both mother and daughter were also shrewd businesswomen. A'Lelia had been managing the business since they opened a second office in Pittsburgh in 1908. But by the time A'Lelia inherited both the philanthropic and commercial empire that Madam Walker had built, it to some extent it ran itself. By then, A'Lelia could devote herself to her main interests: the arts.

A child of farmers, Madam Walker never forgot her dirt-poor roots, and she was known for her compassion. A'Lelia, on the other hand, was raised with all the money she could ever want. She had never experienced poverty and was never concerned about it in the same way her mother was. A'Lelia was generous to her employees and to others as it struck her fancy, but two-thirds of her inheritance already went to a charitable foundation so she did *not* have to worry about charities as such.

Carl Van Vechten described A'Lelia in his 1926 novel about Harlem which caused a tremendous controversy because of its title *Nigger Heaven,* a slang term for both Harlem and the balcony where blacks usually had to sit:

"To be sure, she had never been conspicuous for benefactions to her race. On the other hand, she could be counted on for occasional splurges when a hospital was in need of an endowment or when a riot in some city demanded a call for a defen[c]e fund."

Though that description may have been fictitious, it shows the spontaneity that marked Walker's munificence. Though Van Vechten thought the portrait of Walker in his book was anything but flattering, Walker liked it. They were great friends, even afterward.

Walker has suffered by being compared to her mother, a truly great philanthropist. Madam Walker helped many black artists directly. She paid for singers such as Louis Deppe to study with Caruso's coach and architects such as Vertner Tandy to design her Villa Lewaro mansion. She made many direct grants to individuals and regular grants to organizations. But also with over half of her annual income already earmarked for philanthropic projects, A'Lelia probably didn't think she had to worry about building a reputation in that realm.

In life and in history, Walker suffered from most of society's prejudices: She was black, female, lesbian, and nouveau riche just to *start* the list.

As noted, the Harlem Renaissance in general has suffered from historic racism. Not nearly enough research on it has been done, not nearly enough understanding of its importance has filtered out to the general public. Of Walker, this is doubly true. Had she been a white male, she would have been taken much more seriously, her life and work diligently noted by authors and diarists, journalists and historians who would have brought it to light.

Compared to Paris, its participants, and its paltry influence on the modern world she undoubtedly would have better survived the "test of time."

Walker was also looked down upon because of her background. Even though A'Lelia graduated from college, her mother's washerwoman roots were never forgotten. To quote Anderson:

"Not everyone in Harlem society was impressed by A'Lelia's glamour and money or by her connections among artists and intellectuals. There was an old upper crust that positively despised her.

" 'Quite often, when the matter of her social leadership was mentioned among certain people,' the *Amsterdam News* said in 1931, 'there were those who smiled scornfully; and one knew that they were thinking of other women whose brilliantly intellectual qualities, highly polished and superficial culture, so-called background, or supposedly great family inheritance perhaps better qualified them to be society leaders.' "

Not only has Walker suffered in posterity, she suffered, as well, during her lifetime. She was also looked down upon because her skin was dark. In an era when light-skinned blacks (such as the mulattos of the "Blue Vein Circle") gladly "passed as white" and were at the top of a caste ladder in the African-American and the Anglo world, she was at the bottom of the heap.

Because of her African features, she was also considered ugly.

Though photographs of her make it clear that she was quite beautiful, she clearly did not fit into the conventions of beauty of the day. Called an Amazon for more than one reason, she was six feet tall and buxom. To add to her height, she often wore a jeweled turban.

As the character Adora Boniface in Carl Van Vechten's novel, she was described as:

". . . even beautiful, in a queenly African manner that set her apart from the other beauties of her race whose loveliness was more frequently of a Latin than an Ethiopian character."

To make matters worse, Walker also carried a riding crop. And as if *that* weren't enough, Faderman quotes a black lesbian of the day as saying that Walker had private sex parties at her Edgecombe Avenue apartment.

"But she threw other kinds of parties as well. Mabel Hampton, a Harlem dancer in the 1920's who attended some of Walker's less formal gatherings with a white lesbian friend, remembers them as 'funny parties—there were men and women, straight and gay. They were kind of orgies. Some people had clothes on, some didn't. People would hug and kiss . . . and do anything they wanted to do. You could watch if you wanted to. Some came to watch, some came to play. You had to be cute and well-dressed to get in.' "

Race, sex, class, looks, sexual orientation, sexual politics—Walker suffered from the stigma of them all. By definition, minorities, women, and lesbians are relegated to the lower, least-important rungs of history. As such, Walker's life and achievements are a history lesson in more ways than one.

The Dark Tower

Walker's influence on the Harlem Renaissance began with the ongoing series of parties she began holding as soon as she moved to Harlem in 1913 and lasted until her untimely death in 1931. During these years, she also created a formal salon named The Dark Tower, which later became a restaurant and nightclub. Nonetheless, her regular "at-homes" at her townhouse and weekend parties at her country estate Villa Lewaro made up the backbone of her contribution.

Like Mabel Dodge Luhan's Greenwich Village salons of the previous decade, Walker was considered the hostess of the day, rivaled only by

Carl Van Vechten at the opposite end of town. In his autobiography, Langston Hughes wrote about both:

"Carl Van Vechten and A'Lelia Walker were great friends, and at each of their parties many of the same people were to be seen. . . . At cocktail time, or in the evening, I first met at his house Somerset Maugham, Hugh Walpole, Fannie Hurst, Witter Bynner, Isa Glenn, Emily Clark, William Seabrook, Arthur Davison Ficke, Louis Untermeyer, and George Sylvester Viereck."

Walker's guests included such notables as filmmaker Robert Mamoulian, cosmetics queen Helena Rubinstein, surrealist Salvador Dali, and cartoonist Miguel Covarrubias.

Like Natalie Barney who relied on writers and Gertrude Stein who relied more on artists, Van Vechten and Walker also attracted slightly different crowds. Van Vechten pulled the writers while Walker's group was more upscale. Possibly because of her wealth and her sexual orientation, her salon also attracted the European aristocracy. She was friends with Lady Nancy Cunard, Sir Osbert Sitwell, and Dame Rebecca West, as well as the English Rothschilds. French princesses and Russian grand dukes were frequent guests; so, too, Princess Murat who, after meeting Walker and companion Mayme White, decided to spend a few more months in New York.

One of the most often cited anecdotes about Walker's life tells of the crown prince of Sweden, who was also Walker's guest—in a manner of speaking.

That particular evening, there were so many people at Walker's, the press of bodies so great, that by the time he arrived, even he, a crown prince couldn't get in the door. When Walker relayed the message through his servant that though she was terribly sorry, there really wasn't much she could do except open a bottle of champagne and send it down to the prince.

Like any good host, Walker invited the right people, provided the atmosphere and the mix, circulated for a bit, then let the combination work its magic.

Like gay culture itself, Walker's salons were also known for the cross-section of people who attended. Everyone from bankers to bohemians to titled aristocracy came to them. Blanche Dunn, one of the most beautiful women of the day and a courtesan of the highest rank, was one of Walker's regular guests as was Mac Stinnett, a well-known bootlegger, who often worked as her social secretary.

An artist quoted by Lewis said of her salon when she died:

"Those Thursday afternoons with her were looked forward to with eagerness; for one could forget the cares and worries of the day while listening to the piano music of Carol Boyd and Joey Coleman; watching Al Moiret and Freddie Washington dance beautifully through her charming rooms; hear Alberta Hunter sing in her most intimate manner."

With invitations coveted and people always turning up unannounced, her soirees regularly filled her adjoining brownstones and then some. In keeping with the times, they were invariably frenetic because of the amount of liquor consumed.

In Van Vechten's novel that features A'Lelia as a character, the free-flowing quantities of drink at the Villa Lewaro mansion, in an era when drink was allegedly hard to come by, were described:

"One party which had driven down in a great Packard announced its advent by tossing sundry empty gin bottles out into the drive. Another case of this favourite beverage, however, had immediately been opened in their honour. Gin, indeed, flowed as freely as if there had been a natural spring of it, while whisky, Scotch, rye, and Bourbon was almost equally plentiful."

Though her literary connections were not as solid as Van Vechten's (she ran a cosmetics, not a literary, empire) she was regarded as one of the "greatest salon-keepers in Harlem," according to Lewis, for one very important reason. At her salons, black artists were free to mingle socially, perhaps for the first times in their lives, with white agents, critics, editors, and publishers—people who could help their careers. Most black artists felt comfortable coming to A'Lelia's salon in Harlem. All the local artists had to do was walk down the street. For Van Vechten's downtown gatherings they had to travel to a part of town in which they weren't always welcome.

While that may not seem controversial today, "mixing the races" was truly revolutionary then. It broke long-standing taboos in the U.S. of not mixing blacks and whites for even a game of cards.

As if breaking that taboo weren't difficult enough, the worlds from which everyone hailed were extremely different. The salon was considered stiff beyond measure by such bohemian artists as Richard Bruce Nugent. For white writers like Van Vechten, however, who created such lurid portraits of Harlem in *Nigger Heaven,* the world above 125th Street was much more wild and free than the one he actually lived in. For many whites, going uptown was undoubtedly a chance to "let their hair down."

According to Faderman, it's clear that blacks were not always as liberal as whites assumed them to be, especially when it came to sexuality. As usual, racism was rearing its ugly head though few people on the light side of the color barrier realized it.

As the twenties wore into the thirties, more whites joined the Harlem bandwagon not necessarily because of art or music but because of fashion. Slumming became more common, and fewer blacks felt comfortable participating as a result.

After Walker moved to Edgecombe Avenue, Walker's salon became more of a combination restaurant and nightclub than an open house. Unfortunately, it had little chance of lasting success as it opened three days after Black Thursday—the Wall Street crash of October 1929, which brought about the end of the Roaring Twenties. A few years later, there wouldn't be enough money for anything, much less entertainment.

Named after a gossip column in the black magazine *Opportunity,* the salon's formal opening had poetry lettered on the walls by gay writers Langston Hughes and Countee Cullen. Some artists didn't feel welcome, however. The Dark Tower was too formal, too white, too expensive, thought artist Nugent, who arrived at the opening without socks or tie, and was horrified at the prices charged for food and the number of rich whites.

"The artists left hungry," he said.

Like all of Walker's movements, the opening of the Dark Tower was covered in the emerging black press. Harlem's leading gossip columnist, Geraldyn Dismond, wrote it up for the *Inter-State Tattler,* a weekly newspaper that ran seven years and covered black social life in the major cities as well as New York.

Ever the astute businesswoman, Walker was probably just cashing in on the nightclub phenomena that was making owner after owner in Harlem the talk of the town. She had initially offered the studio and tower to a group of artists. But after waiting for a reasonable period of time, during which even Nugent admitted the free-flowing quantity of liquor turned the artists into a bunch of squabbling drunks, she hired a decorator and created her own plans.

And part of the problem with any salon in the U.S. is that it operates in a vacuum without the centuries of tradition behind it that French ones have. In addition, the salons of the Harlem Renaissance were somewhat different from their French counterparts. With much less emphasis on literature and so much more emphasis on music, it's not surprising that Walker's would eventually become a nightclub rather than a proper salon. But in Harlem that's where the action was, where the future of culture lay. As such, nightclubs were one of the most important elements of the scene.

Duke Ellington got his start at Barron Wilkin's and Gladys Bentley at The Clam House. Many others, such as Ethel Waters and Bill "Bojangles" Robinson were regular attractions at the most famous club of all, The Cotton Club. Countless others, whose names are no longer remembered, whose titles are forgotten, created the breakthrough in music that was such an important stepping stone to today's pop music scene.

Songs that are still heard today were written in this era. "You Made Me Love You," "All of Me," "Am I Blue?" and "Who's Sorry Now" are not only standards of cabaret singers worldwide but regularly turn up in movie soundtracks as well as in many jazz repertoire.

By 1930, Walker spent all her time in Harlem and decided she should sell Villa Lewaro, the mansion her mother had built in the country. She wrote to Van Vechten that it was silly to hold on to it for sentimental reasons. Though she did not find a buyer, she allowed the contents to be auctioned off in December. Like the auction after Natalie Barney's death at which people cried and identified possessions Natalie willed them that her estate wouldn't let them have, Bessye Bearden, a friend of A'Lelia and mother of artist Romare Bearden, said that those who had come up there for weekends "stood with wet eyes and looked on."

Aubusson tapestries, Hepplewhite mahoganies, the library, the billiard table, everything went. To quote from Anderson:

"The sale included the enormous oil paintings, costly lamps of Chinese jade, both green and white; several silver services; whole sets of china, tea sets of silver with Chinese dragons swallowing the sun; a Japanese prayer rug, for which Madam Walker paid $10,000, and countless pieces of ivory."

Nine months later, A'Lelia was dead. On a night in August 1931, she attended a small party in New Jersey where she had a stroke and died a few hours later. She was forty-six years old.

Like her daughter Mae Walker Robinson's wedding, ready a decade earlier, her 1931 funeral was the social event of the season. Another of the what Anderson calls the "great funerals of Harlem," it rivaled Florence Mills's in 1927, Bert Williams's in 1922, and, of course, her own mother's in 1919.

Though people had mixed feelings toward Walker during her life, in

death she became as respectable as her mother. Ten thousand people
filed by the casket to pay their respects as Walker lay in state.

The funeral was by invitation only and invitations were at a premium.
So many people came that "hours before the funeral, the street in front
of the undertaker's chapel was crowded. . . . Once the vast honorary
pallbearers had marched in, there was a great crush at the doors. Muriel
Draper, Rita Romilly, Mrs. Roy Sheldon and I," wrote Hughes, "were
among the fortunate few who achieved an entrance."

The most famous black clergyman of the era, The Reverend Adam
Clayton Powell, Sr., gave the eulogy. Hughes wrote:

"We were startled to find De Lawd standing over A'Lelia's casket.
It was a truly amazing illusion. At that time *The Green Pastures* was
at the height of its fame, and there stood De Lawd in the person of
Rev. E. [sic] Clayton Powell, a Harlem minister, who looked exactly
like Richard B. Harrison in the famous role in the play. . . . Now, he
stood there motionless in the dim light behind the silver casket of
A'Lelia Walker."

Despite the odd resemblance, it was a momentous occasion. Black
educator, reformer and friend of her mother, Mary McLeod Bethune
also spoke.

Even in death, Walker knew how to throw a party. The four Bon
Bons, who had often performed at her parties, sang Noël Coward's
"I'll See You Again," swinging it slightly, "as she might have liked
it," said Hughes.

Hughes's own poem "To A'Lelia," specially written for the occasion, was read by a close gay friend, Edward Perry.

When the cortege moved to the cemetery, one of the most famous
black aviators of the day, Colonel Hubert Julian, paid a last tribute,
flying silently overhead to drop a wreath on the grave.

Wrote Hughes:

"[Walker's death in 1931] was really the end of the gay times of
the New Negro era in Harlem, the period that had begun to reach its
end when the crash came in 1929 and the white people had much less
money to spend on themselves, and practically none to spend on Negroes, for the Depression brought everybody down a peg or two. And
the Negroes had but few pegs to fall."

Walker's death might have been the end of an era, but that era lives
today in music and has left the modern world a legacy that would have
shocked the society of the day.

In 1925, six years before Walker's death and a few days after the first literary awards banquet given by the black magazine *Opportunity,* a reporter for the New York *Herald Tribune,* wrote:

"One of fate's quaint but by no means impossible revenges [would be] if the Negro's real contribution to American life should be in the field of art."

The writer undoubtedly thought the statement terribly outrageous. But time was on Harlem's side, at least in art, if not economics. At the cusp of the twenty-first century, seeing how much life has changed, how much contemporary art and popular culture worldwide owe to African-Americans, it's clear that the African-American influence has been one of the greatest contributions to American culture, that it flowered first in Harlem, and that A'Lelia Walker was a great part of it.

A'Lelia Walker

1867 Madam C. J. Walker (nee Sarah Breedlove) born

1885 A'Lelia (named Lelia) Walker born in St. Louis

1905 Madam Walker starts black beauty products business in St. Louis

1907 Madam Walker moves headquarters to Denver

1908 A'Lelia graduates from college and joins Madam Walker to open a second office in Pittsburgh which A'Lelia manages as well as training center for black beauticians called Lelia College

1910 Madam Walker sets up laboratories and second training school in Indianapolis

1911 New Jersey girl arrested for doing the "turkey-trot" and singing "Everybody's Doing It"

1913 A'Lelia moves to New York City and becomes known as a hostess for parties at her apartment
James Reese Europe's Clef Club orchestra plays Carnegie Hall

1917 Silent Protest down Fifth Avenue against lynching and anti-black riots by whites across the country

1918 Villa Lewaro, Madam Walker's posh Hudson River mansion, completed

1919 The Hell Fighters march through Harlem for the Armistice
Madam Walker dies, leaving A'Lelia one of the largest fortunes of any black woman in the country

1923 The $60,000 wedding of A'Lelia's adopted daughter, Mae Walker Robinson, is biggest social event of Harlem season.

1925 Alain Locke's *The New Negro* published
     Countee Cullen writes the poem *What Is Africa to Me?*
     Josephine Baker's Révue Nègre takes Paris by storm
1926 Paul Green's *In Abraham's Bosom* wins the Pulitzer Prize
     White Harlemite Carl Van Vechten's *Nigger Heaven* published
1927 Duke Ellington's *Black and Tan Fantasy* performed
1928 A'Lelia Walker starts formal salon at apartment on West 136th
     Street
1929 Wall Street crashes on October 24, Black Thursday
1930 Walker moves salon to Edgecombe Avenue apartment and turns
     it into a combination restaurant and nightclub
1931 A'Lelia has a stroke and dies a few hours later. She was 46
1932 Lois Maillou Jones *The Ascent of Ethiopia* painted
1934 Aaron Douglas paints *The Aspects of Negro Life* mural
1935 The first group exhibit of African American art at a major Ameri-
     can museum is held at the Museum of Modern Art
     Blacks riot in Harlem
1940 Langston Hughes's autobiography, *The Big Sea,* published

Chapter Eleven

ANNA FREUD

"I'm not a lesbian; I just fell in love with another woman."

"I'm not gay; I'm married. I only sleep with men occasionally."

Until gay liberation in the 1970's, that was the standard answer of millions of gay men and lesbians. That was the situation Anna Freud, founder of child analysis, daughter of Sigmund Freud, faced when asked the question everyone wanted to know: Was she gay?

Undoubtedly, Anna Freud would have said no, despite a twenty-five-year relationship with Dorothy Tiffany Burlingham, the daughter of famed stained glass maker Louis Comfort Tiffany. But she had little choice.

Then, the 1950's were in their full glory. Red-baiting and Communist witch hunts were at their height. To the general population, second only to a pinko was a pervert. Even among intellectuals, homosexuality was still considered a psychological aberration, a case of "arrested development" as the Freudians put it, despite Freud himself saying all people were bisexual. The problems of homosexuals, he felt, were the fault of society. But not until 1973 did the American Psychological Association take homosexuality off the "sick" list. Anna Freud didn't need to add "dyke" to the names she'd already been called.

By that time, she had already been through the major professional battle of her life—a battle that got so personal, so nasty, that opponents were saying she wasn't fit to be an analyst.

As if that weren't enough, she faced another, equally serious, problem. Her first child-therapy success, Dorothy Burlingham's eldest son, Bob, was having troubles not only with the manic-depression that eventually killed his father but with homosexuality itself.

Anna Freud did what many lesbians still do today when faced with the loss of career, credibility, finances—she chose the closet. How deep that closet was, whether she denied her homosexuality even to herself, is something we will never know.

But such are the workings of the unconscious, whose strange machinations we take for granted today.

It wasn't always that way, however. We believe in the unconscious because Anna's father, Sigmund, unearthed the concept.

In fact, the existence of the unconscious is so much a part of today's world, it's difficult to imagine how truly revolutionary it was then. In their day, Freud's theories created as much controversy as Darwin's theory of evolution. Disciples might have come from all over the world to study with "Herr Professor," but it took three decades before Freud's startling ideas would become part of the commonly held notion of reality.

At first, people were truly frightened there could be a side to themselves—especially one that controlled their behavior—they didn't know was there and they fought the notion tooth and nail.

The nineteenth century was one of the most sexually repressed eras in history. The thought of a hidden self that was angry and hateful or, worse, sexually aggressive and pleasure-oriented, was loathsome. Freud's followers were hated and reviled. And because Freud based many of his conclusions on observations about himself, the attacks were viciously personal. Freud was called everything from a pervert to a monster and a sex maniac.

Even today, Freud is not the most popular of thinkers. For most women, the concept of penis envy is ludicrous. Few women actually want a penis, though most would gladly take the automatic authority that goes with the added appendage. It's clear today that the young women Freud analyzed were not jealous of the body but the political and economic freedom that went with it. But that was before the idea of "sexism" had been invented, before the inequalities of patriarchal society were beginning to be questioned. "Power envy" would have been a better term but that's hindsight.

The most serious flaw in Freud's work, at least as it affects women, however, was the failure to recognize sexual abuse. We know today that women in the U.S. are victims of molestation and incest at a phenomenal rate. Whether Jeffrey Moussaieff Masson is correct when he states in *The Assault on Truth* that Freud deliberately covered up the evidence at hand when faced with a barrage of criticism from his colleagues, we'll never know. But Freud certainly helped set the tone of disbelief that continued until the early 1980's.

What we are beginning to realize now is that a taboo against incest doesn't exist. Fathers, brothers, uncles, victimize their female relatives in horrifying numbers. The taboo is against *talking* about incest, against confronting the aggressor and putting him in jail. It would take nearly a century of fighting for economic freedom (and position in society) before such profoundly personal and wrenching issues of female sexual bondage could be brought to light.

With these issues as stumbling blocks, it is sometimes hard to understand how much Freud actually contributed to the modern world and that, skewered as it was, his work did have an enormously positive impact.

Anna said that she was born in the same year as psychoanalysis. To understand the daughter, it helps to understand the father. The year of her birth, 1895, was the year that Sigmund discovered the meaning of his dreams, what became the philosophical underpinning of the study of the unconscious.

The youngest of six children, Anna was a bright, precocious handful. Even as a toddler, she was proud of her "naughtiness." According to Elisabeth Young-Bruehl's biography, at age three Anna remarked: "On birthdays, I am usually rather good," a striking contrast to the adventurous self she usually displayed, the self her father loved best. He, too, had been adventurous and wild as a youth. So much so, he told his fiancé that it was best he marry her (and not her sister) because he and her sister were too much alike. What they each needed for a happy life was someone of the opposite temperament, the steadying influence given by their respective, complementary fiancées.

Anna grew up in relative comfort, though the family was still moving up the financial ladder (and would never get that far). Freud was barely a professor at Anna's birth, though he was already taking in clients and beginning to lay out the philosophy that would eventually make him famous. Anna was five when his first book, *The Interpretation of Dreams (Die Traumdeutung)*, created a sensation.

Like Virginia Woolf, Anna did not go to the "gymnasium" and felt the lack of a classical education all her life. But from childhood on, Anna listened to discussions about the workings of the human mind.

From her father's comments on human behavior at the dinner table to the Wednesday night meetings of the newly formed Vienna Psychoanalytic Society held in Freud's library, Anna absorbed psychological concepts and terms.

Biographer Uwe Henrik Peters describes the truly unique quality of Anna's upbringing in "Anna Freud: A Life Dedicated to Children":

"While still young she was introduced to her father's complicated theoretical system and was able to absorb it without difficulties. From the very beginning she thus treated Freud's theoretical constructs (such as the unconscious) . . . as real data, as if they were palpable objects rather than theory."

But Anna had to test her own wings before coming home to roost. For five years she taught elementary school—until she realized that what she really wanted to be was a psychoanalyst "like her dear Papa."

During those five years, however, she laid the foundation for her life's work. Even though she became a psychoanalyst, she and Dorothy Burlingham would run nurseries and schools for fifty years that combined analysis with teaching.

Like many gay women, Anna had conflicts with her "femininity" during her early adult years. At one point, Sigmund wrote to her:

"We will notice a change when you no longer withdraw from the pleasures of your age but gladly enjoy what other girls enjoy. One hardly has energy for serious interests if one is too zealous, too sensitive, and remains removed from *one's own life and nature*; then one finds oneself troubled in the very things one wishes to take up."

Anna eventually did resolve the problem of being true to "one's own life and nature," but it was not until she met Dorothy Burlingham nearly a decade after that letter was written.

While teaching, Anna began analysis with her father, took seminars, and went on psychiatric rounds with the doctors at the local hospital. But she was also beginning to be dissatisfied with teaching. Eventually she realized she had to change. Once she saw her true path in psychoanalysis, it was fairly easy to change fields—all she had to do was change her personal analysis to a training one. One of the basic tenets of psychoanalytic training is the understanding of one's own nature discovered through analysis. Though it may seem odd today to be in analysis with one's father, there were few analysts in those day and none better than Sigmund Freud. Also there were no ethical guidelines against analyzing family and friends. The early founders of the field were happy to analyze anyone who crossed their path—and quite often did. They started by analyzing each other.

In fact, they were so oblivious to the implications in those days that Anna became involved with Dorothy Burlingham through analyzing Dorothy's children. She not only analyzed two of the four children she helped raise but called herself the children's "psychological" mother. It wasn't until 1935, more than a decade after she began the analysis with son Bob, that analysts began to question whether they should be treating people close to them.

Years later, the complications of having been analyzed by her father—the impossibility of complete honesty and the lack of transference, a supposed key to success—became apparent, and came back to haunt her. But by then, the "damage," as they say, was done.

Beyond Analysis

"Beating Fantasies and Daydreams," Anna Freud's first paper, dealt with the ways people tried to stop masturbating. "Self-abuse" was thought to be not only immoral but dangerous. It could lead to insanity, lesbianism, and death, as well as acne, halitosis, and constipation! Despite analysis, Anna was apparently as guilt-ridden as anyone when it came to the joys of "self-love." Being an analyst, Anna used the fantasies leading up to the event (and the "punishment" she then had to "inflict") to write about the mind. The paper was a reponse to one of her father's a few years earlier about sadomasochistic fantasies. Anna used the paper as a requirement for admittance to the Vienna Psychoanalytic Society.

Thus began Anna Freud's work in psychoanalysis, work that would lead to the creation of the field of child therapy.

Anna quit teaching to open a practice during the economic crisis that followed World War I. Food was scarce, clients scarcer. Friends sent "CARE" packages of food; Freud had even fewer clients than before which hadn't been many to start with. Worse, a flu epidemic was sweeping the world, killing twenty million people, including Anna's sister, Sophie.

Despite the hard times, Anna's family did not object when she left a secure income to open a practice, the income from which was never certain. Like Freud, she saw patients at home, which at least meant she didn't have the added expense of an office. She also brought in money translating articles for the local psychoanalytic journal.

Though Anna always bristled at the suggestion that Dorothy Burlingham's money made her life easier, when Dorothy first brought her eldest son and her daughter to Anna for treatment of the psychological problems resulting from their father's mental illness, mother's separation, and Bob's asthma, Anna's finances began to look up. When Anna accepted Bob as a patient, Dorothy moved the family lock, stock and barrel to Vienna. Soon, another American family moved to Vienna to have their children analyzed by Anna too. Dorothy then went into analysis herself with Theodore Reik and to complete the circle, she eventually trained with Freud Père to become an analyst.

Freud said in a letter to his son-in-law, to quote from the biography of Dorothy Burlingham by her grandson, Michael, *The Last Tiffany*:

"Anna is treating naughty American children."

What Freud didn't say was "naughty, *rich*, American children."

According to her grandson, Dorothy rented the "mansion of a Hungarian prince, fully furnished with extensive grounds." Dorothy also had a car, a rarity at the time, which allowed them to sightsee. By spring, some six months later, they were "making regular excursions to the Vienna Woods, their discussions leading the women over carpets of wild strawberries and patches of melting snow to 'lonely, beautiful spots.' "

We can imagine the attraction between Anna, whose dark Eastern European sense of authority was just what Dorothy needed. For though Dorothy had money, she had been through the mill psychologically. As a girl, she had sworn she would never put up with the abusiveness that marked the worst side of her father. She married a brilliant, sensitive man only to discover over time that his worst moods matched her father's depths of abuse. She chose to escape with four young children in tow but she had to travel all the way to Vienna before she found a home.

Anna was younger and had much less actual experience, but she'd seen the depths of human nature and was wise beyond her years. And she believed in change, in the ability of analysis to make life better, if not actually good. We can imagine Dorothy breathing a sigh of relief as she rested her head on Anna's shoulder. She had finally found someone to trust.

For Anna, the youngest of six, the one left out of family outings because of her age, the one ignored at dinner because she was too young to understand, having someone believe in her, someone look up to her and respect her, was the best gift anyone could give. It was a match Aphrodite herself would have been proud of, a match that lasted the rest of their lives.

Herr Professor was also entranced by this American who owned her own car and chauffered them on trips around town and country. He even gave Dorothy an opal brooch.

Anna wrote to Max Eitingon, her therapist:

"I think sometimes that I want not only to make them healthy but also, at the same time, to have them, or at least have something of them, for myself. . . . I have this dependency, this wanting-to-have-something—even leaving my profession aside—in every nook and cranny of my life."

Anna wanted what most people want—a family of her own. By then, Dorothy had moved to a wine merchant's mansion but she soon moved to the flat above the Freuds at Berggasse 19. Dorothy had the flat renovated, adding a fireplace, new plumbing and wiring as well as a direct phone line between Dorothy and Anna's bedrooms so they could "chat privately after retiring for the night."

The children ran up and down the stairs between the two flats. The two families began to eat together and vacation as one.

During summer vacations, an opening in the hedge connected their villas. Anna led Dorothy and "the Four" in Viennese pastimes: climbing mountains, swimming lakes, and playing nightly games of checkers. She made up stories to amuse them, telling them that Dorothy's daughter Mabbie got her blue eyes because God gave her a piece of sky to look out of. And like her father had done before her, Anna took them mushroom hunting and taught them how to find the meadow fungi that hid at the foot of black pine trees.

Freud later wrote Eitingon that Anna was further from marriage than ever, "totally absorbed in her friendship with Dorothy." Mother Martha, who was not terribly demonstrative to Anna, signed letters to "my dearest Dorothy" with "a hug."

It must have been quite a scene—at least on the therapy front. In his biography, Peters says that Anna's famous case, the Devil Girl, was actually Dorothy Burlingham's daughter. According to Anna's notes, six-year-old Mabbie felt she had a devil inside her who made her want to say and do "evil things." After working with her to let the devil out, at least in therapy where she could talk about the hostility "the devil" felt, the child began to feel free to express herself in other ways.

"In the absence of external condemnation, the child lost all modera-
tion, carried over into her home all the ideas previously expressed only
during analysis, and completely revelled, as she had with me, in her
anal preoccupations, comparisons, and expressions. The other members
of the household soon found this intolerable; especially on account of
the child's behavior at the dinner table, they lost all appetite."

In a few days, the girl went from being a seemingly nice child to a
self-satisfied monster.

It must have been quite an experiment in child-rearing. Luckily, Anna
had the confidence of her closest friend for one of her first and possibly
most outrageous attempts at child therapy. Grandson Michael wrote:

"Dorothy was no doubt relieved to surrender to Anna a share of her
parental responsibility and authority. Having shouldered it alone for
over four years and, in Bob's case, to such unhappy ends, she virtually
hurled herself into the role of cooperative parent, Anna's confidence
irradiating her pockets of doubt. . . . Charged with custody of one of
'the greatest secrets of nature,' their enthusiasm seemed boundless. Dorothy was young, Anna still younger; they shared that enthusiasm."

Anna eventually solved the problem by telling Mabbie that she had
broken a promise they made from the first, that the devil could come
out in therapy—and only therapy. Faced with the threat of ending their
special time together, the child agreed to show that particular self only
during "their lessons," as they called therapy sessions.

In 1927, Anna and Dorothy took their first vacation alone. In 1930,
they bought a house in the country for weekends and summers.

Now comes the "L" question. Despite "the persistent rumor that
the friends were lesbians," biographer Elisabeth Young-Bruehl in
"Anna Freud" insists that Anna and Dorothy's relationship was
"chaste," though how she can make that claim—unless she spent nights
with them—is amazing. Biographer Peters sidesteps the question. Only
Burlingham's grandson deals with it in any serious way, calling them
"the oxymoron, intellectual lesbians." Intellectual lesbians or not, at
least one guest at their country house was shocked to find "only one
double bed in the only bedroom in the house."

But the emphasis on sexuality misses the point anyhow. Burlingham-
Freud fit the continuum of romantic friend-lesbian relationships that
began centuries earlier and runs through the personal denial of the mid-
twentieth century up to the political awakening of the post-Stonewall
era, when gays and lesbians began not only to demand rights but to
define themselves for the first time.

Anna's response to lesbianism is typical of the era. Prior to the work of sexologists like her father and Havelock Ellis, women could live their whole lives together without anyone thinking twice. When the sexologists began saying that women not only *had* sex but *enjoyed* it, women who lived together were suddenly looked at askance. They were dirty, filthy, evil.

Amazingly enough in retrospect, the women who epitomized the "romantic friends" movement and were idealized by thousands of women in England and Europe, lived their whole lives as "man and wife" in the most obvious way imaginable. Looking at photographs of the Ladies of Llangollen today with Lady Eleanor Butler in top hat and tails, they are clearly a butch-femme pair in the traditional lesbian manner.

The general public didn't think anything of it, however, until people like Anna's father began theorizing about women's sexuality and exposed the deceptive innocence of the romantic friendships.

For the record, the word "homosexuality" wasn't coined until 1869, and "heterosexuality" at the end of the century, which originally meant "bisexual." Not until the early part of the twentieth century did scientists officially create two kinds of relationships and classify them as "normal" and "abnormal." Prior to that, everyone had known that men sometimes loved men and women sometimes loved women—but it was not regarded as an illness, however distasteful it might have seemed. It was not until the twentieth century that the world was divided into an "us" and "them" sexuality.

Dorothy and Anna saw themselves as twins, as perfect complements in an "ideal friendship." The need to prove (or disprove) a sexual component is a ruse that keeps women out of the historic lesbian fold. It also misses the most obvious aspect of lesbian relationships, the "intellectual" side. To quote from grandson Michael:

"Life with Anna offer[ed] productivity and self-respect."

Productivity and self-respect—the two most important components of lesbianism for any woman, whether she is a biological or political lesbian.

For most women, self-respect comes first, affection, loyalty, trust, and respect come second. Sex comes distant third—unless the couple has just met, and even then, is often a minor part of an attraction. Whether heterosexuals project their own fear of hedonism on lesbians or whether sex really is the basis of heterosexual relationships, it certainly is not the basis of lesbian ones, even today when there is so much emphasis on lesbian sexuality.

For Anna, meeting Dorothy Burlingham was also professionally re-warding. Two years after meeting her, Anna wrote her first book, *Intro-duction to the Techniques of Child Analysis,* a training manual on child therapy. (Dorothy did not publish her first book on twins until after the war—where she had had a chance to study four sets of identical twins, two pairs of nonidentical ones, and a set of triplets! Her elder sisters had also been twins.)

It's not necessary to go into detail about the theories in Freud's 1927 book except to say that her emphasis on the role of environment in the child's life put Anna at odds with some of the leading psychoanalysts of the day. Other analysts such as Melanie Klein were claiming that the child's inner life, that his (or her) drives, were completely indepen-dent of *anything* outside the child's mind. People today realize that this is nonsense, but at the time, it was one of the main lines of psychoana-lytic thought.

And Anna Freud was one of the first people to say that the child's environment had an impact. As is accepted today, Freud stressed that the parents needed to be involved with the therapy and the child needed to learn to fit this new knowledge into the larger context of family, friends, and school.

Freud also introduced the idea of play therapy and drawing as a way to get through to children, whose use of language and understanding of self is extremely limited, if not nonexistent. But before that, Freud underwent a vicious personal and professional attack.

The 1927 meeting of the British Psychoanalytic Society was con-vened to refute Anna Freud's newly published book. Held in London, at the home of Freud's child-therapy rival, Melanie Klein, and run by a jilted suitor, Ernest Jones, the symposium trashed not only Anna's ideas but her professional competence. Klein had already set herself up as the new Freud by saying that all childhood behavior stems from aggression. Saying she was "more Freudian than Freud," Klein rewrote history, erasing Anna's place as pioneer in the field. One of the speakers even went so far as to say that Freud was not even competent to talk about Freudian theory because she had been analyzed by her father and had had an "incomplete analysis" as a result.

Always thinking of psychoanalysis first, Anna Freud never answered the charges directly. She cared too much for the fledgling field to create a rift between the British and Viennese analytic societies by defending herself.

This ongoing clash caused Anna grief for years, however, especially after she emigrated to England to escape the Nazi takeover of Austria. Although she disagreed vehemently with the Kleinian school, she did not want to seem ungracious by attacking the very people who had given her refuge in her hour of need. Only the passage of time proved the "Continental school" of child development correct.

No wonder Anna Freud, when faced with homosexuality in herself and her adoptive family, would want to sweep it under the carpet. All she needed was another reason for the critics to dismiss her.

The *Anschluss*

Sigmund Freud was used to being called names. But when the National Socialists took power in Germany, the name-calling was taken to new lows not just for therapists but for anything "Jewish." Suddenly, psychoanalysis was a "Jewish invention." During the war, German psychoanalysis was called the "science of the soul."

Analysts were so fearful by 1932 that some refused to stay for the yearly group photo at the German Psychoanalytic Society meeting. Scared of the political turn of events, some fled, others emmigrated to England, France, and the U.S. After the war when German and Austrian therapists had scattered across the West and beyond, the originals were instantly spotted by their thick European accents. By then, they were respected, for they were the founders. But during the Nazi era, it was a very different story.

Because he was Jewish, Anna's brother, Oliver, lost his job in Berlin. In 1933, during one of those *kristallnachts* that Germany later became so infamous for, Freud's books were burned at a massive bonfire in Berlin, a city that had once been filled with clubs and bars, a city that had once been home to a gay liberation movement.

Despite signs they should leave, Sigmund said he'd rather stay in Vienna. He was old, he was in constant pain, dying of the cancer he'd been fighting for nearly two decades. He also felt that they would be protected by the Austrian tendency to ambling inefficiency, that nothing untoward would happen in Austria even if the Nazis took over. Even today, Austrians pride themselves on their *Lebenskunst,* or art of living. They hoped to wait it out, though everyone in the German and Viennese analytic societies was talking about getting out before it was too late.

On March 12, 1938, the Germans occupied Vienna. The next day Nazis broke into Freud's flat and stole the family's savings, six thousand shillings. According to Young-Bruehl, the only thing that saved the flat from the complete destruction that usually accompanied a visit from the stormtroopers was Mother Martha's dignity and courage. Treating them like welcome guests so unnerved the ruffians that they left without tearing the place apart. That same day, Nazis broke into Anna's brother's shop in Vienna and destroyed it. That night, the Vienna analytic society called an emergency meeting, urged every analyst to flee, officially disbanded, and decided to locate future headquarters "wherever Sigmund Freud was."

Ernest Jones raced to Vienna from London. A disciple of Freud and later biographer, Jones was one of a raft of past suitors, none of whom had measured up to either Freud or Anna's exacting standards for a mate. About one such man, Anna said she got the better end of the bargain when she put the kibosh on the relationship because he only ended up marrying someone else while she got a large German shepherd named Wolf instead! Nonetheless, Jones came to Vienna to help both Sigmund and Anna.

Princess Marie Bonaparte came from Paris to see what she, as royalty, could do to protect the Freud family. Dorothy Burlingham was in touch with the American ambassador almost daily.

But they couldn't just pack and get on a train. They had to have entry visas and work permits from the English as well as permission to leave from the Austrians. In fact, many Jews were refused just such help and died at the hands of the Germans precisely because other governments wouldn't give them refuge.

It took nearly three months of waiting for the necessary papers to arrive. During that time they didn't know whether they would live or die. While they waited, they sorted through their papers and prayed.

In the meantime, the Germans closed the psychoanalytic publishing house run by the Viennese association that was located a few doors down from the Freud's home and confiscated all books and manuscripts.

A week after the *Anschluss,* Anna Freud was arrested by the Gestapo. Princess Bonaparte went down to the station to join her, but the Nazis didn't want anything to do with someone on a diplomatic passport. Left sitting in a corridor, Anna realized that if she was not interrogated that day, she would probably disappear in the night, never to be seen or heard of again.

She decided to act fast. Jumping up, she began walking when a group of alleged political dissidents were brought down the hall. She joined them in an attempt to be questioned and released. When asked about the radical political group she belonged to, she gave details of the Vienna analytic society, how they met every Wednesday night, published books and answered letters from analysts all over the world. It seemed tame enough to the Gestapo and she was released that evening. But the terror she felt never left until she was able to cross the border to freedom. Faced with the thought of actually losing "his only true son," as Freud called her, Sigmund realized for the first time how truly dangerous the situation was.

The day Anna was incarcerated, another more grisly band of Nazis paid a visit to the Freud residence. And this time, they weren't so polite. They tore linen out of cupboards, threw things on the floor, and made the true terror of their power felt. Martha tried to scold them into submission but it did no good.

That day, the Germans officially dissolved the Vienna Psychoanalytic Society though the group itself had already beat them to it.

For three months, the Freuds waited and wondered if they would be able to escape. They sorted through the papers of the Psychoanalytic Society, hoping to transfer its operation to London for the duration of the war.

Tante Minna, Martha's nearly blind sister, was given permission to leave first. Dorothy Burlingham took her to London in May. Anna's brother and sister's families were allowed to leave next. On June 4, eighty-three days after the harassment of their family began, Anna, Sigmund, and her mother, Martha, were finally given permission to go.

Of the Freud family, only four elderly aunts were left behind. Thinking they were too old to be moved, too old to be a threat, too old to be harmed, the Freuds left them behind. All four, Anna found out later, were killed in the camps. Marie died at Theresienstadt, Rosa at Auschwitz, Dolfi and Pauline at Treblinka. After the war, Anna vowed she would never return to Vienna. Only in 1971, more than three decades afterward—when it would have been too embarrassing to refuse the honor being bestowed—did she set foot on Viennese soil again.

The London Years

In 1939, England declared war on the Germans. The Germans retaliated by destroying whole sections of London. The East End was practically demolished. Young men went off to fight. Anyone who could leave went to the country. Many women who couldn't afford to leave were killed by bombs or separated from their children by the fires and chaos that followed the *blitzkrieg* attacks.

Though they could have taken refuge in the U.S., Anna and Dorothy stayed in London, setting up a home for children separated from their parents because of the war. It followed the lines of the school they had run in Vienna for children who were in analysis and was the first formal test of their teaching and child-rearing methods.

Later called the Hampstead War Nurseries, it housed 120 children from working-class sections of London worst hit by the bombs whose children suffered most from the psychological trauma.

For weeks, people had taken shelter in subway stations. It was safe underground, but trains ran until 1 A.M., making sleep impossible.

Even from the relative safety of suburban Hampstead, Anna described an air raid, taken from Peters:

"The sound of falling bombs was continuous, the crackling of fires which had been started could be heard in the distance, and again all these sounds were drowned by the incessant droning of airplanes which flew over London, not in successive waves as in former raids, but in one uninterrupted stream from 9 o'clock in the evening until 5 in the morning."

The Germans invented psychological warfare. They sent planes which dropped bombs that didn't explode but sounded the same as they whistled through the air. Night-long air raids were part of the weapons the Nazis hoped would wear down the English.

But neither Anna nor Dorothy were beaten. During the five years they ran the nurseries, they even wrote a book about the residential care of children. Anna did most of the writing from an analysis that Dorothy, the statistician, had compiled by comparing individual data collected on cards. They also trained child analysts at the nurseries.

After the war, the Hampstead Child Therapy Course became the "Mecca for the psychoanalytic treatment of children." During the war years, Anna also began working with *The Psychoanalytic Study of the Child,* the American journal which, over the next twenty years, would disseminate her theories of child development to the world.

At the beginning of the war, Dorothy decided to go back to New York for the birth of Mabbie's child. She expected to spend a few weeks there, since the U.S. had not yet entered the war. Little did she know when she left that she would spend nearly eight months attempting to get back to Anna once travel restrictions were placed on all nonmilitary personnel. Though it was a trying time for both, the separation marked a turning point in their lives.

While she was gone, Dorothy had a flirtation with a younger man. (Her husband, after years spent in mental institutions, committed suicide in May 1938. Despite a lifetime of therapy, Mabbie would also commit suicide eventually. She, too, succumbed to the manic-depression that also killed her father.)

Because of the honesty of their relationship, Dorothy told Anna about her feelings—and her confusion. In her letters, she questioned her motives from every angle, including the fear of committing herself to Anna as well as the opposite fear that something would happen to them while they were apart. On New Year's Day, when the usual letter from Anna didn't arrive, Dorothy panicked. The letter was delayed by the chaos caused by the war, but it made Dorothy realize what she'd done. What if Anna was so angry she never forgave her? What if she lost Anna, the mainstay of her life? Suddenly, she knew how much Anna meant to her. She wrote, quoting from Young-Bruehl:

"You know from my letters that I was afraid—afraid of complications, afraid of being forced apart—but it was only now that I was shocked into realizing that I might really lose you—and that the consequences might ruin my life and ours together."

Dorothy later said that theirs was the "most precious relationship" she had ever had. Anna agreed. Four months later, eight months after they said goodbye, Dorothy sailed to Genoa, took a train north to France, crossed the Channel, and finally got back home. Dorothy returned to the flat at 2 Maresfield Gardens, a few doors down from the Freud house at Number 20. Their commitment was certain; they would never be parted again. After the war, they bought a house in the country for weekends and one in Ireland for the summer.

Sigmund died in 1939, a year after they emmigrated. Martha and her sister, Minna, both died in 1941. In the middle of her life, Anna finally was relieved of her position as the unmarried daughter responsible for the care of her elderly relatives.

In many ways, Anna's life was more Victorian than twentieth century. For nearly two decades, she cared for her father while he wasted away from the cancer that eventually killed him. From the first, she had been the one to take care of him. Left in a room at the hospital during his first operation in Vienna sixteen years earlier, when Anna came to visit she found Freud covered in blood. When he started to hemorrhage, no attendants could be found. In fact, he would have died had she not been there. After that experience, Anna spent the night at the hospital herself to make sure he got the care he needed.

During the subsequent operation (and fifteen more), Freud had a large section of his jaw and cheek removed. Anna was the only person who could help him insert and remove the painful prosthesis he wore from then on. Freud had trouble talking and was too embarrassed to be seen in public. Anna became his ambassador to the world, and as the years went by, she became the spokesperson for psychoanalysis itself.

But she paid a heavy price for her devotion to her family. Not until both parents were gone could she and Dorothy live together. Not until their mid-fifties were the two women free to live with each other.

After the war, Anna came down with pneumonia. She was no longer young and had been working and writing, taking dictation for her father as he struggled and pushing psychoanalysis for more than thirty years. Dorothy's health had never been good. She suffered from the debilitating effects of tuberculosis until drugs were finally discovered that could keep it in check. For the first time, they began to relax and travel extensively—to Europe, to Greece to be with Princess Bonaparte, to America where Anna began to lecture.

But even declining health couldn't keep the women from the driving force of their lives: the study of children. In 1952, they were able to get enough money to set up a formal clinic which became their research center for the next quarter century. Using data gathered over the years filed under such headings as anxieties, defenses, and transference, they formulated an index which could be used to compare individual character traits. Burlingham took charge of the index and the publication of papers based on their findings. The two women also created a Developmental Profile for comparison of a child's development with the normal stages, and Anna herself devised a questionnaire, called the Diagnostic Profile, to diagnose a child's problems instantly instead of the months of meticulous observation it usually took—getting to what Anna said was the crux of child psychology: "Whether the child needed analysis or the mother needed a housekeeper."

After her father's death, Anna also started to come into her own as a world-renowned analyst and theoretician. She became one of the leading spokespeople for the psychoanalytic movement and therapy in general. Though she hated dealing with the press and Dorothy hated traveling by anything other than boat, Anna began to lecture and tour.

In the later years, Anna—whose inner life had been mined for analytic theory first by her father and then by herself—became very protective of her privacy. Inaccurate biographies of Sigmund Freud appeared, including one written by a psychologist of a rival school which caused Anna tremendous distress. When articles came out speculating on Sigmund's use of cocaine for medical purposes and a rumored affair with his wife's sister, Anna completely closed off. What mattered most to her was their theory, not their life story. In fact, being included in a book of lesbians would probably make her turn over in her grave. In the 1950's, she began studying (and trying to cure) male homosexuality.

Anna continued to write throughout her life. An astute and farsighted thinker as well as a very clear writer, her work eventually filled eight volumes. The ramifications of one of her last works still is being felt in the courts and social service agencies today.

Toward the end of her life, she and Dorothy collaborated with Albert Solnit and Joseph Goldstein on three books whose titles all include the phrase "the best interests of the child." The authors argue that the child's interest must remain paramount, above and beyond that of the parents, even if it is in complete opposition to the parents. They posited the concept of the "psychological" parent, a situation Anna knew well, of course, having been one herself to the four Burlingham children. Courts today are still wrestling with the problem of what is best for the child, especially in a society as mobile and complex as today's.

In 1979, Dorothy died with Anna sitting quietly beside the bed. Always striking to the core, Anna, who had written earlier that the only way to overcome grief was to incorporate the deceased into one's own psyche, now wrote that no matter how much therapy one has had, death and loneliness always feels like abandonment. On Dorothy's death, grandson Michael told Anna, to quote from Young-Bruehl:

"You were everything to her and she had a most wonderful life with you; how fortunate she was in finding and capturing someone like you."

Anna sold the house in Ireland, not wishing to go there alone.

The latter years were filled with concerns about the clinic she and Dorothy had founded. Who would take over when they were gone? How would it survive financially? A bequest from actress Marilyn Monroe, who had been analyzed by a friend and colleague of Anna's, solved many of her financial worries. Eventually, she found another, younger director to take over.

Nearly three years after Dorothy's death, Anna suffered a stroke. She said of the massive struggle to regain the use of her limbs; "I am glad Dorothy did not see me like this, she would have minded so."

On October 9, 1982, she, too, died in her sleep but her ideas have become part of our lives.

Anna Freud

1891 Dorothy Tiffany Burlingham born in Manhattan

1895 Anna Freud born in Vienna

1900 Sigmund Freud's *The Interpretation of Dreams* starts the field of psychoanalysis and psychology

1922 Anna Freud becomes a member of the International Psychoanalytic Association

1925 Anna Freud meets Dorothy Burlingham who starts her eldest son in therapy with Freud

Burlingham goes into analysis with Theodor Reik

Freud starts a *kinderseminar* with Burlingham

1927 *Introduction to the Technique of Child Analysis* published; Anna and Dorothy go on first vacation together

1936 *The Ego and the Mechanisms of Defense* published

1938 Hitler invades Germany; Anna arrested and interrogated by the Gestapo; the Freud home ransacked by the S.S. The Freud family emigrate with Burlingham to England

1939 Sigmund Freud dies

1941 Freud founds Hampstead Child Therapy Clinic with Burlingham

Freud also moves in with Burlingham after mother and aunt die

1942 *Young Children in Wartime* by Freud and Burlingham published

1944 *Infants Without Families* by Freud and Burlingham published

1971 Returns to Vienna for first time since the Anschluss

1979 Dorothy Burlingham dies; her ashes are laid in the Freud crypt

1982 Anna Freud dies at 86

Chapter Twelve

VITA SACKVILLE-WEST

Vita Sackville-West was a well-known writer of bestsellers. Like many writers, she wrote about what she knew best—her life. Old-fashioned today, her novels nonetheless make fascinating reading because they chart Vita's love life for some twenty years.

And what a love life it was!

Like Natalie Barney, Vita had both great loves and liaisons, many women and a few men. The best known love affair, thanks to the recent BBC series *Portrait of a Marriage,* was with Violet Trefusis, a childhood friend. A tempestuous, stormy affair, the relationship lasted three years and nearly broke up Vita's marriage.

Her liaison with Virginia Woolf, another great love, was shorter physically but lasted for the rest of their lives. They had a literary love affair that tied them together in a way that not even emotion could.

Except for Violet, Vita turned most lovers into friends. Dorothy Wellesley, who followed Violet, became a great gardening buddy. But like Natalie Barney, Vita could go through affairs fairly quickly to create a wide but close circle of friends.

In the year 1928, for instance, Vita was seeing the novelist Margaret Goldsmith Voigt (they were writing each other daily) when Vita met and seduced Hilda Matheson. (A portrait of Vita as the character Hester Drummond was included in Voigt's novel *Belated Adventure.*)

Dumped by Vita, Margaret wrote:

"My darling, do you understand? There can be no question of emotional alimony from you to me.'' (Quoted in *Vita, a Biography of Vita Sackville-West* by Victoria Glendinning.)

Though still in love with Vita, Margaret was resigned to a friendship, if that was all she could get.

Vita met Hilda when she appeared on a BBC discussion program Matheson was in charge of. Vita appeared on the BBC with Hugh Walpole and stayed the night with Hilda ''to discuss the show.'' Hilda ''called in sick'' the next morning.

That year, Vita not only saw Margaret but also spent time with Virginia (who got jealous when she found out Vita had gone on vacation with Hilda) and her old friend Dottie Wellesley (who also complained of Vita's coldness). As if that weren't enough, they all knew one another and commiserated about Vita's wanderlust. To quote Glendinning:

'' 'Darling,' wrote Hilda to Vita after [Hilda] had seen Dottie, 'why is there this legend that you are so detached about people? I noticed Margaret Goldsmith elaborated it, and Dottie seemed to assume it.' ''

During this same time, Vita was also trying to get rid of Mary Campbell, the poet Roy Campbell's wife. Another old flame, Geoffrey Scott, died of pneumonia in New York.

Vita loved whoever it was passionately, devotedly—when she was with them—and practically forgot them when she wasn't. In addition to an ongoing series of *rondeles,* she also became involved with a lesbian couple at one point.

Though her books do not chronicle her love life in this kind of detail, they do follow her affairs as they developed. *Challenge,* one of her first novels, was about her affair with Violet Trefusis. She used the ''male side'' of herself for the character Julian.

Because of the lack of psychological knowledge and the strict gender restrictions of the day, Vita was stuck thinking she had a ''dual nature,'' one male and one female, instead of realizing she was what we'd now call a strong woman. During her years with Violet, she passed as a man so that she and Violet could tour England and the Continent unmolested.

Had they been discreet, it probably wouldn't have mattered. But they stayed in hotels and ate at restaurants their family and friends frequented. Dressed as a soldier with her hair wrapped in a bandage from an alleged war wound, Vita caused a scandal wherever they went.

Like many lesbians up to the middle part of the twentieth century, Vita was torn apart by the seemingly opposite side of her nature. She also bought into then-current theory that lesbians were men trapped in women's bodies.

As a result, she believed the part of her which wanted to succeed and be recognized as an author had to be the lesbian male side—and she believed that the part which loved women was also male. Because of the strict gender codes of the day (women still wore dresses and few had careers), this false dichotomy plagued her all of her life.

Five years after her marriage to diplomat Harold Nicolson, she began to take her lesbianism seriously. She fell madly in love with Violet. During that on-again, off-again three years, Vita had to decide how she was going to live her life.

Vita loved her childhood chum and wanted to run away with her. But she also wanted to be recognized as a writer and to retain her position as an aristocrat in British society. By then, Vita had also two children: Ben, who would become a scholar as well as gay; and Nigel, the founder of the publishing house of Weidenfeld and Nicolson, who would chronicle Vita's love affairs in the 1973 book *Portrait of a Marriage*.

By the time Vita became involved with Violet, she also knew that Harold, too, was gay.

Being male, Harold could be more circumspect. He had a career to think of and could easily divide his life between home and *l'amour* (even when he lived with his boyfriend). Vita found it impossible to do that at first. Eventually, however, she realized that Harold was a refuge from the complicated entanglements her love life created. And she realized she could have a home and a place in society as well as an escape from passion when her ardor cooled. But in the early days of her marriage, she didn't know that.

When she realized she loved Violet, Vita wanted Violet and Violet alone. For three years, she left Harold and the children to fend for themselves—only to change her mind and return. From the time she began to court Violet in 1918, she left husband and home for weeks at a time, traveling with Violet to Paris, Monte Carlo, Venice, and Avignon.

For three years, she loved both Harold and Violet—and couldn't make up her mind which she wanted more. A month after leaving Harold to be with Violet, she would return home in despair. Two weeks later, she would realize she'd made a mistake and leave again. Harold tried to be patient. After all, he had his boyfriend. But Vita wasn't being discreet. She was constantly seen passing as a man in places they both frequented. And she went through money like crazy. In Monte Carlo, she gambled and had to pawn her jewelry to pay the hotel bill. It was most embarrassing for Harold, a member of the diplomatic corps.

Also, the children missed her. They had servants and governesses, but Ben was becoming withdrawn. Harold was afraid he would end up with emotional problems if they were both gone all the time.

Violet was going through her own emotional turmoil. Not yet married, she was still financially dependent on her parents. Her mother, Alice Keppel, had been the mistress of Edward VII when Violet was young. But being the mistress of the king was one thing; Violet's family was not about to stand for the kind of scandal she was creating with Vita. (Ironically, Camilla Parker-Bowles, the woman who has created such a scandal for the British monarchy today, is actually related to Violet Trefusis. Violet's mother was Camilla's great-grandmother.) Back then—before the press became the moral watchdog for a public that expects middle-class values of its monarchy—being the mistress to the King was an honor, part of a long tradition.

When the king died, his "unofficial widow," as Alice Keppel was called, took both Violet and her sister Sonia to Ceylon for an extended period of mourning. At the turn of the century, the British aristocracy was very sophisticated when it came to such liaisons. Nonetheless, England has never been tolerant of homosexuals, whether part of the monarchy or not.

Violet tried to force Vita's hand by marrying Denys Trefusis during one of their tiffs. By marrying Trefusis, Violet hoped to gain economic freedom. She had also extracted a promise of celibacy from him—at least in relation to her. But Violet was playing both ends against the middle.

Until the day of the wedding, Violet begged Vita to rescue her from her "fate.' To quote a dramatic letter from Glendinning, which shows how seductive Violet could be:

"Cast 'side the drab garments of respectability and convention, my beautiful Bird of Paradise, they become you not. Lead the life Nature intended you to lead. Otherwise Mitya, you'll be a failure—you who might be among the greatest, the most scintillating and romantic figures of all time, you'll be 'Mrs. Nicolson, who has written some charming verse.' "

Little did Violet know then that Vita would never be known as "Mrs. Nicolson" and that she would become one of the most romantic figures of all time, despite her marriage.

But jealousy did win that round and got the upper hand as Violet had hoped. Vita wrote to Harold that she was absolutely terrified of what she would do, that she must join him in Paris to avoid making a scandal at the wedding.

Vita might have been escaping to Paris for the wedding, but Paris was also one of the couple's honeymoon destinations. As soon as Violet and Denys arrived, Vita appeared, claimed Violet, and took her to a hotel room to make love. Though the three of them had actually enjoyed one another's company prior to the wedding, Vita couldn't stand the thought of Violet being married. In fact, Violet had often told Vita how much her two loves were alike, how Vita would be as adventurous as Denys—if only she were male.

Night after night during the honeymoon, Vita sat alone at a table at the Ritz watching Violet and Denys. Toying with her food, she was eaten up by misery. But that affair was the only time she would let herself be carried away. From then on, she would be the pursued.

For Vita, Violet's marriage was the beginning of the end. The break, however, did not come quickly. The two decided to elope. But by then, they had husbands in tow, who hired a private plane to bring them home. They found the women on Valentine's Day, 1920. Under pressure, the two gave in.

A few days later, Vita received the galleys of *Challenge,* the novel she had written about Violet. When Vita saw it in print, she was horrified. It was too autobiographical to be published. She stopped the publication in both Britain and America. She had it printed privately instead—but stored it in a safety deposit box. It wasn't published publicly until 1974, a decade after her death.

Vita's homecoming lasted little more than a month. Violet went to Avignon, where Vita joined her. Eventually, Harold and Denys decided to let the cards fall where they might.

Vita and Violet saw each other for a year after that, but the relationship, which had always been fraught with emotional torment, eventually began to wear on both. Vita was wracked by the guilt of being gay and the thought of forfeiting her family.

She couldn't face losing her place in society and her hope for fame as a writer. After a year of indecision, she broke it off. If only she had been born male, as she should have been!

Vita did see Violet again, but only rarely. Violet went to the Continent to live and Vita channeled her energy into her work. She wrote an unpublished autobiography which son Nigel eventually turned into *Portrait of a Marriage*.

Vita also retreated to her garden. She had been to Constantinople when Harold was attached to the Foreign Office there and had brought back ideas on gardening she had seen there—of the wildness and the neglect that could be part of nature's beauty.

For Vita, Long Barn, the home they bought after they married, was the first chance to try out some of the things she had seen in the East. When Harold was posted in Teheran in 1925, Vita would have another chance to see the famed gardens of the Middle East.

When she took to her bed, ill, depressed, unable to go on after the break with Violet, the garden became her source of solace. Thinking of the magical world she could create in flowers and shrubs and trees—a world that would never make the demands that people made, a world that would only give and give in return—she began to come to. In fact, Vita turned to the land which was her ancestral heritage. To quote from Jane Brown's book, *Vita's Other World, a Gardening Biography of V. Sackville-West*:

"And being Vita, she turned to a source she knew well, she planted 'flowers that English poets sing'—roses, daffodils, iris, wallflowers, love-in-a-mist, borage, lavender, stocks, columbine, poppies and hollyhocks."

She turned to the garden, the never-ending round of the seasons, and it began to heal her lovesick heart. Vita had already given up Knole, her family estate. She could not bear to give up everything else for love. She wanted too much from society, fame as a writer and a home that could make her feel rooted to the earth.

The garden was Vita's solace during times of stress. During World War II, the love she had for the land, the trees, the wild animals, even the ramshackle buildings, became poignant with the threat of German bombs always on them. When Dorothy Wellesley, the gardening buddy who replaced Violet, succumbed to alcoholism, Vita used the recurring cycle of the seasons to help her remember that life goes on. When Virginia Woolf succumbed to madness and committed suicide in 1941, Vita found the will to go on through gardening.

Virginia's death was a particularly crushing blow. By the second world war, they were not as close physically or socially as they had been. Vita never felt comfortable in Virginia's witty Bloomsbury crowd. Vita felt slow and stupid amid their bright chatter. But the relationship between them had grown in one of the best ways a relationship can—in a meeting of the minds. So much so that Virginia played almost as large a part in Vita's life as Harold.

Orlando

When Vita first met Virginia Woolf in 1922, both were drawn to the literary passion in the other. At the time, Vita was one of the best writers of the day. Virginia was considered an upstart experimentalist—so much so, that in one issue of the *New York Evening Post* literary review, Vita's now-forgotten novel *Seducers in Ecuador* got high praise and top billing while Virginia's classic *Mrs. Dalloway* got a lackluster review at the bottom of the same page. It wasn't until Woolf published the 1928 novel *Orlando* about Vita that Woolf became the respected author she is today.

No matter what the public thought, there was no question in the minds of either woman, however, who the literary genius was. Despite Vita being ten years older, she sat at Virginia's feet both literally and figuratively. Virginia was the mentor, Vita the student.

They first met at a dinner given by Virginia's brother-in-law, Clive Bell. Shy and nervous around such artistic company, Vita fingered her trademark rope of pearls so much that she broke one off and dropped it in her dinner plate. Nonplussed by her *faux pas*—the mark of a true aristocrat, Virginia noted—Vita asked for some liqueur.

At first, Virginia herself felt "shy and schoolgirlish" in Vita's presence. But by the end of the evening, she could see Vita as she truly was—a grenadier whose passions traced back five hundred years to become as romantic as old yellow wine.

Vita wasn't the only one with a great imagination. Virginia was well known for being hot and cold toward people, depending on which part of the manic-depressive cycle she was in at the time. If you hit her on a particularly manic day, she would fantasize about you so much, making up stories in her head as you talked, that she would think you were absolutely marvelous and rave about you to everyone. Then, if she spent time with you next on a "down" day, she'd wonder why she ever thought you were interesting at all.

Virginia asked Vita to write something for her. Vita wrote back from her vacation in Italy, to quote from Glendinning:

"You asked me to write a story for you. On the peaks of mountains, and beside green lakes, I am writing it for you. I shut my eyes to the

blue of gentians, to the coral of androsace; I shut my ears to the brawl-
ing of rivers; I shut my nose to the scent of pines; I concentrate on my
story. And you.''

Their "affair" probably lasted less than a year, though they remained
close until Virginia's death twenty years later. Vita called her love for
Virginia, "absolutely true, vivid and unalterable." Her son, Nigel, writing about them in *Portrait of a Marriage* said that their relationship
was so deep, to call it an affair would be a "travesty."

From the beginning, however, there was the problem of Virginia's
"nerves." She had already had two breakdowns, the first after being
molested as an adolescent and the second immediately after her marriage to Leonard. Though married, their relationship after one attempt
at sex was apparently based on affection—and a publishing partnership—rather than sex.

Vita wrote Harold that she feared what might happen if she and
Virginia actually became lovers. Virginia had had a previous woman
lover, but nonetheless, two breakdowns after sex was not a comforting
thought. By then, Harold knew their own relationship could withstand
lovers, but he, too, worried about Virginia, as well as Virginia and
Leonard. He wrote that tempting Virginia to bed was like "smoking
over a petrol [gas] tank.''

Vita's letters to Harold reveal the fear and the excitement of her
newfound relationship with Virginia in addition to her growing com-
radeship with Harold. To quote from Nigel's book:

"I love Virginia—as who wouldn't? But really, my sweet, one's love
for Virginia is a very different thing: a mental thing; a spiritual thing,
if you like, an intellectual thing, and she inspires a feeling of tenderness
. . . owing to her funny mixture of hardness and softness—the hardness
of her mind, and her terror of going mad again.''

Despite the disclaimer, Vita had already thrown caution to the wind
and bedded Virginia. In the same letter, she writes:

"I am scared to death of arousing physical feelings in her, because
of the madness. I don't know what effect it would have, you see: it is
a fire with which I have no wish to play. . . . I have gone to bed with
her (twice), but that's all."[!]

At her best, Virginia was ethereal and cerebral. For the sensuous and
earthy Vita, the physical relationship was apparently not that satisfying.

But like so many lesbian couples even into the twentieth century, the
sexual aspect of the relationship was not of primary importance. Their
bond was based more on intellect and shared passions. They enjoyed

each other's company, but more important, admired each other's minds. Their relationship eventually turned into a friendship deepened by a professional collaboration which lasted nearly two decades. Until Woolf's death, she published Vita's books at the Hogarth Press, founded with Leonard, that only barely disguised Vita's tempestuous love life.

Both wrote novels about the other.

Vita wrote the early Bloomsbury-style novella *Seducers in Ecuador* to woo Virginia—and to show her talent. Even then, Woolf was a fierce literary watchdog who became known for her criticism over the years. (At one point, she was miffed that Vita wanted Harold to look at her poems before she submitted the manuscript to Virginia. Virginia wrote asking why Vita wanted a "diplomat" for a literary critic.)

Two years after they met, Virginia published *Seducers* and cemented their long literary collaboration.

Virginia returned the favor by writing *Orlando*.

Written in Woolf's densely melodious prose, *Orlando* captures Vita's feelings about her "dual-nature" by making her both a man and a woman in the novel as the eras move on. In a nod to Virginia's historian father, it also traces the family history of the Sackvilles—and that of England itself. Set (at first) in Elizabethan times, the novel takes a mythical nobleman through four centuries.

A scribbler himself, Orlando meets famous writers of the day, including "Bill" Shakespeare and "Kit" Marlowe. But like a butterfly pinned into a collection box he finds himself transformed into a woman by the time he/she gets to one of the most oppressive eras for British women, the Victorian. By using a magical gender change to compare sex roles in different eras, Woolf captures Vita's masculine courage and verve— and the freedom she would have had as a man as compared to the restrictive bounds she was forced into as a woman.

After a week-long trance, Orlando wakes up female:

"He stretched himself. He rose. He stood upright in complete nakedness before us, and while the trumpet pealed . . . we have no choice but to confess—he was a woman.

"The sound of the trumpets died away and Orlando stood stark naked. No human being, since the world began, has ever looked more ravishing. His form combined in one the strength of a man and a woman's grace.

"Orlando had become a woman—there is no denying it. But in every other respect, Orlando remained precisely as he had been. The change of sex, though it altered their future, did nothing whatever to alter their identity. Their faces remained, as their portraits prove, practically the same. His memory—but in future we must, for convention's sake, say 'her' for 'his,' and 'she' for 'he. . . .' "

The book actually had photographs of Vita dressed as a woman—and a man.

When Vita later began doing a weekly literary show on BBC radio, she reviewed Woolf's *A Room of One's Own*. With her usual sense of irony, Virginia wrote to Vita on hearing it, to quote from Glendinning:

"I thought your voice, saying Virginia Woolf, was a trumpet call, moving me to tears; but I daresay you were suppressing laughter. It's an odd feeling, hearing oneself praised to 150 million old ladies in Surbiton by one with whom one has watched the dawn and heard the nightingale."

Odd, indeed, but that is one of the more delicious feelings associated with secret love.

Like Natalie Barney, praising lovers, reviewing their work and writing about them was part of Vita's life.

And Virginia and Violet weren't the only ones to inspire books. Vita also wrote a *Harper's Bazaar* short story in 1930 about her affair with Mary Campbell, the poet Roy Campbell's wife. Though the jealous husband in this collage—as Vita called her whirling round of lovers—never committed suicide, a few others did threaten to do so. From Violet to Geoffrey Scott, who divorced his wife for Vita—only to realize that Harold was a much less demanding husband who would let Vita have complete freedom—lovers pulled out all the stops. But it never did any good. Vita went her way and hoped for the best, which is what usually happened. It would have been so embarrassing, so dreadfully un-English to commit suicide, no one ever did despite the threats.

While "Orlando's" novels are forgotten today, "he" also wrote biographies, starting with "his" own family, *Knole and the Sackvilles*. *Pepita* is about Vita's Spanish grandmother, a famous dancer, from whom Vita felt she inherited her wild and tormented gypsy nature.

Vita also wrote three biographies of women: one of Aphra Behn, the playwright and novelist who was the first woman in England to support herself as a writer; the second, of St. Joan of Arc, the cross-dressing soldier who drove the English out of France in the fifteenth century; and the third of St. Teresa of Avila, who loved a female cousin, but, times being what they were, founded a religious order.

Vita's books sold, but her poetry drew the honors. *The Land* won the Hawthornden in 1927 and *The Garden* the prestigious Heinemann twenty years later. To celebrate the first, Vita planted her own "hawthorn den" of hazels and poplars. For the second, she used the prize money to buy hundreds and hundreds of azaleas to go round the moat.

But even as she was winning prizes, Vita's reputation as a writer had begun to dim. Vita had hoped to be the successor of the poet laureate, but her poetry didn't keep up with the times. Lesbian poets such as Edith Sitwell were writing innovative verse that was setting the standard by which modern poetry was judged. In 1922, T. S. Eliot's breakthrough poem, "The Wasteland," set the tone—and changed the subject matter forever—to one of a jangled urbanism. Twenty years later, Vita was still writing about land.

After *The Garden* won the Heinemann in 1946, "Orlando" never published another poem. She continued to write novels, but the pleasures of rural life became "the scribbler's" main subject—and her columns became her métier. When Vita died in 1962, the love of the Sackville land that had once ranged over more than half of what is now East Sussex, the love that shown so clearly in her gardening columns filled seven volumes.

An Open Marriage

Vita was born at the end of Queen Victoria's reign, an era second only to the Puritan one as England's most sexually repressed. But the mores of the times hardly touched the English aristocracy. In Vita's social circle, marital infidelity was so acceptable that her mother had brass plates installed on bedroom doors for name cards—to keep confusion at bay during midnight amours.

After he tired of her mother, Vita's father, Lionel, took up with Lady Constance Hatch. Not to be outdone, her mother not only became involved with the wealthy bachelor Sir John Murray Scott, but helped sustain the family's dwindling fortune by having him add a codicil to his will giving her £50,000 once they got involved. He also paid for a house for Victoria in Mayfair and, according to Glendinning, dealt directly with her husband Lionel to set it all up. Growing up, Vita spent summers at Murray's estate, Sluie. In later years, Victoria was also connected to the landscape architect Sir Edwin Lutyens, whose collaborations with Gertrude Jekyll did so much for English romantic gardens. McNed, as he was nicknamed, helped Vita and Harold lay out the garden at their first home, Long Barn.

Early on, Vita and Harold learned that you could put on a public front for the world and still have a private life.

The difference, however, between the aristocratic tradition and theirs was that they were both gay. But unlike gay writers such as Winifred Ellerman, known as Bryher, and Robert McAlmon, whose relationship was purely one of convenience, theirs began with love. Neither realized their homosexuality until their children had already been born. After a few difficult years trying to integrate a love life into their marriage, they realized they could be secret gay allies in a hostile, heterosexual world. Eventually, they created a marriage that allowed them both freedom while adding to bonds that held them together.

The most obvious bond was the children, but a less obvious one was the building of a home that each could return to for sustenance. In the end, they became the closest of friends whose shared dreams held them together.

There were probably other reasons their relationship worked. For some reason, homosexual relationships tend to be less proprietary than heterosexual ones. Though it can be fierce at first, jealousy does not seem to last quite as long in gay relationships. Whether male or female, gay relationships often meld the past with the present, merging current loves with former ones.

Unlike her parents whose relationship ended bitter and strained, Vita's relationship with Harold was a model of understanding, companionship, and shared interests. As can be seen from their letters about Virginia Woolf, they even asked each other's advice on love affairs and commiserated over heartaches.

Admittedly, they never lived together as such. Harold always had a separate residence even if he was only working in London. Even when he was in England, he only came home on weekends. At Sissinghurst, Vita worked in her tower while Harold had his own study in a separate building. (Even the children had their own building at Sissinghurst). And of course, they had separate bedrooms.

If anything, their relationship shows the terrible price most people paid for being gay. If anything, they were probably the lucky ones, two who managed to integrate their homosexuality into their lives without having to move to foreign countries to get away with it. But then, perhaps some gay instinct drew them to each other, or some "gay sensibility." Her "coming out" in the "matrimonial fishpond," as Vita called her debut, wasn't as bad as it might have been since Edward VII died shortly before—putting "a damper on society life," as Glendinning says. Six years younger than she, Vita sought out Harold from the pack. He was different, somehow unlike the run-of-the-mill men she was meeting. Only later would she find out why. At the time, he seemed "alive and charming," "dark and grave" all at once.

Perhaps without even knowing they were gay, they sought out the gayness in the other—Vita was drawn to the "femme" in Harold; Harold to the "butch" in her. Once they had committed themselves to the relationship, however, they were determined to make it work.

Unlike Natalie Barney or Gertrude Stein, they did not have the courage to chuck it all for a passing love. They wanted to be part of English society in a way they would never have been able to had they been honest about their sexual orientation.

Eventually, they triumphed in spite of making a very difficult choice. But they also suffered, at least at first, because of this decision.

In fact, if there is a morality play in this book, a lesson to be learned from our ancestors, it is in Vita and Harold. Though everyone wants to see themselves as courageous, most people, whether gay or not, are so worn down by the dictates of society—and by the grind of earning a living, if nothing else—they often live lives of quiet desperation, or lives tranquilized by alcohol, work, or other addictions. Vita and Harold chose the seemingly "easy" road of playing it straight and keeping their sexual orientation quiet. But it is also the one that, gays now are discovering, bears the heaviest psychological price—that of lying about one's self. Though it's hard to tell because Harold didn't write nearly as much, especially about his feelings, Vita seems to have suffered the most. In her novel *All Passion Spent,* she describes male-female relations:

"[The man] . . . would continue to enjoy his free, varied and masculine life with no ring upon his finger or difference in his name to indicate the change in his estate; but whenever he felt inclined to come home she must be there, ready to lay down her book, her papers or letters. . . . It would not do, in such a world of assumptions, to assume she had equal rights."

Vita did not have equal rights, that was clear. There was no way she could in her day and age. But that didn't stop her fighting for them.

No matter what she wrote, Vita never changed her name. All her life she was known as Vita Sackville-West. Anyone who made the mistake of calling her "Mrs. Nicholson" got an icy stare.

Nor did Vita drop everything for Harold. Unlike most diplomatic wives, she did not do "the career jaunt" and join him at his posts. Nor did she campaign when he was running for Parliament. She had her own life—her writing, her garden, her friends. Though she did make room for Harold when he was home. Many was the lover who suddenly found themselves in the middle of an emotional if not physical *ménage à trois* when Harold arrived. Because they did love each other in their own odd way.

They also eventually became the center of the other's life. By the time they grew old, they were like most elderly couples—worrying about who would go first and how the other would survive.

The need for solid roots was perhaps the key for both.

The loss of her home, Knole, might be hard to fathom in these mobile times, but it was so great, Vita said it took away part of her self away. Vita expected to live at Knole all her life; her ancestors had lived there for four hundred years. She said she wanted to die the day she had to give it up. Almost everyone close to her recognized what it meant to her.

Violet Trefusis wrote:

"It is almost as though the places have generated the people; equipped and apposite, they have sprung spontaneously from the background which created them. It was necessary to see Vita at Knole to realize how inevitable she was."

Virginia Woolf also recognized that Knole was part of Vita's sense of self. In *Orlando,* she wrote that from the highest point at Knole, "nineteen English counties could be seen beneath; and on clear days thirty, or perhaps forty, if the weather was very fine"—a slight literary exaggeration that makes the point even more strikingly.

As Virginia implied, the history of Knole was the history of England itself, only slightly revised. For Knole not only consisted of towers and turrets.

"The heath was theirs and the forest, the pheasant and the deer, the fox, the badger and the butterfly," wrote Woolf.

And it was true. In later years, when Vita re-created Knole at Sissinghurst she didn't care how much anger she caused the local gentry. Once a fox got safely to her land, the "game" was over. There was no hunting at Sissinghurst because Vita had the power to protect the animals on her land—and she did. Vita herself wrote of the love of the land a family estate can inspire in the novel *The Heir.*

Perhaps more than anyone, Harold understood Vita's love of Knole and the immeasurable grief she felt at its loss; Harold had his own loss in that regard.

Being a diplomat's son, he had never been in one place long. Born in Teheran, he traveled so much in his young years that he felt like a stranger in his own land. As much as Vita, though for opposite reasons, he longed for a home of his own, a place he could put down roots. He wrote, to quote from Jane Brown's *Vita's Other World, a Gardening Biography of V. Sackville-West*:

"My father during all the years of my childhood and boyhood lived abroad. . . . Behind this exotic tapestry was a gap of which only today am I fully conscious. What I really wanted was to see the trees grow year by year in fields that had known me since I could not walk. I wanted to come back after long absence and . . . rejoice to think that willow-cuttings had shuffled into willow coppices of their own. I longed instinctively to feel a little less un-English in my own country, a little less foreign when abroad. I wanted to feel . . . the son of some hereditary soil."

Their marriage soon became the calm at the center of their existence. So much so, that they actually had the nerve to do a radio talk show about marriage in which they argued that to be successful, the man had to develop his feminine side and the woman her masculine one. They should have known—being gay—that particular gender road was a well-traveled one.

According to their son Nigel, their love might be a recipe for success in any partnership:

"Each loved most in the other the qualities she or he did not possess, Vita his leniency, Harold her wildfire romanticism, and it amused them to identify the differences between them in order to highlight the qualities they shared."

A very good prescription for anyone, gay or straight.

In the gardens they built, the homes they restored, Vita and Harold's yearnings dovetailed. But it wasn't easy. They worked hard, day after day, year after year, staying in touch by letter and phone, telling each other their innermost thoughts and secrets to keep them connected.

And they worked hard to create a home by restoring Sissinghurst, a dilapidated wreck they bought in 1930. Abandoned two hundred years earlier, it was in such a state of disrepair it took more than a year to bring it to a livable condition and more money than they had paid to begin with. The "garden" was an overgrown rubbish heap, full of old boots and bedsteads, ploughs and sardine tins.

But Vita had to have it. She wrote, to quote from Glendenning:

"The place, when I first saw it on a spring day in 1930, caught instantly at my heart and my imagination. I saw what might be made of it. It was Sleeping Beauty's castle."

Harold did some research and found it had belonged to an ancestor of Vita's. It wasn't as grand as Knole but it had once been part of her ancestral heritage and was almost as old. They began the slow process of creating what has since been called a house built for a garden.

When they finished, they had four main buildings at the north-south and east-west ends of the main courtyard, numerous gardens, a double row of pleached lime trees, a nut orchard, another grove of trees, and a moat. Vita bought another parcel and added a lake for wild geese.

And they had statues, not corny cement gnomes or even life-size replicas but actual antiques. In the garden Vita saw from her tower was an art Deco nude they called "the Virgin." Reflected double in the moat was, fittingly enough, a statue of Dionysus for Harold—also in its naked glory.

Vita's Other Passions

Vita Sackville-West had many loves in her life but none greater than Knole, the family mansion. The thousand-acre estate had been in her family since Queen Elizabeth I gave it to one of *her* favorites, Thomas Sackville. Like the Churchills, who were given the castle at Blenheim as a sign of affection between Queen Anne and Sarah, the Duchess of Marlborough, estates were part of the trappings of royal favor in the past.

Not quite as grand as Windsor Palace, Knole was a castle nonetheless with towers and turrets and battlements closing not just one but a numerous courtyards. The buildings alone spread over six acres. A self-sustaining village, the estate had a forge and saw mill, paint and carpentry shops, hot houses and orchards, as well as vegetable gardens and pastures, fields of grain and everything else needed for the family and sixty (or so) servants. Even today, Knole is one of the largest estates in England.

As a child, Knole was as much of a companion as Vita's parents. Built as a fortress at a time when the nobility was still killing each other for property rights, there were secret staircases leading to other parts of the palace in which to play hide-and-seek from unlucky governesses. A child with a great imagination, Vita would take refuge in chapels at the end of endless corridors when sworn ancestral enemies were closing in.

The place was so huge that one winter Vita found a stag in one of the halls. He had taken refuge from a storm, his antlers spread out like a candelabra above his head. He was almost as startled as Vita.

As an only child, Vita's other companions were her ancestors, rows and row of portraits whose double-hung faces lined the galleries, faces she knew so well she said "they almost spoke."

Life for young Vita was lonely with Lord and Lady Sackville. As was typical of her day and social class, there was a constant stream of governesses, none particularly to Vita's liking. Her father put her to bed at night with maxims such as "Never start a letter with the word 'I.' "

As is typical of many gay children who never fit in with their family, Vita's frou-frou mother tried to dress her in party gowns covered with cloth wisteria blossoms. As an adult, Vita shocked everyone by creating a costume of riding breeches, lace-up boots (usually with a garden tool stuck in the top), a silk blouse, and rope of pearls. At a time when women didn't wear pants, Vita wore the outfit everywhere, though she would borrow dresses to receive awards and meet dignitaries. No matter how much money she made, she couldn't see spending it on clothes when she could be buying bulbs or something for the garden.

Vita loved with abandon, though, whether it was women or song, buildings or gardens. Besides Knole, she had two other inanimate loves: poetry and gardening. Of the three, only gardening was faithful to her.

Because she was a woman, she realized—about the time she was an adolescent—that she could never inherit Knole. The title and estate could only pass to a male, the brother of her father. Despite the fact she was the only child of the third Baron of Sackville, at age thirty-five she had to hand over the keys to her uncle Charles. Years later, after Knole had been passed to his son, the cousin asked if she would like to have it back. (Unlike Vita, Eddy didn't think much of it. To him, Knole was large and drafty and didn't have any "mod cons.")

At the risk of sounding melodramatic, it broke her heart to say no, but she did. Once Vita left Knole in 1928, she only visited it occasionally. Once she and Violet broke up, they only saw each other a few times over the course of the rest of their lives. It was too painful to do anything else. Like Violet, the loss of Knole became a major part of Vita's life.

But Vita wanted to be known for her second love, poetry, and over the years that, too, disappointed her. Unlike her novels, which were popular, her poetry was outdated even as she wrote it. Stylistically, she wrote in rhymes and long, epic poems when the style had already gone to the more free-flowing, unrhymed short stanzas we have today. Not only was her style passé, but she wrote about subjects that were out of fashion, too. She was still writing about the round of the seasons at a time when alienation had become literature's main focus.

Of her three great loves, the garden gave as much back to her as she gave to it—or more. Vita never wanted to be known for her garden but it turned out that was where she made her lasting mark.

In fact, she *hated* the weekly garden columns she wrote, though her skills as a writer showed nonetheless. For nearly twenty years, her discoveries (and her poetic way of expressing them) delighted readers. For thousands of readers, her columns in the *New Statesman* and then the *Observer* were part of the Sunday morning ritual—even for people who didn't garden.

Robin Lane Fox explains best:

"They were read not only by fanatical gardeners but by thousands of wishful-thinking fellow-travellers who liked to entertain a good idea and by the many non-gardeners who liked an elegant performance."

The closest equivalent today is probably Miss Manners, whose columns are read not only for their wit on questions of etiquette but for their ironic take on life. Vita's articles were much more than a gardening column. Through them, she popularized some of the greatest ideas of the English romantic style of the previous centuries. From William Kent to Gertrude Jekyll and Sir Edwin Lutyens, William Robinson (who was actually closest to Vita's own heart), and Albert Reginald Powys, Vita wrote about flowers as if they were people, landscapes as if toys to be played with and the land itself as if it were a great love.

In writing about a sombre corner, Vita shows how sensuous she could be:

"For the plants involved are all on the mournful side. Sullen and sombre beauties, they have the dark richness of some fruits, certain plums for instance, and 'Black Hamburgh' grapes, and the inside of figs.

"*Veratrum nigrum* . . . throws up a very sinister-looking spire, four to five feet high, tightly clustered with myriads of tiny, almost black flowers, as though a swarm of bees or flying ants had settled all the way up the stem. Nobody could possibly describe it as pretty, but it has . . . its somewhat perverse charm.

"I recommend this queer, murky, murderous corner . . . a corner that should be visited when the sky is lurid with an impending thunderstorm."

Vita was a night owl who walked in the garden on the full moon, looking at the white flowers sparkling in the strangely silver light. From one such walk, she decided to plant an all-white garden that she could look down on from the tower where she had her study.

With flowers as with people, though, Vita could be ruthless. She would find just the right flower for the right place, a flower that would not only grow but look as if it were meant for that spot and that spot alone. She would cut a flower or leaf and hold it in place to see if it could fit in. If it did, she would give it a try. But if it didn't look right once it was in, it didn't matter. If it wasn't growing to its potential, if it didn't turn out as she expected, she would rip it out without a second thought—much like tiresome, too-demanding lovers. Her gardeners must have had wonderful gardens of their own—purely from her castoffs.

But the timeless beauty she and Harold created at Sissinghurst, their last home, was a joy not just for gardeners but for tens of thousands who visit it annually (or read about it in books). Together, they left the world a legacy of ephemeral yet eternal beauty that perhaps because of its impermanence is even greater. Vita wanted to go down in history as a poet but such is the irony of fate.

The Sissinghurst Garden

When Vita began writing her columns in 1938, she had been gardening for nearly twenty years and had had nearly a decade to test her ideas at Sissinghurst. In that time, she had visited gardens across England and Europe as well as the Middle East. It was only in her mid-forties, however, that she had the chance to put those ideas on paper. She wrote in one of her early articles, to quote from Glendinning:

"I believe in exaggeration; I believe in big groups, big masses; I am sure that it is more effective to plant twelve tulips together than to split them into groups of six; more effective to concentrate all the delphiniums into one bed than to dot them about at intervals of twos and threes"—though for Vita, a group of twelve meant "twelve hundred." At one point she counted the bulbs she had ordered that year: nearly twelve *thousand*.

Before she got out of bed in the morning, she made copious notes concerning ideas for the garden. Now she began to keep a more organized diary. By then, she also had gardeners, three full-time and one part-time. Sissinghurst was already a masterpiece but Vita continued to perfect it. That February, she put thirty roses in the orchard, as well as "some climbers into the trees." Sissinghurst would later become famous for the climbing roses that embraced the trees.

That year, she also opened the garden for a fund-raiser one weekend. Reflecting on the event that saw a thousand gardening enthusiasts and made Vita feel like an "old Tory squire," she wrote that though the garden was at its best in June with irises, roses, peonies, and delphiniums, it must be planted so that there would always be something spectacular every season, not just for her own pleasure anymore but for that of the public.

Though done in the English romantic style, Sissinghurst was laid out in the formal manner like most European gardens to Harold and Albert Powys's design. Harold said, to quote Fox:

"Sissinghurst . . . has a succession of privacies: the forecourt, the first arch, the main court, the tower arch, the lawn, the orchard. All a series of escapes from the world, giving the impression of cumulative escape."

The "architectural" effects such as the neatly trimmed hedges that created an almost Celtic circular Rondel at the center of the rose garden were Harold's. But the romantic plantings which made it so famous were Vita's. By 1939, to quote from Anne Scott-James's book about the garden itself, there was "a Sissinghurst way of combining plants and Sissinghurst conceits and fancies." And it was clear for all to see then and now. Even today Sissinghurst is the most visited garden in England.

At one point, Vita judged a local gardening competition. Upon choosing the favorite garden, she was told by the delighted owner that it had been planted "to her specifications" from her columns and talks.

Not all of Vita's ideas were original. She got most from Gertrude Jekyll and William Robinson. But her ability to explain them to the public in a grand way popularized many of them. Referring to her own projects (and doubtless remembering her father's nighttime axiom), she would write: "If there happens to be a moat nearby," never "At Sissinghurst, I" though Sissinghurst was the place her ideas were tested and discarded or allowed to come to perfection, the landscape where the moat was part of a romance with nature gone wild.

Vita loved the land in a sensual way. And her columns show it. They sound as if she is in love with each and every plant, each and every nook and cranny. In her columns, she let her emotionalism, her love of color and touch run riot, one reason why her writing is so inspiring. The poet in her made the articles sparkle.

She called magnolias "great white pigeons settling among dark leaves" and likened sweet woodruff to "those enormous eiderdowns that one finds in old-fashioned French hotels," to give just two examples.

Though she did not invent it, Vita popularized the idea of using one color scheme for a garden.

Every section of the house was a separate building. To get from the tower to the bedroom, from the living room to the kitchen, she had to walk through a garden. One moonlit war-time night, she became inspired by the beauty of white flowers suddenly taking on a completely different hue—as if they were different plants. After the war, she put in "the pale garden I am now planting under the first flakes of snow," which became the most famous garden of all, the white one. She wrote to Harold during the war of her plan:

"All white flowers, with some clumps of very pale pink. White clematis, white lavender, white agapanthus, white double-primroses, white anemones, white lilies including giganteum in one corner, and the pale peach-coloured pulverulenta."

Harold responded, to quote Brown:

"How these things take one away from the sorrow of war."

The war did halt everyone's plans. Units practiced rifle drills in the courtyard, ate meals in the dining hall, and used the tower for a lookout. But Vita was willing to do whatever she could to protect the land she loved. She became an unofficial night watchman, making rounds to see that every house, every barn, was blacked out to hide it from the Nazi bombing raids. She wrote, to again quote Brown:

"Every evening I go my rounds . . . to see that the blackout is complete. . . . Not a chink reveals the life going on beneath those roofs, behind those blinded windows; love, lust, death, birth, anxiety, even gaiety. . . . Alone I wander . . . I might be a badger or a fox . . . I think of all the farms and cottages spread over England sharing this curious protective secrecy where not even a night-light may show from the room of a dying man or a woman in labour."

Sissinghurst was in the flight path of the bombers going to London. The living room was sheeted with asbestos; putty was put in the corners to make it airtight. Everyone was fitted with gas masks. Harold told her to be ready, to pack the car with her jewels, diaries, and clothes.

She never did. Instead, she got suicide pills from a Swiss doctor in case Hitler got as far as Albion's green and gentle shore.

After the war, Sissinghurst opened year round. Visitors dropped money in an "honesty" box and came any day they liked. It was Knole all over again. As a child, Vita had given guided tours to visitors and later wrote a guidebook to Knole's history and treasurers.

At first Vita jokingly called the visitors "the shillings," after the amount of donation asked, but when the numbers rose to ten thousand annually, she was grateful to be able to plow back every penny into the garden.

Vita found she liked showing off the garden, more so than the nerve-wracking energy it took to be witty with the literati, an art she never did master. She was no good at small talk and felt dreadfully self-conscious when talking about culture. The garden was a different matter, however. It was a less conscious part of her, somehow part of her soul. She wrote of the visitors:

"It is a real experience to open one's garden to the public. . . . You share your personal delight; the scheme you have built up for ten, twenty years becomes part of the pleasure of inquisitive eager gardeners."

Vita took ideas from other gardens, such as Hidcote Manor to which Sissinghurst is often compared, but she went beyond current trends to create a style that is truly unique. The way she combined plants was what set Sissinghurst apart.

The plants themselves were (and still are) overgrown to the point of wildness. Climbing roses cascade off brick garden walls to meet gardens of roses underplanted with tulips and lilies and peonies which spill out to borders of cyclamen, violets, and lavender. The paved stone walks were overgrown with thyme and pennyroyal, which, give off the scent of mint and herbs. Roses climbed the trees. Between the trees, daffodils, jonquils, and narcissus carpeted the ground. With a artist's eye to color and design, Vita turned a bed between one garden and the next into a "Persian carpet of creeping purple, white and red thymes with a few crocus," wrote Brown.

Being such a part of British history, Vita also brought back old flowers and herbs, including old roses. These are shaped more like flat dogwoods or round cabbage roses than modern, taller floribunda or tea roses. Old roses have more fragrance but bloom less often. Their canes are more pliant, giving the shape of the bush a delicate, even wispy look.

She used only the original colors of flowers unless the modern variety was truly spectacular. She crossed many modern flowers off her list, such as blue primroses, because she felt they had gone too far afield of the original color and no longer looked "right." The herb garden in 1948 had "herbs of yore," herbs that few gardeners other than herbalists grow, including elecampane, costmary, woad, herba barona, vervain, and wormwood, as well as six varieties of thyme out of the twenty-four she tracked down over the years from literary references and old gardening books.

During the 1950's her gardening correspondence grew voluminously, Vita answered every letter. Some ideas such as growing strawberry grapes which tasted of alpine strawberries brought truckloads of mail and endless requests for cuttings.

Another time, a single comment set off a furor. When she mentioned that taking cuttings and seed (or digging up flowers in the wild) should be done whenever possible, it brought a tirade from a local nursreyman who said she was encouraging people to steal his livelihood. His letter in turn brought a deluge of mail from people telling him how often they had gone to a nursery and how much they'd spent over the years because of Vita's inspiration.

She got thank-you notes. One reader, to quote from Fox, showed how much she was admired:

"To be offered a rose by a great poetess as the morning sun lights up the breakfast-table is a delightful experience."

The 1950's brought distinguished guests, including Princess Margaret and the Queen Mother. For the visit Vita allegedly donned a dress.

Always the butch, she cared little about furniture or clothes, though she hardly had to worry about furniture. She inherited heirlooms from Knole when she married that furnished both Long Barn and Sissinghurst. But when she had money, she spent it on the garden. She borrowed evening dresses so frequently, it finally became so embarrassing that Harold insisted she buy one of her own. Even then, she was appalled at the price and calculated how many tulips she could have bought for the same sum.

The garden and the life she created with Harold eventually brought them both comfort. After Harold quit his job at the Foreign Office and had no idea how he was going to make a living, he wrote of their life and their choices, to quote Brown:

"Louise during the day has been spreading out the carpets from Streatham. They are moth eaten but superb. It is typical of our existence that with no settled income and no certain prospects, we should live in a muddle of museum carpets, ruined castles and penury. Yet we know that all this uncertainty is better for us than dull and unadventurous security. After dinner we discuss the front at Sissinghurst. We decide to plant a wall of limes, framing the two gables and the arch. . . . That is our life. Work, uncertainty and huge capitalistic schemes. And are we wrong? My God! We are not wrong!''

Despite the pleasures of Sissinghurst and fame enough for parodies in *Punch,* the 1950's brought sorrow as well. Harold, who had been a member of parliament for more than a decade, lost his seat in 1948. He, too, turned to scribbling full-time and wrote a number of books before his death in 1968.

But time was catching up with them both. Harold found Vita sobbing in the garden one day, her back aching so badly, she could hardly bend over to work. She did not know what she would do if she could no longer find solace in the garden. In fact, she had some years of gardening left. And before she died of cancer, she wrote of what it meant to her, slightly paraphrased:

''Gardening is a luxury occupation; an ornament, not a necessity, of life. . . . A useless member of society, considered in terms of economics, [the gardener] must not be denied her rightful place. She deserves to share it, however humbly, with the painter and the poet.''

In these days, which are often filled with tension and noise, metal and plastic, chaos and violence, walking in a garden, working in a garden, even sitting in a garden, can give us a sense of peace found few other ways. At a time when we are able to experience the grandeur of nature only rarely, a garden can put us in touch with our true mother, the earth, and remind us of the place we come from and return to, a place more eternal than any of us will ever know, a place whose body gives us life, whose presence sustains us.

Vita Sackville-West

1882 Virginia Woolf born in London
1886 Harold Nicolson born in Teheran
1892 Vita Sackville-West born at Knole, Kent, England
1913 Marries Harold, gay diplomat
1914 Vita gives birth to Ben

1917 *Poems of West and East* published
Vita gives birth to Nigel

1918 Vita begins affair with Violet Trefusis (nee Keppel)

1919 *Heritage* published

1921 *Orchard and Vineyard* published
Affair with Violet ends

1922 *The Heir* published
Knole and the Sackvilles published
Vita meets Virginia Woolf

1923 *Challenge* about affair with Violet, withdrawn from publication, printed privately

1924 Bloomsbury-style novels *Seducers in Ecuador* about Virginia Woolf published by Woolf's Hogarth Press

1925 Vita Goes to Teheran with Dorothy Wellesley to visit Harold

1926 *The Land* wins the Hawthornden Prize for poetry
Passenger to Teheran published

1927 *Aphra Behn* published

1928 Knole passes to Vita's uncle
Virginia Woolf's *Orlando* about Vita published

1929 Harold quits the Foreign Office

1930 Vita and Harold buy Sissinghurst

1931 *All Passion Spent* published

1933 *Collected Poems* published

1935 Harold elected to House of Commons

1936 *Joan of Arc* published

1941 Virginia Woolf commits suicide

1943 *The Eagle and the Dove* published

1945 Sissinghurst Gardens opened to public year round

1946 *The Garden* wins the Heinemann poetry prize.

1948 Harold loses seat in Parliament

1951 *In Your Garden* published

1953 *In Your Garden Again* published

1955 *More for Your Garden* published

1958 *A Joy of Gardening* published

1961 *No Signposts in the Sea* published

1962 Vita dies of cancer at age 76

1968 Harold dies

BIBLIOGRAPHY

JANE ADDAMS

Addams, Jane. *Newer Ideals of Peace*. New York: The Macmillan Co., 1907.

——————. *Twenty Years at Hull House*. New York: The Macmillan Co., 1910.

——————. *The Second Twenty Years at Hull House*. New York: The Macmillan Co., 1930.

Cook, Blanche Wiesen. *Female Support Networks and Political Activism: Lillian Wald, Crystal Eastman, Emma Goldman*. Los Angeles: Chrysallis magazine, 1977.

Davis, Allen F. *American Heroine; The Life and Legend of Jane Addams*. New York: Oxford University Press, 1973.

—————— and Mary Lynn McCree. *Eighty Years at Hull House*. Chicago: Quadrangle Books, 1969.

Johnson, Geoffrey. *Sisterhood Was Powerful*. Chicago: *Chicago Magazine*, Nov. 1989, p. 192.

Linn, James Weber. *Jane Addams.* New York: Appleton-Century, 1935.

Tims, Margaret. *Jane Addams of Hull House,* London: George Allen & Unwin Ltd., 1961.

NATALIE BARNEY

Chalon, Jean. *Portrait of a Seductress, The World of Natalie Barney.* Translated by Carol Barko. New York: Crown Publishers, Inc., 1979.

Jay, Karla. *The Amazon and the Page: Natalie Clifford Barney and Reneé Vivien.* Bloomington: Indiana University Press, 1988.

Klaich, Dolores. *Woman Plus Woman.* Tallahassee: Naiad Press, 1989.

Livia, Anna. *A Perilous Advantage, The Best of Natalie Clifford Barney.* Edited and translated by Anna Livia with introduction by Karla Jay. Norwich, Vermont: New victoria Press, 1992.

Wickes, George. *Americans in Paris.* New York: Doubleday & Company, Inc., 1969.

————————. *The Amazon of Letters, The Life and Loves of Natalie Barney.* New York: G. P. Putnam's Sons, 1976.

JAMES MIRANDA BARRY

Dekker, Rudolf M. and Lotte C. van de Pol. *The Tradition of Female Transvestism in Early Modern Europe.* New York: St. Martin's Press, 1989.

Rae, Isobel. *The Strange Story of Dr. James Barry.* London: Longmans, Green and Co., 1958.

Rose, June. *The Perfect Gentleman*. London: Hutchinson & Co. (Publishers) Ltd. 1977.

Sullivan, Louis. *Information for the Female-to-Male Crossdresser and Transsexual*. San Francisco: L. Sullivan, 1985.

Woodhouse, Annie. *Fantastic Women, Sex, Gender and Transvestism*, New Brunswick: Rutgers University Press, 1990.

SYLVIA BEACH

Beach, Sylvia. *Shakespeare and Company*. New York: Harcourt Brace World Inc., 1956.

Benstock, Shari. *Women of the Left Bank, Paris, 1900–1940*. Austin: University of Texas Press, 1986.

Fitch, Noel Riley. *Sylvia Beach and the Lost Generation*. New York: W. W. Norton & Company, 1983.

Monnier, Adrienne. *The Very Rich Hours of Adrienne Monnier*, translated by Richard McDougall. New York: Scribners, 1976

ANNA FREUD

Burlingham, Michael John. *The Last Tiffany: A Biography of Dorothy Tiffany Burlingham*. New York: Atheneum, 1989.

Mason, Jeffrey Moussaieff. *The Assault on Truth, Freud's Suppression of the Seduction Theory*. New York: Farrar, Straus and Giroux, Inc., 1984.

Peters, Uwe Henrik. *Anna Freud, A Life Dedicated to Children*. New York: Schocken Books, 1985.

Sayers, Janet. *Mothers of Psychoanalysis: Helene Deutch, Karen Hor-*

ney, Anna Freud and Melanie Klein. New York: W.W. Norton & Company, 1991.

Young-Bruehl, Elisabeth. *Anna Freud*. New York: Summit Books, 1988.

ALICE HAMILTON

Grant, Madeleine P. *Alice Hamilton, Pioneer Doctor in Industrial Medicine*. London: Abelard-Schuman, 1967.

Hamilton, Alice. *Exploring the Dangerous Trades: The Autobiography of Alice Hamilton, M.D.* Boston: Little, Brown and Company, 1943.

—————————. *A Woman of Ninety Looks at Her World*. Boston: The Atlantic, 1965.

Sicherman, Barbara. *Alice Hamilton, A Life in Letters*. Cambridge: Harvard University Press, 1984.

Smith-Rosenberg, Carol. *The Female World of Love and Ritual*. Minneapolis: Signs: Journal of Women in Culture and Society, 1975.

HAMILTON, EDITH

Hamilton, Edith. *Mythology*. New York: New American Library, Inc., 1940.

—————————. *The Echo of Greece*. New York: W. W. Norton & Company, Inc., 1957.

—————————. *The Greek Way*. New York: W. W. Norton & Company, Inc., 1930.

—————————. *The Roman Way*. New York: W. W. Norton & Company, Inc., 1932.

Reid, Dorothy. *Edith Hamilton: An Intimate Portrait*. New York: W. W. Norton & Company, Inc. 1967.

FLORENCE NIGHTINGALE

Cook, Sir Edward Tyas. *A Short Life of Florence Nightingale*. New York: The Macmillan Co., 1925.

Huxley, J. Grant. *Florence Nightingale*. New York: Putnam, 1975.

Myron, Nancy and Charlotte Bunch, Eds. *Women Remembered, A Collection of Biographies from The Furies*. Baltimore: Diana Press, 1974.

Strachey, Lytton. *Eminent Victorians*. London: Chatto & Windus, 1918.

Woodham-Smith, Cecil. *Florence Nightingale*. New York: McGraw-Hill Book Company, Inc. 1951.

VITA SACKVILLE-WEST

Bell, Quentin. *Virginia Woolf, A Biography*. New York: Harcourt Brace Jovanovich, Inc., 1972.

Brown, Jane. *Vita's Other World, A Gardening Biography of V. Sackville-West*. New York: Viking, 1985.

Fox, Robin Lane. *V. Sackville-West, The Illustrated Garden Book, A New Anthology*. New York: Atheneum, 1986.

Glendinning, Victoria. *Vita, A Biography of Vita Sackville-West*. New York: Quill, 1983.

Jullian, Phillipe. *Violet Trefusis: A Biography, including correspondence* with *Vita Sackville-West*. San Diego: Harcourt Brace Jovanovich, 1985.

——————————— and John Phillips. *The Other Woman: A Life of Violet Trefusis*. Boston: Houghton Mifflin, 1976.

Nicolson, Nigel. *Portrait of a Marriage*. New York: Atheneum, 1973.

——————————— and Joanne Trautmann. *The Letters of Virginia Woolf,* Vol. III. New York: Harcourt Brace Jovanovich, 1977.

Nicolson, Philippa Ed. *V. Sackville-West's Garden Book*. London: Michael Joseph, 1968.

Sackville-West, Vita. *The Illustrated Garden Book, A New Anthology by Robin Lane Fox*. New York: Atheneum, 1986.

———————————. *The Letters of Vita Sackville-West to Virginia Woolf,* edited by Louise de Salvo and Mitchell A. Leaska. New York: William Morrow, 1985.

Virginia Woolf. *Orlando*. New York: Harcourt Brace Jovanovich, Inc., 1928.

M. CAREY THOMAS

Finch, Edith. *Carey Thomas of Bryn Mawr*. New York: Harper & Brothers, 1947.

Stein, Gertrude. *Fernhurst, Q.E.D., and Other Early Writings*. New York: Liverwright, 1971.

LILLIAN WALD

Brown, Judith. *Immodest Acts, The Life of a Lesbian Nun in Renaissance Italy*. Oxford: Oxford University Press, 1980.

Coss, Clare. *Lillian Wald, Progressive Activist.* New York: Feminist Press at CUNY, 1989.

Curb, Rosemary and Nancy Manahan. *Lesbian Nuns: Breaking Silence.* Talahassee: Naiad Press, 1985.

Duffus, Robert Luther. *Lillian Wald, Neighbor and Crusader.* New York, The Macmillan Company, 1938.

Siegel, Beatrice. *Lillian Wald of Henry Street.* New York: Macmillan, 1983.

Wald, Lillian. *The House on Henry Street.* New York: Dover Publications, Inc., 1971.

West, Celeste. *A Lesbian Love Advisor.* Pittsburgh: Cleis Press, 1989.

A'LELIA WALKER

Anderson, Jervis. *This Was Harlem.* New York: Farrar, Straus & Giroux, 1982.

Bundles, A'Lelia Perry. *Madam C.J. Walker.* New York: Chelsea House Publishers, 1991.

Dallas Museum of Art. *Black Art, Ancestral Legacy: The African Impulse in African-American Art.* New York: Harry N. Abrams, Inc., 1989.

Erenberg, Lewis A. *Everybody's Doin' It: The Pre-World War I Dance Craze, the Castles and the Modern American Girl.* New York: Feminist Studies, Fall 1975.

Faderman, Lillian. *Odd Girls and Twilight Lovers.* New York: Columbia University Press, 1991.

Hughes, Langston. *The Big Sea, An Autobiography of Langston Hughes.* New York: Alfred A. Knopf, 1940.

Kellnor, Bruce. *The Harlem Renaissance: A Historical Dictionary for the Era.* New York: Methuen, 1984.

Lewis, David Levering. *When Harlem Was in Vogue.* New York: Alfred A. Knopf, 1981.

Morris, Lloyd. *Incredible New York.* New York: Random House, 1951.

Notable Black American Women. Detroit: Gale Research Group, 1992.

Van Vechten, Carl. *Nigger Heaven.* New York: Alfred A. Knopf, 1926.

AND . . .

Corinne, Tee. *Women Who Loved Women.* Portland: Pearchild, 1984.

Elliman, Micheal and Frederick Roll. *The Pink Plaque Guide to London.* London: GMP Publishers Ltd., 1986.

Faderman, Lillian. *Surpassing the Love of Men.* New York: William Morrow, 1981.

Greif, Martin. *The Gay Book of Days.* Secaucus: Lyle Stuart, 1982.

Grier, Barbara and Coletta Reid. *Lesbian Lives, Biographies of Women from "The Ladder."* Oakland, Calif.: Diana Press, 1976.

Lesbian History Group. *Not A Passing Phase: Reclaiming Lesbians in History 1840–1985.* London: The Women's Press, 1989.

Notable American Women, 1607–1950. Cambridge: Belknap Press of Harvard University Press, 1971.

Raymond, Janice G. *A Passion for Friends.* Boston: Beacon Press, 1986.

Rich, Adrienne. *Compulsory Heterosexuality and Lesbian Existence.* Minneapolis: Signs: Journal of Women in Culture and Society, 1980.

Uglow, Jennifer S. *The Macmillan Dictionary of Women's Biographies.* New York: Macmillan, 1982.

INDEX

A Few Sonnet-Portraits of Women (Stein), 182

A Lesbian Love Advisor (West), 125

A Perilous Advantage (Livia), 181, 184

A Room of One's Own (Woolf), 270

A Tribute (Branham), 160

A Woman Appeared to Me (Vivien), 183

Abbott, Bernice, 213

Academy of Women, 194–95

Addams, Jane, 18, 93–112, 113, 130, 131, 138, 151, 156

accomplishments during World War I, 107–11

in Europe, 100–101

lifetime accomplishments, 110–11

poem by, 106

relationship with Alice Hamilton, 139

relationship with Ellen Gates Starr, 94–98

relationship with Lillian Wald, 117–18

relationship with Mary Rozet Smith, 105–107

Albermarle, Lord, 36

Alice Hamilton, a Life in Letters (Sicherman), 136

Alice Hamilton, Pioneer Doctor in Industrial Medicine (Grant), 146

All Passion Spent (Sackville-West), 273

The Amazon of Letters, The Life and Loves of Natalie Barney (Wickes), 180

American Legion, 110

Amsterdam News, 234

An Intimate Portrait (Reid), 160

Anderson, Jervis, 218

Anderson, Margaret, 206

Andrews, John, 140

The Angel and the Depraved (Delarue-Mardrus), 183

The Anschluss, 253–55

Antheil, George, 209, 211

Anthony, Susan B., 77, 142

Arthur, Helen, 114, 124–25

The Assault on Truth (Masson), 245

Association of Practical Housekeeping Centers, 122

Baker, Josephine, 221–22

Balch, Emily Greene, 151

Barnes, Djuna, 183, 195

Barney, Albert Clifford (father), 183

Barney, Alice Pike (mother), 183

Barney, Laura (sister), 183

Barney, Natalie, 19, 83, 177–99, 203, 236, 239

childhood, 183–84

education, 185

on marriage, 181–82

relationship with Janine Lahovary, 197–98

relationship with Liane de Pougy, 179–81

relationship with Renée Vivien, 185
relationship with Romaine Brooks, 195–96
salons, 191–94
Barry, James (Irish painter), 26
Barry, James Miranda, 17–18, 21–45, 72
  career, 21, 28–33
  career setbacks, 38–40
  court-martials, 39–40
  death of, 44
  education, 29–30
  enemies of, 32–33
  at leper colony, 32–33
  medical theories, 27–28, 41
  meeting with Nightingale, 42–43
  in military, 30–33
  performing Caesarean section, 31
  personal life of, 34–38
  at prison, 33
  reforming crusades, 28
  relationship with Charles Somerset, 36–37
  relationship with Mrs. Fenton, 36
  at St. Helena, 38–40
  as sportsman, 37
Beach, Eleanor (mother), 204
Beach, Sylvester (father), 204
Beach, Sylvia, 18, 201–15
  childhood, 204
  education, 205
  experiences during World War II, 212–14
  relationship with Adrienne Monnier,
    201–203
  relationship with James Joyce, 205–209
Bearden, Bessye, 239
"Beating Fantasies and Daydreams"
  (Freud's first paper), 247
Behn, Aphra, 270
Belated Adventure (Voigt), 261
Bentley, Gladys, 221, 239
Bethune, Mary McLeod, 240
The Big Sea (Hughes), 232
Bishop, Sophie, 25–26
Black Art, Ancestral Legacy (Gaither), 219
Blackwell, Elizabeth, 120, 142
Bonaparte, Marie, 254
Bonheur, Rosa, 23
Bonnierre, Suzanne, 211
Bowen, Louise deKoven, 105, 151
Bradley, Katherine, 19
Branham, Grace, 160
Brewster, Mary, 121
British Army hospital at Scutari, 57–58
Brooks, Romaine, 177, 186, 195–96, 197

Brown, Jane, 266, 275
Brown, Judith, 114
Bryher, 19, 210, 212
Bryn Mawr School for Girls, 88, 165–67
Buchan, Lord, 27
Burke, Edmund, 27
Burleigh, Margaret, 105
Burlingham, Dorothy Tiffany, 18, 243, 246,
    247, 248–52, 254, 256–57, 258, 259
Bussy, Dolly, 184
Butler, Edward, 97

Caesarean section, 31
Caillavert, Arman de, 193
Califia, Pat, 177
Campbell, E. Simms, 223
Campbell, Mary, 262, 270
Carlini, Benedetta, 114
Carter, Hilary Bonham, 66–67
Castles, 218
Catt, Carrie Chapman, 108, 151
Challenge (Sackville-West), 262, 265
Chalon, Jean, 182, 188, 191, 193, 194
Chicago magazine, 96
Chicago School of Civics and Philanthropy,
    107–108
Chicago Tribune, 209
Child labor, 98
Children's Bureau, 94
Christianity, 20
Civil Liberties Union, 110
Civil War, 23
Clarke, Mary, 49, 51, 192
Clarkey. *See* Clarke, Mary
Claudine series (Colette), 182–83
Clermont-Tonnerre, Lily Duchesse de, 177,
    197
Cleyrergue, Berthe, 189, 192, 193
Clough, Arthur Hugh, 63
Codman, Armory, 154
Codman, Katy, 154, 155
Colette, 182
Communes, 118
Cook, Blanche Wiesen, 106, 113, 115, 122,
    125
Cooper, Edith, 19
Copland, Aaron, 209
Cornell University, 81
Coss, Clare, 117
The Cotton Club, 239
Covarrubias, Miguel, 223
Crawford, J.L., 229

Crimean War, 57–62
  Nightingale running hospital during, 57–62
Cross-dressing, 23–25, 79
Crowley, Aleicester, 206
Cullen, Countee, 222, 238
Curb, Rosemary, 114
Custance, Olive, 181, 188
Cutpurse, Moll. *See* Frith, Mary

Dahomey (play), 223
Dancing, 217–18
Dangerous Trades (Oliver), 139
d'Annunzio, Gabriele, 196
The Dark Tower, 235–39
Daughters of the American Revolution, 110
Davies, Christian, 23
Davis, Allen F., 101, 105, 107
De Lawd, 240
Debuts, 51
Dekker, Rudolf, 22, 24, 34, 35, 37
Delarue-Mardrus, Lucie, 183
Democracy and Social Ethics (Addams), 108
Deppe, Louis, 234
Depression, 128
  affect on the Harlem Renaissance, 224–27
Dickinson, Emily, 48
Dictionary of the Harlem Renaissance (Kellner), 224
Dildos, 35
Dilling, Elizabeth, 93, 110
Dismond, Geraldyn, 230, 238
Distressed Gentlewoman's Hospital, 56, 58
Dock, Lavinia, 113, 114–15, 132
Donnelly, Lucy, 135–36
Douglas, Aaron, 223
Douglas, Alfred, 181
Drag ball, 232
DuBois, W.E.B., 225
Duffus, R.L., 119, 122
Dunn, Blanche, 236

East, Mary, 30
The Echo of Greece (Hamilton), 171, 173, 174
Eighty Years at Hull House (Davis and McCree), 94, 101, 105
Eitingon, Max, 249
Eliot, T.S., 178, 194, 271
Ellerman, Winifred, 272
Ellington, Duke, 239
Ellis, Havelock, 83, 251
Embattled Paradise (Skolnick), 118

Eminent Victorians (Strachey), 53
Erant, 153
Erenberg, Lewis A., 217
Estella, Mme., 229
Europe, James Reese, 221
Evans, Edward de Lacy, 35
Exploring the Dangerous Trades (Hamilton), 137, 140, 156, 161

Faderman, Lillian, 170, 219, 230, 235, 238
Fane, Mae, 230
Fantastic Women (Woodhouse), 24
Fauriel, Claude, 51
The Female World of Love and Ritual (Smith-Rosenberg), 138
Fenton, Mrs., 36
Fernhurst (Stein), 83
Fielding, Henry, 23–24
Finch, Edith, 73, 75, 79, 82, 85, 87, 90
Finnegans Wake (Joyce), 213
First International Congress of Women, 108
Fitch, Noel Riley, 204, 207, 208, 209, 212
Florence Nightingale (Woodham-Smith), 48
Flower, Lucy, 147
Fox, Robin Lane, 278, 280
France, Anatole, 193
Freud, Anna, 18, 66, 160, 243–60
  caring for Sigmund, 257–58
  childhood, 245–46
  experiences during the *Anschluss*, 253–55
  first paper, 247
  on lesbianism, 251
  in London, 255–56
  relationship with Dorothy Burlingham, 248–52
Freud, Sigmund, 217, 243
  experiences during the *Anschluss*, 253–55
  theories, 244–45, 252
Freund, Gisèle, 211
Frith, Mary, 23
Fuller, Loie, 204

Gaither, Edmund Barry, 219
The Garden (Sackville-West), 270
Garrett, Mary, 18–19, 71, 73, 83, 88–89, 163, 165
Garvey, Marcus, 225
The Gay Book of Days (Grief), 36
Gay culture. *See* Homosexual culture
Germain, André, 192
Gershwin, George, 220
Gide, André, 211

Gilbert, Susan, 48

Gilder, Rosamond, 169

Gilpin, Charles, 223

Girton College, 86

Glendinning, Victoria, 261, 262, 264, 267, 270, 271, 272–73, 275

Goldstein, Joseph, 259

Good Housekeeping, 219

Gourmont, Remy de, 190–91

Gramont, Elisabeth de, 177, 187

Grandjean, Anne "Jean Baptiste," 35

Grant, Madeleine, 143, 146, 153, 154, 162

The Greek Way (Hamilton), 170, 172

Green, Paul, 223

The Green Pastures (play), 223, 240

Grew, Mary, 105

Grief, Martin, 36

Guardian (Fitch), 207

Gwinn, Mamie, 18–19, 71, 73, 74–76, 82–83, 85, 87, 88

Hackett, Francis, 93

Hall, Helen, 131

Hall, Radclyffe, 179, 183

Hamilton, Alice, 19, 99, 104, 108, 111, 130, 135–57, 161, 163, 164, 165, 174

  accomplishments, 156

  childhood, 141–42

  education, 143–45

  at Harvard University, 154

  at Hull House, 139, 145–47

  investigating munitions, 153

  relationship with Jane Addams, 139

  relationship with Julia Lathrop, 146–47

  relationship with Mabel Kittredge, 151–52

  research on lead poisoning, 148–51

  trip to Belgium, 152

  trip to Russia, 155–56

Hamilton, Edith, 19, 88, 135, 136, 141, 142, 143, 144–45, 156, 159–76

  accomplishments, 174–75

  at Bryn Mawr prep school, 165–67

  education, 163–65

  interest in Ancient Greece, 170–75

  relationship with Doris Fielding Reid, 159–60

  writing career, 169–70

Hamilton, Gertrude (mother), 141, 142

Hamilton, Margaret (sister), 90, 135, 136, 143, 156, 162

Hamilton, Mary "George," 23, 34–35

Hamilton, Montgomery (father), 141, 161

Hamilton, Norah (sister), 137, 143, 151, 156

Hampstead War Nurseries, 256

Hampton, Mabel, 235

Harlem General Hospital, 224

Harlem Renaissance, 219–24, 225

  the Depression's affect on, 224–27

  Walker's influence on, 235–41

Harper's Bazaar, 270

Hayward, William, 225

Hazenplug, Frank, 93

Heap, Jane, 206

Hemingway, Ernest, 209, 210

Henderson, Fletcher, 221

Henry Street Settlement, 113, 128

  fortieth anniversary of, 131

Herbert, Liz, 56, 65

Herbert, Sydney, 55, 58, 59, 64–65, 67

Heterosexual culture, difference from homosexual culture, 16–17

Heterosexuality, 251

Hickok, Lorena, 124

Hicks, Alice, 72

Hodder, Alfred, 82

Homosexual culture, 20, 170–72

  difference from heterosexual culture, 16–17

Homosexuality, 251

Homosexuals, male, 84

The House on Henry Street (Wald), 126, 130

How, James. *See* East, Mary

Howland Institute, 79

Hughes, Langston, 222, 227, 232, 236, 238, 240

Hull House, 93–94, 99, 103, 110–11, 113

Hull House Maps and Papers, 146

Hunter, Alberta, 221

Hurston, Zora Neale, 223

I Remember (Barney), 183

Immodest Acts, The Life of a Lesbian Nun in Renaissance Italy (Brown), 114

In Abraham's Bosom (Green), 223

Incredible New York (Morris), 218

Indiscreet Memories (Barney), 183

Industrial medicine, 141, 151

International Congress of Women 1915, 151

The Interpretation of Dreams (Freud), 245

Inter-State Tattler, 238

Intimate Letters to the Amazon (Gourmont), 191

Introduction to the Techniques of Child Analysis (Freud), 252

Jackman, Harold, 226
Jackson, Bessie, 221
Jane Addams of Hull House (Tims), 105, 146
Jay, Karla, 178, 179, 194
Jazz, 220–22
Jekyll, Gertrude, 271
Joan of Arc, 270
John Hopkins medical school, 88
Johnson, Geoffrey, 96
Johnson, Georgia Douglas, 222
Johnson, James Weldon, 222
Johnson, Malvin Gray, 223
Johnson, Samuel, 44
Jones, Ernest, 252, 254
Jones, Lois Mailou, 223
Joyce, James, 205–209, 210, 213
Julian, Hubert, 240
Jullian, Philippe, 194

Kelley, Florence, 99, 100, 113, 114, 115–16, 151
Kellner, Bruce, 224
Kenney, Mary, 101–102
Keppel, Alice, 264
Kereiwinieo, Ralph, 35
Kimbal, Ethel "James Hathaway," 35
Kittredge, Mabel Hyde, 114, 122–23, 138, 151–52, 155
Klaich, Dolores, 192
Klein, Melanie, 252
Knole Estate, 274, 276–77
Knole and the Sackvilles, 270
Koestler, Arthur, 212

The Ladies Almanack (Barnes), 183, 195
The Ladies' Home Journal, 218
Ladies of Llangollen, 48, 83, 251
Lady Chatterly's Lover (Crowley), 206
Lahovary, Janine, 177, 197–98
The Land (Sackville-West), 270
Landsberg, Clara, 136
Lasker Award, 156
The Last Tiffany, 248
Lathrop, Julia, 94, 99, 100, 111, 138, 146–47
Lead poisoning, 148–51
Leaves of Grass (Whitman), 209
Lelia College, 229
Léon, Paul, 213
Leper colony reform, 32–33
Les Ruches, 184
Lesbian Nuns: Breaking Silence (Curb and Manahan), 114

Letters to the Amazon (Gourmont), 191
Lewis, David Levering, 221, 227, 232, 236
Lewis, Lloyd, 104
Lewisohn, Alice, 113, 116–17
Lewisohn, Irene, 116–17
Lewisohn, Leonard, 116
Lillian D. Wald, Progressive Activist (Coss), 117
Lillian Wald, Neighbor and Crusader (Duffus), 119
Lillian Wald of Henry Street (Siegel), 121
Linck, Catharine, 35
Linn, James Weber, 100, 104, 106, 107
Livia, Anna, 181, 184, 196
Lobdell, Lucy Ann "Joseph," 35
Locke, Alain, 222, 223
Loeb, Betty, 121
London Daily News, 67
Loulan, JoAnn, 177
Lutyens, Edwin, 271

M. Carey Thomas of Bryn Mawr (Finch), 73
McAlmon, Robert, 272
McCree, Mary Lynn, 101, 105
McDowall, Helen, 113
McIntosh, Millicent Carey, 167
The Making of Americans (Stein), 178
Malone, Annie M. Turnbo, 228–29
Manahan, Nancy, 114
Manchester Guardian, 28
Marinoff, Fania, 226
Marks, Jeannette, 156
Martineau, Harriet, 67
Masson, Jeffrey Moussaieff, 245
Materia Medica (Dock), 114
Matheson, Hilda, 261, 262
Meade, Gertrude, 75
Medicine, industrial, 141, 151
Memorial Institute for Infectious Diseases, 140
Mentor-student relationships, 159–60
Milhaud, Darius, 220
Military service, 23
Mill, John Stuart, 27
Millay, Edna S. Vincent, 230
Millett, Kate, 13
Mills, Florence, 222
Milnes, Richard Monckton, 53, 54
Miranda, General, 26–27
Miss Kirkland's School for Girls, 95
Miss Porter's Girls School, 163
Modern literature, 209

Monnier, Adrienne, 18, 201–203, 206, 209, 210, 211–12, 214
Monroe, Marilyn, 259
Morgan, Agnes, 125
Morgenthau, Rita Wallach, 113
Morris, Lloyd, 218
Morris, William, 94
Mrs. Dalloway (Woolf), 267
Munitions, investigating, 153
Murat, Princess, 236
My Friend, Julia Lathrop (Addams), 100
Mythology (Hamilton), 171, 173

NAACP, 233
Neighborhood Playhouse Theater, 117
New Statesman, 278
New Thoughts of an Amazon (Barney), 191
New York East Side Neighborhood Guild, 99
New York Evening Post, 267
New York *Herald Tribune*, 224, 241
The New York Times, 225, 229
The New York Times magazine, 104
Newer Ideals of Peace (Addams), 108
Nicholson, Henry, 48, 49
Nicholson, Marianne, 48, 49, 56
Nicolson, Harold, 263–65, 272–76
Nigger Heaven (Van Vechten), 233, 237
Nightclubs, 239
Nightingale, Fanny (mother), 49, 54
Nightingale, Florence, 19, 47–69, 126, 137
  accomplishments, 67–68
  battle with family, 54–55
  career, 56
  debut, 51
  meeting with Barry, 42–43
  relationship with Hilary Bonham Carter, 66–67
  relationship with Sydney Herbert, 64–65
  return to London after war, 62–68
  running hospital during Crimean War, 57–62
Nightingale, Parthe (sister), 54
Nightingale, W.E.N. (father), 49, 56
Notable American Women, 95, 228
Nuclear family, 118
Nugent, Richard Bruce, 237, 238
Nursing, 53
  public health, 122, 126

Observer, 278
Odd Girls and Twilight Lovers (Faderman), 219

Odyssey, 171
Oliver, Thomas, 139
The One Who Is Legion, or A.D.'s After-Life (Barney), 183
Opportunity, 238, 241
Orlando (Woolf), 267, 269–70

Palmer, Evalina, 185
Panmure, Lord, 65
Paris, France, 203
Parker-Bowles, Camilla, 264
Peace and Bread in the Time of War (Addams), 110
Pepita, 270
The Perfect Gentleman (Rose), 25
Perkins, Frances, 111, 156
Perry, Edward, 240
Peters, Uwe Henrik, 246, 249, 250, 256
Phossy jaw, 140
Porgy (play), 223
Portrait of the Artist As a Young Man (Joyce), 206
Portrait of a Marriage (Nicolson), 263, 266, 268
Portrait of a Seductress (Chalon), 188
Pougy, Liane de, 177, 179–81, 185
Pound, Ezra, 194
Powell, Adam Clayton, Sr., 240
Prison reform, 33
Prophets of Israel (Hamilton), 173
Prostitution, 22
The Psychoanalytic Study of the Child (Freud), 256

Rae, Isobel, 26, 37, 43
Raglan, Lord, 42
Rainey, Ma, 221
Randolph, A. Philip, 225
Ray, Man, 213
Récamier, Julie, 192
The Red Network (Dilling), 93
Reflections of an Amazon (Barney), 194
Reid, Doris Fielding, 19, 135, 136, 159–62, 163, 167, 168–69, 174
Reik, Theodore, 248
Reinhardt, Max, 222
Rhoads, James E., 87
Roaring Twenties, 217–19
Robeson, Paul, 223
Robinson, Bill "Bojangles," 225, 239
Robinson, Mae Walker, 239
Rogers, Julia, 75

"Romantic friendships," 79, 83–84
Roosevelt, Eleanor, 124
Roosevelt, Franklin, 153
Rose, June, 25, 37
Russell, William Howard, 58

Sacco and Vanzetti, 1920 case of, 154
Sackville-West, Vita, 19, 261–85
    childhood, 271
    and gardening, 278–79
    and the Knole Estate, 276–77
    and poetry, 277–78
    relationship with Harold Nicolson, 263–65,
        272–76
    relationship with Violet Trefusis, 263–65
    relationship with Virginia Woolf, 267–70
St. Teresa of Avila, 270
Sapphic Idyll (Pougy), 180, 182
Sappho, 178
Saunders News Letter, 28
Savage, Augusta, 223–24
Scatterings, 189
Schiff, Jacob, 121
School of Social Service Administration of
    the University of Chicago, 108
Schuria, Henrica, 35–36
Schuyler, George S., 226
Scott, Geoffrey, 262, 270
Sea Wall, 168
Seducers (Woolf), 269
Seducers in Ecuador (Sackville-West), 267,
    269
Sexual abuse, 244–45
Sexual liberation, 187, 219
Sexual Politics (Millett), 13
Shakespeare and Company, 204, 210–14
Shakespeare and Company (Beach), 202, 214
Shilleto, Violette, 185
Sicherman, Barbara, 135, 136, 139, 145, 146
Siegel, Beatrice, 121
Sissinghurst Estate, 275–76
    garden, 279–84
Sitwell, Edith, 218, 271
Sitwell, Osbert, 218, 229
Skolnick, Arlene, 118
Slobo, Dr., *See* Slobodinskaya, Rachelle
Slobodinskaya, Rachelle, 143–44
Smash, 79
Smith, Ada "Bricktop," 222
Smith, Lillian Arkel "Col. Sir Victor
    Barker," 35
Smith, Mamie and Bessie, 221

Smith, Mary Rozet, 18, 93, 97, 104–107,
    109, 111, 131
Smith-Rosenberg, Carol, 105, 138
Snell, Hannah, 24
Social work, 99
Socialism, 94
Solnit, Albert, 259
Somerset, Charles, 36–37
South Halsted Street (Chicago), 102–103
Spokesmen for God (Hamilton), 173
Staël, Madame de, 193
Starr, Ellen Gates, 18, 93, 94–98, 147
Stein, Gertrude, 83, 193, 203, 236
Steinbrugge, Camilla, 212
Sterling, Anthony, 59
Stevedore (play), 231
Stinnett, Mac, 236
Strachey, Lytton, 53, 184
The Strange Story of Dr. James Barry (Rae),
    26
Studies and Preludes (Vivien), 182
Sylvia Beach and the Lost Generation
    (Fitch), 204

Taft, William Howard, 147
Tandy, Vertner, 234
Tarn, Pauline, 182, *see also* Vivien, Renée
The Female Husband (Fielding), 23
Theater, black, 223
This Was Harlem (Schuyler), 226
Thomas, Dr. (father), 74, 78, 81
Thomas, Edna, 223, 230–31
Thomas, Lloyd, 231
Thomas, M. Carey, 18–19, 71–91, 165
    accomplishments, 90
    at Bryn Mawr, 82, 85–90
    childhood, 77–78, 84–85
    cross-dressing, 79
    early education, 78–80
    education, 80–82
    relationship with Bessie, 79
    romantic friendships, 82–85
    at University of Leipzig, 74–76
    at University of Zurich, 76–77
Thomas, Mary (mother), 78, 79, 81
Thomson, Virgil, 178, 209
Thoughts of an Amazon (Barney), 184, 191
369th Infantry, 225
The Times, 58
Tims, Margaret, 105, 146
Tipton, Billy, 22–23, 35
Tolstoy, Leo, 106

Toynbee Hall, 96, 99
*The Tradition of Female Transvestism in
　Early Modern Europe*, 22
Transvestites, 24, 34
Trefusis, Denys, 264
Trefusis, Violet, 261, 262, 263–65, 274
Turner, Kate Scott, 48
Twenty Years at Hull House (Addams), 95,
　101, 107
Twose, George Mortimer Randall Plantegent,
　93

Ulysses (Joyce), 204, 205, 206–207, 210, 214
University of Leipzig, 74–76
University of Michigan, 143
University of Munich, 145
University of Zurich, 76–77

Valéry, Paul, 194
van de Pol, Lotte, 22, 24, 34, 35, 37
Van Vechten, Carl, 226, 233, 235, 236, 237
Vanity Fair, 227
The Very Rich Hours of Adrienne Monnier
　(Monnier), 201
Vita, a Biography of Vita Sackville-West
　(Glendinning), 261
*Vita's Other World, a Gardening Biography
　of V. Sackville-West* (Brown), 266,
　275
Vivien, Renée, 177, 178, 182, 183, 185, 188
Voigt, Margaret Goldsmith, 261–62
von Tisza, Stephen, 109
von Zuylen de Nievelt, Helene, Baroness,
　188

Wald, Julia (sister), 120
Wald, Lillian, 19, 110, 113–33, 138, 151, 217
　accomplishments, 132
　after World War I, 129–32
　relationship with Florence Kelley, 115–16
　relationship with Jane Addams, 117–18
　relationship with Lavinia Dock, 114–15
　relationship with Mabel Hyde Kittredge,
　　122–23
Wald, Max (father), 119
Wald, Minnie (mother), 119

Walker, A'lelia, 19, 217–42
　funeral of, 239–40
　influence on the Harlem Renaissance,
　　235–41
　relationship with Edna Thomas, 230–31
Walker, C.J. (mother), 227–29, 233, 234
Walker, Mary Edwards, 23, 118
Walker Hair Parlor, 230
Washington, Sarah Spencer, 229
The Wasteland (Eliot), 271
Waters, Ethel, 239
Weaver, Harriet, 206, 208
Well of Loneliness (Hall), 179, 183
Wellesley, Dorothy, 261, 262, 266
West, Celeste, 125
When Harlem Was In Vogue (Lewis), 221,
　226
White, Mayme, 230
Whitehaven News, 28
Whitman, Walt, 209
Who's Who in Pacifism, 130
Wickes, George, 180
Wilde, Dolly, 177, 187
Wilde, Oscar, 189
Willard, Frances, 142
Wilson, Woodrow, 90
Windows on Henry Street (Wald), 131
Witness to the Truth (Hamilton), 173
Wollstonecraft, Mary, 27
The Woman Way (Hamilton), 172
Women's Peace Party, 108
Wong, Nadine, 177
Woodham-Smith, Cecil, 43, 48, 51, 52, 59,
　62, 63, 65
Woodhouse, Annie, 24
Woodhull, Victoria, 186
Woolf, Virginia, 56, 261, 262, 266–70, 274
Woolley, Mary, 156
Works Progress Administration (WPA), 231
Wright, Richard, 214
Wyndham, Olivia, 231

Yarros, Victor, 143
Young-Bruehl, Elisabeth, 245, 250, 254, 257,
　259

*Last night on the board
I wrote*

*Ya
Toc*